POPCORN
AND
Sexual Politics

Movie Reviews by Kathi Maio

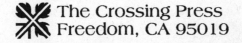
The Crossing Press
Freedom, CA 95019

For My Mother, Esther V. Maio

and in memory of my Grandmothers,
Christine A. Campana and Maria A. Maio
—Strong women, all.

Cover design by Janice Angelini
Cover photo by Dennis M. Wade

Printed in the U.S.A.

Acknowledgements:

My gratitude, again, to all the wonderful women of *Sojourner: The Women's
Forum* (42 Seaverns Avenue, Jamaica Plain, MA 02130). *Soj.* truly is a "forum"
where women can write it the way we see it—and not just about movies.
Working for the feminist press has never paid the rent, but it has provided me
with a shelter of at least equal value.

In my case, I cover the bills with a full-time job as a reference librarian.
I would be a sniveling ingrate if I didn't also publicly acknowledge all my co-
workers at Sawyer Library. I'd especially like to thank Elisa McKnight, one
of my partners in Reference, and Assistant Director Jim Coleman. Jim is my
immediate supervisor, as well as a good friend, and his support is what makes
it possible for me to be a librarian *and* a writer.

To Dennis M. Wade, my thanks for the author photo—and for so much
else over the last eighteen years.

Cataloging-in-publication data

Maio, Kathi, 1951-
    Popcorn and sexual politics : movie reviews / Kathi Maio.
      p. cm.
    Includes index.
    ISBN 0-89594-469-3 -- ISBN 0-89594-468-5 (pbk.)
1. Women in motion pictures.   2. Sex role in motion pictures.
3. Motion pictures--United States--Reviews.   I. Title.
PN1995.9.W6M335 1991
791.43'652042--dc20

                                    91-8500
                                    CIP

Contents

vii **Preface**

1 **Introduction**

7 **A Fine Romance**
8 *Pretty Woman*
15 *Earth Girls are Easy*
20 *Ghost*
27 *White Palace/ Tune in Tomorrow*
35 *Chances Are/ See You in the Morning/ Skin Deep*

45 **The Lost Race of Hollywood**
46 *A World Apart*
54 *Shag*
61 *A Dry White Season*
67 *Bagdad Cafe*

75 **The New "Woman's Film"**
76 *Beaches*
82 *Working Girl*
88 *Mystic Pizza*
93 *Steel Magnolias*
99 *Blue Steel/Impulse*

111 Losing Out and Getting Even

112 *The Good Mother/The Accused*

121 *Shame*

128 *She-Devil*

134 *Heathers*

141 Motherhood in Patriarchy

142 *Men Don't Leave*

150 *Look Who's Talking/Immediate Family*

158 *Postcards From the Edge*

166 *Mermaids*

173 With Friends Like These...

174 *Another Woman*

181 *Betsy's Wedding*

186 *Strapless*

193 *Cookie*

199 A Real Class Act

200 *Driving Miss Daisy/Stella/Stanley and Iris/*
     Where the Heart Is

217 Index

PREFACE

The response to my first collection of film reviews, *Feminist in the Dark*, has been extremely gratifying. I'm indebted to all of the readers who've told me that there is a real need for my brand of feminist reviews. And there is nothing I like better than to hear from a reader that "there was *something* about that movie that made me feel uncomfortable, but I couldn't put my finger on it until I read your review." It's an undeniable ego-boost, but what it really means is that I was simply doing my job as a film critic.

My aim isn't to gain the power of suggestion over moviegoers, but rather to help them see through the powerful (often reprehensible) suggestions made by Hollywood about gender, race, and class in this country. There are countless distortions in the mirror images popular film holds up to us. Recognize them and, although they will still be there, they won't be quite as hurtful.

Please don't think that I'm claiming "politically correct" status for my very personal opinions about film. Nothing could be further from the truth. There are as many different opinions and reactions to films as there are people sitting in the darkened theater. There is no right way to see a movie. I hear from the readers of *Sojourner* (where most of the enclosed reviews first appeared) quite often. They let me know, in no uncertain terms, when they think I'm wrong about a particular film. While I would disagree about my being "wrong," I would never disagree that they are *right*. In the parlance of psycho-babble, your feelings are your feelings—especially about the movies. You have a right to them, *and* to express them. And so do I.

The fact is that I have far more respect for the opinions of the so-called "general public" than I do for the opinions of my fellow—most of them *are* male—critics. Even when I can get away from work to attend a press screening, I seldom do. Listening to the distinguished gents of the local media trade snide commentary in the back row never adds to my enjoyment or understanding of the film. (And, sad to say, the same could be said of most of their reviews.)

On the other hand, listening in on the laughter, screams, and stray remarks of a "real" audience enriches the movie for me a great deal. Audience reaction always tells me something important about the film I'm watching. That's why I often quote audience members in my reviews. It's the dynamics of that group experience that is worth the (exorbitant) price of admission—usually even more than the movie itself.

When I heard women's voices yelling "Kill her!" to Michael Douglas as he faced off with Glenn Close at a local cineplex's Saturday night showing of *Fatal Attraction*, I learned something vital about how that movie tapped the misogyny in all of us. And when a friend and I were distracted from watching *The Accused* (see page 115) by several young boys who broke into the theatre expressly to enjoy—with many encouragements to the rapists—the crucial (and, for us, excruciating) gang rape of Jodie Foster, it really was an educational experience. I had living proof that even a fairly sensitive and highly critical depiction of rape can be obscene entertainment for youngsters raised on slasher films and the like. Those boys didn't know how to see violence against women as anything but a good time.

Scary stuff. But other examples of movie eavesdropping provided more cheerful indicators. While the early critical word on *Beaches* (p. 76) was that it was one of the worst movies ever made, I knew it was going to be deservedly successful because I went to see it with general audiences twice, cried each time, and spent the last quarter of the movie listening to the contented weeping of the other women in both audiences. One of my forecast barometers is the tissue test, and *Beaches* was a three-tissue hit, a teary celebration of women's friendships as "The Wind Beneath [Our] Wings."

So, I am not the critic who sits on high, with delusions of being a Roman emperor, pointing my thumb up or down for each fresh movie brought before me. I love the shared experience of movie-watching. My film essays are just my small contribution to the ongoing dialogue.

I feel passionately about movies, and about issues of social equity, not just for women, but for all of us disempowered by this society, and by the social representations we see up on that giant screen. I consider my film writing political, but not, I hope, preachy. I never mean to come off sounding like a polemical treatise or an academic dissertation. My conversational style in these essays is no accident. If I want you to patiently read what I have to say about a movie, the least I can do is keep it readable.

The most accessible of the entertainment arts demands analysis that is, itself, accessible and entertaining. I hope that you find these essays just that.

* * * *

The reviews in this volume are organized in loose subject groupings. The first, *A Fine Romance*, explores the problematic aspects of current film romance.

The second, *The Lost Race of Hollywood*, deals with race and racism in a few recent films. It's no accident that only two of the four films reviewed concede the existence of racism. And those are the two about South Africa. American films, with the exception of the misogynist Spike Lee's, have a hard time admitting that racism is still an All-American experience.

Section three is titled *The New "Woman's Film."* I review weepies and other films produced with a female audience in mind, and two that try to insert women heroes into the male action formula.

Losing Out and Getting Even, the fourth grouping, deals with the theme of women as victims and avengers.

We all know how badly single career women are treated in film. Section five, *Motherhood in Patriarchy*, includes my recent reviews about Hollywood's treatment of movie moms.

As the saying goes, *With Friends Like These...* you don't need enemies. This is a gathering of my reviews of recent works by filmmakers who have been hailed for their positive portrayals of women.

The last essay is a grouping of one. *A Real Class Act* reviews four films, in release at the same time, that examine the lives of the poor, and their relationships with the rich.

INTRODUCTION

Perhaps we should call it The Case of Hollywood's Incredible Shrinking Woman, this continuing diminution of everything female by the American film industry. In front of the camera and behind it, and especially up on the screen, there seem to be fewer and fewer women with less and less power.

The kind of roles I see talented women actors forced to play if they want to work is the aspect of the problem that I'm most familiar with. But that's only part of the Big Picture. In November of 1990, Sharon Bernstein and Elaine Dutka published articles in the *Los Angeles Times* that detailed the problem as a systemic one.

Not one woman studio executive, for example, has final "green-light" power over which movies will be made and which will not. A committee of *Times* writers looked at the output of the Big Eight studios from June through September of 1990 and found that of the 45 films released, only one, Columbia's *Postcards from the Edge* (panned, starting on page 158 of this volume), featured women in the lead roles. And only 16—including *Ghost* (see p. 20)—contained "significant" roles for female actors.

And speaking of female actors, according to the Screen Actors Guild, they're as underpaid as the rest of us. Women earn half of what male actors earn. And the little money an "actress" makes must be gotten while the girlish glow is still on her cheeks. Women land only 29% of the parts in feature films, but women over 40 get only 9% of all the roles in television and movies!

Statistics tell a good bit of the story. The rest can be found by actually examining the movies we see in America. Women are not only given less screen time, when we're up there on the screen we are likely to be portrayed as powerless and ineffectual. We can't change the world. We can't even (as in the case of careerwomen stereotypes like J.C. Wiatt in *Baby Boom*) change a diaper.

Consider how often in the last ten years, in those few instances where we were allowed to see women in courageous starring roles, the character was ultimately portrayed as a victim. *Frances* (1983) and *Silkwood* (1983) are good examples. *Sweet Dreams* (1985) and *A Cry in the Dark* (1988) are later examples from the same "leading ladies," Lange and Streep. Sigourney Weaver's descent into wild-eyed fanaticism, as Dian Fossey in *Gorillas in the Mist* (1988), got her chopped to death. Isabelle Adjani, playing the magnificent and magnificently anguished artist, *Camille Claudel* (1989), ends up destroying her own sculptures, and is finally committed to a mental institution by her family. She lived the last 30 years of her life in confinement.

These stories deserve to be told—although you could argue about the fairness of the telling in a case like the Dian Fossey story—but where are the *triumphant* women heroes to match the winner roles men play constantly? For women it is death or dishonor in the final reel. Such depictions may back up the argument that women are oppressed, but surely these are questionable role models for young girls. (Be courageous! Take risks!....And you too can end up hacked to bits by a machete or locked away in an asylum.)

A talented newcomer like Natasha Richardson may, if she's lucky, end up with an entire career playing sacrificial lambs. She gives a riveting performance in *Patty Hearst* (1989), but it's two hours of rapes in a dark closet and persecution in the courtroom. Natasha played another important (victim) role in 1990, in the screen adaptation of Margaret Atwood's *The Handmaid's Tale*, where she endured more rapes and further domination.

This Volker Schlöndorff film is an impressive one, based on an even more impressive novel, but Harold Pinter's screenplay takes most of the fire out of the character of Kate/Offred by taking away her active past and feminist mother. Richardson's character *does* finally revolt, but her bloody act seems to come out of nowhere.

And did you notice the number the movie marketeers did on this supposedly "ultra-feminist" story? In the film's poster, and later on the video box, our heroine is presented as a demurely seductive cutie, with only a swatch of red drape over her bare bosom. Can the ends justify the means when a sexist marketing strategy is used to sell an anti-sexist film to an unsuspecting public?

But then, maybe this movie isn't so much anti-sexist as anti-totalitarian. The film of *The Handmaid's Tale* ends with Richardson's mountaintop madonna awaiting the birth of her baby, and the return of her man. It's a triumph, of sorts. But one that reinforces both a maternal and romantic obligation on the part of women.

Even if you accept that *The Handmaid's Tale* is, in its own male-filtered manner, sincerely horrified by the threat of a fundamentalist patriarchy that reduces women to baby incubators, many other of today's movies seem to look kindly on the idea. Films like *Three Men and a Baby* (1987) and its 1990 sequel, *Three Men and a Little Lady*, *Look Who's Talking* (p. 152), *Parenthood* (p. 151 and *Immediate Family* (p. 154), all released in 1989, give women little to do besides pop babies, or wish they were popping babies. Yet, with the possible exception of the latter, they all seem to suggest that the only real parenthood is fatherhood. Mom is only important for the first nine months.

Or to sacrifice herself—to the death, if need be—at any point that it seems to serve the child or others. Demi Moore's stirring performance in the pre-apocalyptic horror thriller, *The Seventh Sign* (1988), allows her to play the ultimate Mom. She dies for humankind, Christ, and her newborn son, all in one fell swoop. *Steel Magnolias* (p. 93), the hit weepie of 1989, goes for less spectacular sacrifice. One mother gives a kidney, and her daughter gives up her health, and eventually her life, for the birth of a single boychild. Fathers are seldom expected to prove themselves quite so drastically, yet even in films from "feminist" filmmakers like Alan Alda (see *Betsy's Wedding*, reviewed on p. 181) they remain the central figure of the family.

For a striking contrast to show how movie moms are losing ground in terms of their empowerment to improve their own lives, and those of their children, consider two films made by the same creative team eleven years apart.

Norma Rae was written by Harriet Frank, Jr., and Irving

Ravetch and directed by the late Martin Ritt back in 1979. In it, a poor millworker played by Sally Field (at first a single mom, and later the married mom of a blended family) fights the patriarchy at home and on the job. Her hard-won victories make life better for herself, her family, and all her co-workers. She is unmistakably a film hero.

In last year's *Stanley & Iris* (p. 205), written by the same couple, and directed by the same man, Mom (Jane Fonda) is powerless to improve her own life, the lives of her children, or the lives of the people she works with. Only indirectly, by empowering a new father figure for the family (Robert DeNiro), can Iris make things better. Given the ability to read—a talent Iris has possessed for forty years—there is no stopping Stanley. The smart money stays on the man.

Boys (even ones with green shells) appear as valiant, victorious figures in today's movies with much greater regularity than full-grown women. As I write this introduction, the number one movie in the country, for the umpteenth week, it seems, is *Home Alone*. In this tale of a young boy's initiation into the power of manhood, an eight-year-old saves his home and brings his family back home, together for the holidays. Wee Kevin is quite the mensch. (Poor Iris couldn't even land a better job.) In 1990's other megahit, *Ghost* (p. 20), Demi Moore and Whoopi Goldberg aren't half as resourceful as little Kev. They have to depend on a *dead* man to save them.

Strong, victorious women still exist in film. Just not often enough, and generally not in movies that get much play. The Australian thriller *Dead Calm* (1989) makes a nice change from all the macho thrillers Hollywood produces. Nicole Kidman's wife is as much the self-reliant survivor as her husband (Sam Neill). It is she, alone, who must face off with a homicidal maniac for most of the film—although hubby, wouldn't you know, gets the last save in.

I liked the shock comedy *Heathers* (1989, p. 134) so much because its power politics are right out there in the open, and the young women are as enterprising as the young men. Much of the youthful aspiration, from both genders, is undisguised, status-seeking self-interest. There are a lot of bad choices made. But the narrator/hero, Veronica (Winona Ryder), sides with right *and* might in the end. And in this rare case, that *doesn't* mean that she ends up in some guy's arms.

That's still where most of the happy endings for today's film women come from. *Pretty Woman* (p. 8), the first big hit of

4

1990, does, like *Ghost,* have a woman in a designated "lead" role. But Julia Roberts's heroine is no lead-er. She is a follower. . . of the philosophy that a woman's success is measured by the size of her man's bank account. Her prostitute protagonist is a "fairy princess" as unreconstructed sex object.

Vivian's only major talent is her ability to be just the plaything and accessory Richard Gere's corporate raider "prince" wants and needs. But that's a woman's natural role, isn't it? For her efforts as boy-toy, she'll be allowed to shop 'til she drops. At least until her older man's Jennifer Fever sends his libido hunting for fresher game.

Meryl Streep, in her keynote speech at the Screen Actors Guild's first women's conference this past summer, was none too pleased about that particular box-office hit. As she pointed out, *Pretty Woman* seemed to indicate that "the chief occupation of women on Earth was hooking. And I don't mean rugs." Her speech decried the status of women throughout the film industry, suggesting (only slightly facetiously) that if present trends go unchecked, women will be eliminated from films altogether by the year 2010.

The fact that SAG is now thinking about things like women's conferences, and well-known figures like Streep are willing to go on the record against the sexism in their business community, is our most encouraging sign that things may get better someday.

"We all know what the problem is," said Meryl. Boy, do we. But what, in heaven's name, can we *really* do about it? It's all about power. And, right now, women on the screen and behind the camera have precious little of that commodity.

The success of *Pretty Woman* and *Ghost* will probably force the men with "green light" power to finally admit that there truly is a female movie audience, and that even movie-goers of the male persuasion might be willing to watch something besides macho bloodbaths. On the other end of the product "pipeline," in the next year or so, we'll probably see increasing numbers of films about women characters. But will those characters be movie *heroes*? Time will tell.

One thing you can count on: I'll be watching. Carefully.

A Fine Romance

ROMANCING RODEO DRIVE

Pretty Woman and *Miami Blues*

I greet the release of most movies the same way I welcome to my home the salesmen, politicians, and door-to-door religious fanatics who occasionally bang at my front door: I ignore them in the hopes that they'll eventually give up and go away. This technique works like a charm on people offering you an eternity with God the Father, or 30 days with the *Encyclopedia Britannica*, but it doesn't always work as well with movies.

Sometimes, when you least expect it, a film becomes a mega-hit, and seems intent on setting up permanent residence at every moviehouse in town. You can't escape the big ads that appear, week after week, in the Friday paper. And everybody you know wants to know how you liked it, assuming that you (along with every other member of the viewing public) must have seen it. Eventually, against your better judgment, you figure "Geez, Louise! I better get this over with and see the damn thing."

Pretty Woman is that kind of movie. Except for a few weeks of tough competition from a pesky band of violent adolescent reptiles, this Cinderella story about a working girl and her corporate-raider prince has been number one at the box office since it opened. When most March movies are long gone, it is still grossing about $7 million a weekend. The *Guiness* folks should take note of this one: a street prostitute earning this much for her pimps has got to be some kind of record.

I'd like to think that most of the money from the film is going to Julia Roberts, who with her gawky beauty and knack for comedy puts all the pizzazz into this shamefully ordinary story. Yet I fear that as with far too many hookers, most of the revenues she's producing will go directly to the men behind the scenes at Touchstone/Disney. (What *would* Uncle Walty think about his company making so much money off of a prostitute? He'd be shocked all the way to the bank, I suppose.)

In Pretty Woman, *Vivian Ward (Julia Roberts) listens blissfully, while Edward Lewis (Richard Gere) tells her the three little words that every woman longs to hear: "Time to Shop!"*

Pretty Woman is a film that seems to take pride in its very predictability. Which is one of the main reasons it's doing so well. Fairy tales aren't loved for their originality, after all. This calculated updating of Cinderella tells a story we all know by heart, so what does it matter if the movie itself is heartless? We supply our own emotions to go with the pretty paper dolls, their gorgeous clothes, their sumptuous surroundings and fancy cars. The first line of the movie is, "No matter what they say, it's all about money." And that's as good a summing up of this particular "romantic comedy" as you could ask for.

Edward Lewis (Richard Gere) maintains a professional life that is the perfect blend of old-world viciousness and GQ suavity. He is a corporate raider who invades and pillages other people's companies just like Attila the Hun in an Armani suit. His barbarian approach to big business must have ruined countless lives—a fact that is beautifully soft-pedaled by the movie—but he does what he does with such elegance and such spectacular profits that rich folks, coast to coast, keep him at the top of their A-list.

But, hey, it's lonely at the top. Everyone wants him for

cocktails and caviar, but he can't always get a date. Attila-like tactics may be popular with the boys in the boardroom, but post-feminist gals (unreasonable creatures that they are) expect more sensitivity from an escort. They want respect. They want tenderness. They want more than a hour's notice when they're asked to a party. Poor Eddy! Here he is in Beverly Hills to watch a little polo and steal another company or two and he's just been dumped long-distance by his girlfriend, who is fed up at being at his "beck and call."

Lesser men (i.e., ones with feelings) might be heartbroken, but not our Edward. He borrows his lawyer's expensive sports car and goes joy-riding, losing himself in the wilds of Hollywood. When he stops to ask directions of a Boulevard hooker, Vivian (Julia Roberts), she jumps into the car and into his life.

Every Attila should have a concubine or two. So Edward, although at first reluctant to have anything to do with a street prostitute, soon becomes sold on the idea of establishing a relationship with a woman that is strictly business. For $3,000 Vivian can be his for the week, a sexual "sure thing" who'll make no emotional demands. Vivian's only verboten is lip-kissing. But Edward doesn't want her or any woman to do anything as intimate as kiss him on the lips. And he's sick of women giving him lip about doing what he wants. Vivian's most attractive trait is that she's willing to give good beck-and-call, as long as her efforts are recompensed. And Edward is willing, and easily able, to recompense her handsomely. Clearly, this is the perfect match.

Fledgling screenwriter J.F. Lawton, and his various more experienced script doctors (among them, Barbara Benedek), have somehow touched at the cynical heart of '90s romanticism. Our two lovers experience the redemption of love through the healing power of hard cash. The final product is ingratiatingly sentimental and as phony as a four-dollar bill. This was apparently not Mr. Lawton's original intent.

Director Garry Marshall (*Beaches*, *Overboard*) told the *New York Times* that the original script was "a kind of dark romance" with "a very unhappy ending." But I have a sneaking suspicion that Marshall's idea of an unhappy ending and mine are poles apart. The way he had Lawton's screenplay "lightened up" into a "dream relationship" has a real nightmarish quality.

Pretty Woman has been compared to Shaw's *Pygmalion* and Lerner and Loewe's *My Fair Lady*. It repeatedly borrows from those two precursors, but the differences between Marshall's movie and its models are striking and disturbing. Whether the heroine is a flower vendor or a prostitute is immaterial; it's what the story says about how women improve their lives that bears examination.

Superficially, Eliza Doolittle and Vivian Ward are very similar. Both are given new duds and a glimpse at how the other half lives by an overclass male. Both Henry Higgins and Edward Lewis share power skills with their lovely and spirited protégés. Henry Higgins teaches Eliza about the power of language. And Edward teaches Vivian about the power of the credit card. The most exhilarating scenes in *Pretty Woman* aren't about Vivian learning to love Edward (or vice versa), nor are they about Vivian learning to use the right dinner fork from Hector Elizondo's paternalistic hotel manager. They're about Vivian learning how to shop like a woman who belongs to a rich man, and therefore one who deserves to be "sucked up" to by boot-licking boutique owners.

Edward's approach to uplifting a beautiful street urchin, unlike Henry's, maintains his dominance at all times. When Henry Higgins teaches Eliza how to use language and etiquette it is a power that is hers to keep, and use against him if she chooses. Indeed, when George Bernard Shaw wrote his play, *Pygmalion*, that was exactly what he had in mind. He was shocked when directors and actors suggested that Eliza should actually remain with Higgins at the end of the play. Of course Lerner and Loewe, and later Jack Warner, the movie mogul, eventually had their way with Shaw's story. In the final scene of *My Fair Lady*, Eliza returns to Higgins. The film implies that, like a faithful dog, Eliza will fetch Higgins his slippers for the rest of her days.

Vivian has even less of a chance against the misogynists of Hollywood then Eliza did. The power Edward gives to her, an American Express gold card, is a power Edward can, even expects to, take back from her again. But the filmmakers know enough not to make Vivian the total boy toy. They gloss over the real power politics of the piece with a few scenes in which Vivian flexes her self-respect before a seemingly chastened Edward. And they try to fool us into believing that this is a relationship between equals by having Edward transformed into a nice guy (and humane business person) through Vivian's loving influence.

But how transformed is he, really? He decides not to gut a shipping company owned by James Morse (Ralph Bellamy), but that seems to have more to do with Edward's need to obtain the blessing of a surrogate father than it has to do with his need to be worthy of Vivian's love.

In a telling scene that occurs shortly *after* Edward's enlightenment, his limo-chasing lawyer, Philip (well played by Jason Alexander), assaults and attempts to rape Vivian. Does Edward beat Philip to a bloody pulp? Does he call the cops and assist Vivian in pressing charges? Does he demand that the lawyer, a long-time employee and plundering pal, apologize to the woman he has (supposedly) come to love? He does not. His anger is self-centered. "It's the kill you love, not me!" he yells at Philip. He is outraged that a mouthpiece on a retainer should love him more for his power than for his endearing personality, but he doesn't seem surprised or all that incensed that the little weasel slugged and tried to sexually violate his beloved.

Vivian is too besotted to see that particular warning light. She is deluded by her touching belief in her fairy tale happiness. And the movie's feel-good pay-off would have the audience leave the movie equally deluded. *Miami Blues*, another recent film, is also in part about the delusionary fantasies of a prostitute. But with no happily-ever-afters promised to its lead characters, it isn't doing half as well with its audiences.

Susie, a.k.a. Pepper (Jennifer Jason Leigh), is a Miami hotel hooker sent to the room of a fresh-from-prison psychopath named Junior Frenger (Alec Baldwin). It's been a long time between women for Junior, and it shows. His tentativeness passes for tenderness, and kind-hearted Susie, even more a waif than he, is touched by the joy Junior takes in her. In turn, Junior is as impressed by Susie's talents in the kitchen as he is by her bedroom abilities. Before long, both become caught up in a long-dormant dream of Ozzie and Harriet happiness (minus the kids).

The film's main plot is an occasionally gory police procedural. Sergeant Hoke Moseley (Fred Ward) would like to take Junior down for the murder of a Hare Krishna at the airport, but Junior strikes first. He steals Hoke's badge, gun, and false teeth, and continues with his merry crime spree. The suspense of the film never jells, and too many of the characters (including Ward's Moseley) are given short shrift, but the Bonnie-and-Clyde-go-suburban love story of Susie and Junior is always fascinating.

All of us, even those like Junior and Susie who grew up poor and abused, want the same things out of life. The Edward

In Miami Blues, *Susie (Jennifer Jason Leigh) "want[s] the fairy tale" as much as Vivian does, but she's forced to settle for significantly less from her handsome john, Junior (Alec Baldwin).*

Lewises are just better equipped to get those things through legal means. When Moseley asks Susie why she stayed with Junior, even after she knew he was still robbing and killing, she tells him that she focused on his good qualities. "He always ate everything I cooked for him, and he never hit me," she confides. Susie hoped for more from Junior, but she didn't expect it. And it's her low expectations of her lover that help her survive playing house with such a dangerous character.

The last we see of Susie, she is alone again with a shoebox of cash and meager booty. It's a downer ending compared to Vivian's, who is last seen playing a "princess...saved by the handsome prince" on her fire escape. But I know which one I'd tag as poised for a fall—and it's not sad little Susie, who is left standing on solid ground. She's on her own, but that shoebox is hers. Vivian's situation is much more precarious. The fairy tale claims that she's finally made it. She's got it all, but none of it is really hers.

Pretty Woman makes it very clear that money is power, and that all of the money (minus her $3,000 salary) still belongs to Edward Lewis. Vivian, unlike Shaw's Eliza, is as powerless in her happy ending as she was in the beginning of the tale. Less powerful, it could be argued.

Vivian and her best friend and sister of the streets, Kit (sassy Laura San Giacomo), pride themselves on being independent hookers. They have no pimps, and they call the shots with their tricks. "We say who, we say when, we say how much," is their motto. But if Vivian is swept away in a romantic solution controlled by Edward, then even the power to control her own sex work could be lost to her. She will be the exclusive property of a man who no longer needs to pay her anything.

I don't want to come off sounding too much like Emma Goldman's "The Traffic in Women" in a movie review of a romantic comedy. It is possible, I think, for a relationship between a man and a woman to be one of close (if not *completely* equal) power and veneration. It's just not possible in *this* relationship. It is too unequal from the start, and destined to remain so.

In Vivian's case, I wish Emma Goldman could have had the chance to set her down for a heart-to-heart. A wife "is paid less, gives much more in return in labor and care, and is absolutely bound to her master," Emma wrote in 1911 (quoting Havelock Ellis). Vivian's future may not be as bleak as that of women of Emma Goldman and Eliza Doolittle's generation, but this is still far from a fairy tale world for poor girls with sugar daddy sweetie-pies. Someone should tell Vivian that. And while they're at it, they should warn her not to sign a prenuptial agreement.

A GOOD MAN IS HARD TO FIND
Earth Girls Are Easy

The summer movie season of 1989 leaves us in little doubt that it is still "a man's world." Men? I am too generous. Hollywood is a world of overgrown, hyperactive boys who like to break things—including and especially other people. This isn't new. In fact, as far as I can tell, there will be very little that is new in any way this summer.

Name all the macho movie formulas you've seen a hundred times and hoped never to see again, multiply each by four, and you'll know all you need to know about this summer's movies. Beyond status quo, this stuck-in-a-rut Hollywood season should be branded by women as the Summer of the Repeat Offenders. Be warned, every cineplex marquee will offer a long list of male adventure sequels and tie-ins with nary a significant female lead in the bunch.

Indiana Jones the third is already packing them (but not me) in. And, sliding up the numerical scale, our screens will also be graced with *Ghostbusters II*, *Eddie and the Cruisers II*, and *Lethal Weapon 2*, *Karate Kid III* and *Leatherface: Texas Chainsaw Massacre III*, *Star Trek V* and *Nightmare on Elm Street 5*, *Friday the 13th Part VIII: Terror in Times Square*, and *License the Kill*, the umpteenth James Bond flick. For those who don't like sequels but like their movies to feel nonetheless as familiar as an old semi-automatic, Clint Eastwood will be making the (dying) days of numerous bad guys in *Pink Cadillac*, and in what promises to be the blockbuster and marketing bonanza of the summer, we will also witness the return of *Batman*, the comic book turned TV series turned movie.

Yes, the boys will be bullwhipping, slugging, shooting, kicking, slashing, and beaming one another up this summer. And the women will, for the most part, just stand there, showing cleavage and wide-open baby blues. And for their really big scenes female leads will either scream in terror or sigh

Recording artist, MTV star, and luscious looney-tune Julie Brown lampoons modern romance and southern California life-styles in the frothy film she co-wrote and co-stars in, Earth Girls are Easy.

"My Hero." Repeats of *Roseanne* and *Murphy Brown* beat that kind of trash any day.

It is precisely this kind of cinematic wasteland that makes *Earth Girls Are Easy* look like an oasis of enjoyment. It's fluff. Is it ever. But at least it's female-oriented fluff, more or less. This campy sci-fi semi-musical is the brainstorm of writer, actor, and luscious loony-tune, Julie Brown, and her writing partners (buddy) Charlie Coffey and (now ex-husband) Terrence E. McNally.

Brown, who can now be seen on her own MTV video show, "Just say Julie," was once banned from that station. The video for her novelty hit "The Homecoming Queen's Got a Gun" (a spoof of violent teen flicks in which Debbie, the sweet tiara-crowned teen queen, plays the mad killer) was considered too violent. This from a cable company which proudly broadcasts a steady videotic stream of women playing the sex-slave objects of heavy-metallic domination.

Brown's revenge was her next release off of her *Goddess in Progress* EP. In a number called "I Like 'Em Big and Stupid" Julie made her sassy argument for the efficacy of treating men as mindless sex objects. "Smart guys are nowhere/ They make demands," she complained. "Give me a moron/ With talented hands." Who needs a relationship when you can be "In love til we're done/ Then they're out in the hall"?

While she is far from the image of the traditional feminist, Julie Brown's funny floozy routine is just as far from being a traditional male fantasy. She'll flash a little T & A just as often as she flashes her knowing grin, but she is nobody's babycakes in the woods. She enjoys men on her own terms. And the trappings of pop prettiness are also exhilarating—as long as you let everyone in on the joke.

That same attitude is evident in a movie spin-off from another of Brown's early songs. *Earth Girls Are Easy* tells the story of a Southern California Val-Gal, played by Geena Davis, whose life is changed forever when a trio of furry aliens crash-lands in her swimming pool.

Valerie Dale (Davis) is a nice if naive manicurist who cares about her career. She reads *Nail Technology* and looks forward to a weekend at the Nail Expo and Cuticle Convention. But she is still an old-fashioned girl at heart. She's willing to sacrifice career opportunities and her own comfort if it means winning the approval and romantic attentions of her physician fiance, Ted (Charles Rocket). When Ted becomes distant, Valerie turns to her best friend and boss, Candy Pink (Julie Brown), for aid and advice. As proprietor of the Curl Up and Dye salon, Candy first suggests a total make-over.

Her "vixenizing" complete, Valerie hurries home to set up a by-the-book seduction of her man. But Ted, thinking her out of town at that nail convention, has his own seductions in mind. And the object of his seduction is a cutesy co-worker who is unaware that Ted has already pledged his troth to Valerie.

When her troth is trodden upon, and her romantic evening is ruined, the humiliated Valerie drives Ted from the house, pelting his head with sushi. She then wanders through the house destroying his favorite yuppie toys, singing a torch song that proclaims that she is "stronger than [he] knew."

It is the morning after the big break-up that her visitors from outer space make their big splash-down. That's when the fun really begins.

Earth Girls is a cartoon straight out of MTV land. It is filled with bright-colored silliness, and accompanied by a back-beat of rock music. How could it be else, when Julie Brown's influence is combined with that of director Julien Temple, best known for his work in the rock video field, and in the full-length rock-dominated films *Absolute Beginners* and *The Secret Policeman's Other Ball*? Some of the best scenes in the film are the musical numbers. My personal favorite is Ms. Brown's Beach Blanket Bimbo song, "'Cause I'm a Blond." She struts her way through Zuma Beach proclaiming golden tresses as the key to female success. It's the kind of bouncy burlesque that characterizes Brown's genial brand of satire.

The storyline itself holds fewer surprises as we watch Valerie agonize over whether to take Ted back. She realizes now that he is a scuzzoid (heck, he even has a George Bush sticker on the bumper of his Mercedes), but she despairs of finding anything better. That's where the faint but unmistakable message of this screwball flick comes in. In its own fractured way, the moral of this movie is that women shouldn't settle for less than their self-respect tells them they deserve. "You worked so hard to make Ted happy," Candy tells her. "Who's making *you* happy?"

Why, the captain of the aliens, Mac (Jeff Goldblum), of course. At least he will if he gets the chance. Mac is the strong, silent type, with soulful eyes and a "love touch" that won't quit. And he echoes Candy's encouragement for Val to think more about her own desires and less about pleasing a man. Who says all the good ones are taken? They're just living in another galaxy.

Earth Girls is another of those recent romantic comedies ("Man Bashers" a gentleman friend calls them) that seem to freely admit that human, heterosexual romance look like a miserable proposition for women. Valerie's solution is have her Mr. Right shipped in from another planet, but the film even acknowledges that a girl's odds aren't much better in outer space. Only one of the gents from Jhazzala is any noticeable improvement over his human counterparts. Wiploc (Jim Carrey) and Zeebo (Damon Wayans) are party animals who thoroughly enjoy the sunny hedonism of the San Fernando Valley. They'd much rather get down and get funky than get serious about anyone or anything. By the end of their stay on Earth, they are self-proclaimed "MTV scum."

Evidently, a good man is hard to find anywhere in the universe. And although we're led to believe that Valerie found one of the few floating around, the film never really convinces us that Val and Mac are a match made the heavens. The movie tried to get too much mileage out of the undeniable chemistry between its two co-stars. Davis and Goldblum are married in real life, and they are very sexy and sweet on screen together. But it was lazy of the filmmakers to rely on real-life affinity to carry their love story.

Talk about different worlds! Mac and Valerie have it all over Romeo and Juliet. Their chances for a successful long-term relationship may be slim, but Valerie's gentle and intelligent alien lover seems a significantly better risk as a love-partner than any of the local talent.

Candy is left with all those worthless Earth boys to sort through. But, as played by the sly Julie Brown, Candy faces a romantic future that's far from bleak. A good man may be hard to find, but Candy will surely enjoy the search. And she's not the kind to settle, either.

WOMEN DON'T STAND A *GHOST* OF A CHANCE

Ghost

Being dead isn't so bad, as long as your earthly remains contain the Y chromosome. Men are such valiant, forceful souls that even death doesn't faze them. They can still outwit the bad guys. They can still save the girl. They can still *get* the girl. They can, it seems, act upon their world in a manner almost exactly like their flesh and blood brothers. This summer's *Ghost* and the much less successful *Ghost Dad* are but the latest variations on the theme of male heroics from the hereafter.

Heaven Can Wait (1978), an inferior remake of *Here Comes Mr. Jordan* (1941), allowed a man killed before he was ready to die to take over a new body, and then another, and *live* happily ever after. *Kiss Me Goodbye* (1982), an inferior remake of *Dona Flor and Her Two Husbands* (1978) showed us that a woman can't get rid of a husband, even a dead one, until he's darn well ready to leave her. The TV show *The Ghost and Mrs. Muir* (1968-70), an inferior remake of the 1942 movie of the same name, starred an imperious sea captain, long dead, who still controlled his former household and who still retained so much sex appeal that a living woman couldn't help but fall in love with him. (Of course, Mrs. Muir's love for Captain Gregg may also prove the claim that the *idea* of loving a man is more satisfying than the physical reality, but this would be a less popular interpretation.)

I could think of several additional feel-good movies about male ghostly heroes. And I can recall at least one movie and TV series, *Topper*, in which a man and his *wife* are portrayed as fun-loving phantoms. But, for the life of me, I couldn't recollect a single movie about an active, heroic, sexy *woman* ghost.

A friend, who knows—and remembers—far more about film than I ever will, recollected better. He reeled off a list of a half-dozen films including *Topper Returns* (1941), *Portrait of*

Jennie (1948), and *Maxie* (1985). And yet, upon reflection, none of the movies he named really did the trick for me, although several were real treats to watch again.

Topper Returns comes the closest to presenting a female specter with sex appeal who has fun doing good. Gail Richards (the wise and saucy Joan Blondell) is no relation to Mr. and Mrs. Kerby of the earlier classic. But when she's murdered, she haunts the same fellow, Cosmo Topper (Roland Young). She wants "Toppy" to help her find her killer and protect a woman friend still in danger. Gail is a crackerjack detective. She does such a good job bopping the bad guys and rounding up clues, that you wonder what she needs Topper for. Dead, she's still a daring dame, filled with joie de morte, but she's given no love interest.

Maxie, a flapper starlet's ghost, has a much more active libido, but she doesn't have the 24-carat heart of Topper's friend. Maxie is thinking of no one but herself when she possesses the body of a present-day secretary, Jan (Glenn Close). The dead woman has the hots for Jan's librarian hubby (Mandy Patinkin), but views the woman she exploitively inhabits with contempt. It's never really funny when the greedy Maxie takes advantage of the desperate Jan. That's the main reason the film fails as screwball comedy.

Portrait of Jennie, a sentimental fantasy, is a much different story. It's an endearing movie about enduring love. A painter played by Joseph Cotten finds his muse in a young girl he meets in Central Park. The elusive Jennie (Jennifer Jones) grows up quickly to capture the artist's heart, but there is obviously something other-worldly about her. She's a ghost who moves forward in time to claim her one true love, but she can only tease him with eternity. She can't save herself from certain doom. And neither can he, although (heroic fellow that he is) he tries with all his might.

Jennie is a pure, beauteous, inspiration for a lonely painter. It's a passive role, but a sympathetic one. Too many women ghosts are like the shrew in last year's straight-to-cable fiasco, *She's Back*. She is Carrie Fisher, a gentrifying bitch who is killed by a band of thieves who invade her new home. She wants revenge, but is powerless to do anything but what she did in life, nag her poor (surviving) husband. She browbeats him into becoming a vigilante. But hubby doesn't want revenge. He just wants to get her off his case, and out of his new life.

Noel Coward's *Blithe Spirit* (1945), which is delightfully

funny in that nasty Cowardian way, provided an earlier and much more entertaining version of the wife who haunts to henpeck. Kay Hammond, as Elvira, is certainly an active ghost once she's been summoned up by Margaret Rutherford as Madame Arcati. But her power isn't exactly positive. Still attracted, and attractive, to her re-married husband (Rex Harrison), Elvira is willing to kill him to get him back. And while she's at it, she takes out her husband's second wife, too.

Coward's Spirit may be Blithe, but she is far from angelic. She is more interested in committing murders than solving them. For ghostly purity and valor combined with romantic appeal, you really do have to look to the men. Last winter's *Always*, an inferior remake of *A Guy Named Joe* (1943), was, like *Ghost*, a beyond-death romance between a noble dead guy and his live but lifeless girlfriend.

Mourning may become Electra, but it sure doesn't do much for Holly Hunter. As strong and competent and vibrant as her character is supposed to be, she spends most of the movie grieving over her dead pilot and being manipulated by his ghost. She isn't even allowed the independence of choosing her next lover for herself—Dreyfuss hand-picks his replacement in her affections. And when Holly is in danger, it is her dead lover who rescues her from certain death.

Ghost suffers from the same sexist dynamics as *Always*. But there is one key difference in the two movies. *Ghost* has genuine heart, and its two romantic leads, Demi Moore and Patrick Swayze, produce some real heat in their love scenes together. *Always* can't even manage that. Like most of Steven Spielberg's films, it is chock full of sentimentality but its heart is as cold as ice. Spielberg finds it easy to hide his emotional inadequacy when he works with latex alien puppets and little kids. It is harder to hide his cold-blooded nature when he works with human adult leads.

So *Ghost* is still worth seeing. It is a sappy, suspenseful grab-bag of movie formulas that somehow, despite the odds, works. Comic Relief is appropriately enough provided by Whoopi Goldberg in her best movie role since *Jumpin' Jack Flash*. Demi Moore is luminously sorrowful (and absolutely ravishing in her cropped haircut) as the sculptor, Molly Jensen, who loses her true love in a New York mugging. And that hunka-hunk of burning cowboy dancer, Patrick Swayze, has found his perfect role in *Ghost*.

The two emotions Swayze must regularly convey in this

film are lust (love, if you prefer) and confusion. These he handles with aplomb. Intellect and business acumen are a bit more difficult for him, but since his investment banker character, Sam Wheat, is only alive for the first twenty minutes of the movie, no one is likely to notice how absurd he appears trying to play a high-finance executive. The few viewers who do notice this absurdity will likely forget it during Swayze's scenes with Moore. The man knows how to play a love scene.

It astonishes me to say it, but first-time solo director Jerry Zucker seems to know how to film a love scene, as well. Zucker is best known for his collaborative writing, producing and directing with his brother David and their friend Jim Abrahams. The three are behind the tacky schtick humor of movies like *Airplane!* and *The Naked Gun: From the Files of Police Squad!* I've never been a fan of their work. Their gags (example: a man in a wheelchair is accidentally pushed at a baseball stadium so that he bumps, out of control, down a hundred stairs, crashes into a railing and plummets to the playing field) are the kind of thing that make you gag. Yet Zucker handles the schmaltz of his love story in *Ghost* with surprising sensitivity and a real erotic (not to mention romantic) charge.

As *Ghost* opens, Molly and Sam are leading charmed New York yuppie lives. They refurbish and accessorize their gorgeous Tribeca loft. They go to the theatre. They seduce one another at Molly's potter's wheel, and make love to the original 45 of the Righteous Brothers' "Unchained Melody" playing on their tres chic vintage jukebox. Life is good for these two, until death breaks them up in what appears to be a mugging that got out of hand. Sam's death isn't that simple. On the other hand, it's not that hard to spot the worst villain of the movie. And it's not the latino hood (Rick Aviles) who, fulfilling every WASP's worst urban nightmare, shoots Sam for not surrendering his wallet.

Tony Goldwyn, grandson of mogul Sam, and son of present day producer Sam Goldwyn, Jr., plays *Ghost*'s lead heavy, Carl Brunner, and he's great in the part. Goldwyn makes it clear that Carl's villainy is a just a Gucci-shod baby step past normal yuppie greed and selfishness. And his panic when he realizes how messy clean, white-collar crimes can get is just standard yuppie work stress turned up several notches. Goldwyn only found out about *Ghost* because his wife, production designer Jane Musky, let him read her script: a lucky break for him and for viewers.

Dead, but not gone, Sam is unable to communicate with

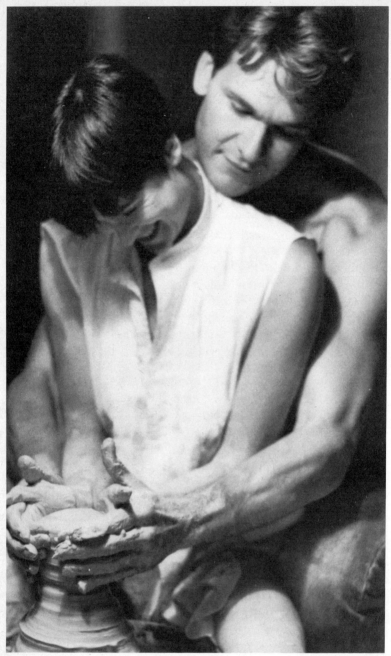

Down and dirty, but oh, so romantic! Molly (Demi Moore) and her lover, Sam (Patrick Swayze), work on centering their relationship at her potter's wheel, in a happy, early scene from Ghost.

Molly until he enlists the help of a psychic named Oda Mae Brown (Whoopi Goldberg). From a long line of clairvoyants, Oda Mae had always believed that the gift of her mother and grandmother had passed her over. Hearing the disembodied voice of Sam speak to her in the middle of a fake seance is a revelation. She isn't the charlatan she always believed herself.

Sam needs Oda Mae to help him protect Molly from the danger he fears will overtake her, but he still remains, at all times, the real hero of the piece. As in *Always*, although we are meant to perceive the female leads, Molly and Oda Mae, as intelligent and resourceful, they can't take care of themselves. They require the almost divine intervention and protection of a dead man.

Molly's weakness as a protagonist is so glaring because she. is forced to spend so much of her time moping around in mourning for Sam. This gives her an air of depressed passivity which would probably not be her character's normal state. Jerry Zucker admitted in a recent interview that he feared that Molly would look too weak, so he had a scene written and shot in which Molly tracks Sam's killer through the streets of Harlem. As racist as that scene no doubt would have played, we might consider it fortunate that Zucker decided to cut it from the final film. And yet, the fact that Zucker decided to cut as "unnecessary" the *one* scene that would have portrayed Molly as a dynamic, brave character tells us something about his attitude towards the women of *Ghost*.

Cutting Molly's big scene was a cop-out. This cowardly *Ghost* is further exposed in the filming of the movie's last love scene. In order that Sam may hold his lost love one last time, Oda Mae permits the ectoplasmic Sam to enter her body. Just when you think you're about to witness something amazing, a same sex, interracial love scene, the filmmakers wimp out in a big way. In violation of their own reality (the only other time Oda Mae is occupied by a ghost—also male—we see *her* body, not the spirit's), Zucker magically transforms Whoopi into Patrick Swayze.

Even if she doesn't get to kiss the girl, Whoopi does get the opportunity to strut her stuff as Sam's reluctant channel. Without Whoopi's comedic flair, Oda Mae could have easily come off as the glorified servant part that she is. Maybe it's only because of her marvelous performance, but the stereotyping of Whoopi's character bothered me less than the racist color symbolism of the quasi-religious Heaven/Hell special effects created by Available Light Limited for *Ghost*.

Those who die, like Sam, in a state of grace are eventually vaporized into white light by snowy globules that look like a celestial version of Lawrence Welk's "champagne" bubbles. The scoundrels of the piece, however, are immediately hauled off to Hades by a band of marauding hooded figures that are entirely—that's right—black. The racist implications of those goblins are almost as reprehensible as the spooked darky role Eddie "Rochester" Anderson was forced to play in *Topper Returns* half a century ago.

I loved the sentimental silliness of *Ghost*. It was the one film I saw this summer that I actually *enjoyed*. Yet I can't help but regret that Jerry Zucker and screenwriter Bruce Joel Rubin were unable to find the inventiveness or courage to go beyond the gender and racial stereotypes that have embodied the out-of-body comedies that came before them.

Even *Ghost Dad*, star vehicle for the ultimate patriarch, Bill Cosby, was more empowering of women than *Ghost*. Although it made the mistake of thinking that any audience could find it humorous that three children should be left orphaned and penniless, at least it gave Cosby's eldest daughter (Kimberly Russell) a key role in saving the day. Would that *Ghost* had given Molly and Oda Mae that much capability.

Hello Again (1987) is still the closest we've come to having a film about a heroic woman ghost. Shelley Long is brought back to life by the love of her sister, does good for herself and others, and makes a new life with a new lover. She's not exactly a ghost, and that's fine. I don't want women to be dead heroes. I want for us to be heroes of our own *lives*.

HERE'S TO YOU,
MRS. ROBINSON

White Palace and *Tune in Tomorrow . . .*

Predatory, yet at the same time pathetic: this is how Hollywood has viewed older women in love with younger men. The double-whammy of sexism and ageism made for some particularly damaging images of women on the screen—images that have mirrored the attitudes of American society.

We've always expected a woman "of a certain age" (say, 35 and over) to be safe and sexless. Her role is maternal (or grandmotherly) and is strictly defined. She should be a quiet, comfortable personage with no needs—sexual or otherwise—of her own. She lives to serve others. Silently, if at all possible.

Mothers who have needs or desires, and vocalize them, are made to look bad in movies. (For an example, think of any kvetching mother in a Woody Allen film. The short he did for *New York Stories* last year, "Oedipus Wrecks," is a concentrated version of his usual mother-hating.) And women, mothers or not, whose needs include sexual desires have been dealt with even more harshly.

In film, a sexual woman above the age of 35 is considered a freak. Men her age, husbands included, are no longer interested in sex with an "old" woman. They want younger women—and get them. And although a man who "robs the cradle" might be considered a "dirty old man," there is more admiration than abhorrence in the label. Society views a 70-year-old man's affair with a 20-year-old woman as an enviable declaration of his power, and therefore, his potency.

Woe to the woman who tries the same thing. To be sexual with younger men has been, according to Hollywood, a female sin punishable by death or dishonor. There have been only rare exceptions over the years. When Mae West encouraged Cary Grant, a much younger man, to come up and see her sometime, she wasn't interested in baking him a batch of brownies. Mae was sexy, but her blatant bawdiness was never threatening because her come-hither looks were played for comedy. And besides, Mae West got to break the rules governing female comportment because Mae West was a law unto herself.

Her screen sisters achieved less autonomy. How sad that right after being dumped by Larry Olivier (for a younger woman), the ailing but beautiful Vivien Leigh ended up playing in *The Roman Spring of Mrs. Stone* (1961). Leigh's character, Karen Stone, is a once-great actress washed up at the age of 45, a "time when Mother Nature catches up with all you old gals." She tries to escape the professional humiliation of a failed play by running away to Rome with her (sweet, kind) *older* husband, who has a heart attack and dies on the plane before they even land.

Karen Stone is left to live an "almost posthumous existence" in Rome until a pimping Contessa (played with malevolent relish by the divine Lotte Lenya) introduces her to a young Italian gigolo, Paolo (Warren Beatty). Karen isn't a complete sap. For a while the plot consists of a "Who's Zoomin' Who" power struggle between the "proud and arrogant woman" and her greedy young lover. But since Hollywood seldom allows a woman her pride, we know that Mrs. Stone will eventually surrender completely to her pathetic need for young Paolo. When she does, he abandons her for a younger woman.

In the movie's final scene, on the same night as her humiliation by Paolo, Karen invites into her home, and presumably into her bed, a young man who lives on the street (or, rather, on the Spanish Steps) outside her pallazzo. This scruffy "boy" is a sinister as well as sensuous figure, and we are led to believe that this young stud will "slit" Mrs. Stone's "throat," rob her, and leave her to die. Karen admits as much to Paolo, earlier in the film. And in that last, menacing shot, as the boy approaches, we hear again (in case we missed it the first time) her words to Paolo that she expects such an end, and will welcome it.

Not all the women who sleep with men young enough to be their sons die for their sins, but most of them live to wish they had. Remember that comedy classic of youthful male disaffection, the early Mike Nichols film that baby-boomers made such a big hit, *The Graduate* (1967)? The film's female lead, Mrs. Robinson (Anne Bancroft), was a villain made infamous on screen and in song. A self-proclaimed "neurotic" and "alcoholic" who seduces the son of her husband's business partner on a sadistic and self-destructive whim, Mrs Robinson is, like Mrs. Stone, incapable of inspiring real affection in her young lover. Ben (Dustin Hoffman) is at first terrified of her. Later, he is thoroughly disgusted by this "broken down alcoholic" he regularly goes to bed with. So much so that he courts her daughter out of spite.

Ben may be a self-centered, sleazy little twerp, but he is also the undisputed hero of this movie. When he and Mrs. Robinson declare war, there is no doubt who will win. When he made off with the beautiful Katharine Ross, right under the nose of her furious mother, Young Benjamin won the admiration of a generation. Mrs. R. loses everything she cares about to that callous *Graduate*; her marriage, her daughter, and her dignified upper-middle-class social standing.

And she, we know, deserves to suffer. To wear jungle print lingerie, to still want sex (especially with a younger man) at *her* age is a violation of nature, as defined by Hollywood. At least, until now.

Imagine my surprise, when two films in the same month show women who want sex—and find it, joyfully, with younger men—as positive, passionate heros. Could it be that now that the baby-boomers are entering middle-age we see things a little differently? Now that we are closer in age to Mrs. Robinson than to Ben, are we, perhaps, a little less eager to dismiss a 40-year-old woman still interested in sex as a "sick and disgusting person"? The jury's still out. But these two entertaining new romances are certainly a hopeful sign.

White Palace, the steamier of the two, is set in present-day St. Louis. It is a love story between a 27-year-old yuppie advertising executive and a 43-year-old burger-joint waitress. Life has been tough on Nora (Susan Sarandon), but she is tough enough to take what ever life hands out and still want more. She may not have seen much of it, but Nora knows how to fully experience joy. Max Baron (James Spader) has had an easier life, but is less resilient. It's two years since an auto accident killed Max's young wife, Janey, and he is still leading a celibate life, emotionally isolated from even family and friends.

Perhaps it's the upheaval of Janey's death that turned Max into an obsessive-compulsive type. More likely, he's always been the kind of guy who can't leave his living room until all the tassels on his oriental rug lay perfectly straight. He's also the kind of guy who would drive miles out of his way to raise a stink at a fast-food restaurant when his big, bachelor-party order is shorted by a few burgers.

That's how Max and Nora meet-cute, although neither of them thinks the other is very adorable at the time. But when Nora sees Max come into her favorite blue-collar tavern later that same night, she makes her move. Max rebuffs it, and when Nora speculates that he must have been recently dumped, he puts on a tragic face and tells her his wife is dead. He expects pity, or an apology, at least. What he gets is a belly-laugh. She lost a son not too long ago, and has no pity for Max. Nor for herself. "What can you do?" she asks, philosophically. "The world spins around."

A capricious universe has clearly brought these two together for some purpose, and Nora thinks she knows what it is. When Max, too drunk to drive home, lies sleeping on her sofa, she makes her move for a second time. Her seduction releases a flood of emotions and sexual desire Max has never before known. Max is at first swept away. Then, reality sets in. What do these two, separated by a generation and the chasm of class, really have in common besides sex?

That's what the rest of the girl-gets-boy, girl-loses-boy, girl-gets-boy-back-again plot is supposed to tell us, but it never really does. Screenwriters Ted Tally and Alvin Sargent spend so much time showing us Odd Couple contrasts in the house-keeping habits of the two lovers (He's a neat-freak, she's a total slob), that they never get to the more important issues. And the big break-up at Thanksgiving dinner never makes a lot of sense. Nora over-reacts in a situation she knew ahead of time would be difficult, and Max does nothing to make things easier for her. As for Max's family, each is a stereotype of an upper-class Jew, and their group portrait creates a cumulative impression that is unmistakably anti-Semitic.

The film's view of Nora comes dangerously close to elitism, too. Although she is braver, stronger, sexier, and more honest than Max (so much so that you wonder why she'd waste herself on this guy), there is much in her portrayal that reinforces the negative stereotype that poor women are sexpot slatterns. It is easy to view Nora as earthy, because she is one step up from dirt. But since Mr. Spader is forced to play yet another of his stereotypically tight-assed yuppies, one shouldn't take Nora's character too much to heart, I suppose. It's stock characters all around. And a ludicrous ending, to boot.

White Palace stands up as an enjoyable film, despite its

Promise her anything, but don't *give her a DustBuster. Anal-retentive yuppie Max Baron (James Spader) learns his lesson the hard way when he falls for Nora Baker (Susan Sarandon) in* White Palace.

many failings, because of the sensitive and sensuous direction of Luis Mandoki (*Gaby—A True Story*) and fine performances by the principal and support players. Eileen Brennan is exquisite in her small role as Nora's psychic older sister, Judy. And, without idealizing her a whit, Susan Sarandon makes Nora a vital and sympathetic woman—a survivor, and then some. Her Nora Baker is no Mrs. Robinson. She is the "aggressor" in her relationship with Max, but she never preys upon him. She deserves all the joy her relationship with Max brings her. The only question is whether Max deserves Nora.

Sarandon is the right age to play Nora, but she may be too thin and beautiful. Even carrying the twenty "extra" pounds she gained while pregnant with her son Jack, born just prior to filming, she is still a far cry from the small-breasted, large-rumped heroine of Glenn Savan's novel. But at least Sarandon's "crow's feet" are there in all their glory. She may be gorgeous, but she is still, clearly and proudly, a woman in her middle years.

Playing a woman of 36 (she is really 42), Barbara Hershey is also a woman in love with a younger man in her new film,

Tune in Tomorrow. And, like Nora, Hershey's character, Julia, is a vibrant and sympathetic woman who deserves her happiness with her 21-year-old "nephew," Martin (Keanu Reeves).

Although the setting and character names have been changed, *Tune in Tomorrow* captures the spirit of the autobiographical novel by the Peruvian novelist, Mario Vargas Llosa, on which it was based. *Aunt Julia and the Scriptwriter* tells the story of the teen-aged Mario, who fell in love with his worldly-wise divorced Aunt (by marriage) Julia, and married her. Such a love affair would turn a few heads today, but it must have been even more shocking in the early '50s, when both the novel and the film are set. Yet the story is no operatic tragedy: it is a light-hearted and romantic fable of love conquering all.

The soap opera aspect of this particular love story is no accident. The tribulations and eventual happily-ever-after of Julia and Martin's relationship reflects the rather fantastical serial that plays on the New Orleans radio station where Martin works as a fledgling newswriter. And the mischievous cupid of Julia and Martin's love story is the fabulously eccentric writer behind the soap opera, Pedro Carmichael (Peter Falk).

Tune in Tomorrow is Peter Falk's movie. Few grizzled pantaloons could wear a French maid's outfit with as much sincerity as this gentleman. Falk's unique look and idiosyncratic acting style are perfect for this dedicated (and not a little demented) artist. Hershey captures her character's brazen insecurity well. And Mr. Reeves (best known for playing airheads or drugged-out dudes in films like *Bill & Ted's Excellent Adventure* and *I Love You to Death*) is absolutely charming and surprisingly effective in the role of the innocent, romantic young Martin. But as good as the performances of the two lovers are, and as engaging as their love story is, their true-to-life characters pale next to the larger-than-life Falk.

But then, *Tune in Tomorrow* is meant to be more than a simple love story. It is an exploration of the cannibalistic relationship of life and art. "Eat or be eaten," Pedro advises young Martin. And Carmichael devours everything and everyone around him to create his colorful melodramas. Read by one set of distinguished character actors, including Richard B. Shull, Pedro's soap opera takes on a life of its own once it reaches the airwaves. The characters of "Kings of the Garden District" come alive, played by several well-known actors, including Elizabeth McGovern, Hope Lange, Peter Gallagher, and John Larroquette.

Tune in Tomorrow tells the story of a young man (Keanu Reeves), who courts and marries his aunt (Barbara Hershey), with the help and hindrance of a cupid-playing scriptwriter (Peter Falk).

Against the backdrop of Pedro's flamboyant cast of high-society screwballs, Julia and her young nephew-lover seem shockingly normal. And so they are. The family may view Julia as a "fallen woman," but she is an angel to Martin, and his perfect life-partner. Still, as rebellious and unconventional as Julia has been in her life, she worries about what others will think of them together. She can already hear people saying "She's too old for him." Martin has no worries. He is confident in their happiness and eager to begin their artistic life together on the Left Bank. "In Paris, *all* the women are older than the men," Martin assures her. "Good for them!" Julia replies.

And that is the attitude of both *White Palace* and *Tune in Tomorrow*. Good for a woman who can find a good man with whom she can share good sex. If the man is a generation younger, so much the better for both the relationship *and* the sex.

It is commonly-held belief that the sexual peaks of men and women occur more than a decade apart, with a man in his teens, and with a woman in her thirties. If there is any truth to this, then "May-December" (although "May-August" would be a more appropriate term) relationships between women and men have a much better chance for sexual compatibility.

Hollywood preaches the opposite because it has a tradition of ageist misogyny to uphold. A man owns his sexuality for as long as he lives. A woman never owns hers. Her sexuality is also a male possession, assigned to her by the patriarchy for as long as her body meets the male criteria for beauty, or for as long as she can bear a man a son. An openly sexual older woman defies the male definition of female sexuality. She is no dewy virgin and no baby machine. She is a woman of experience and as such she is a woman of power.

And that is why Ben, Mike Nichols, and all the other lads of Hollywood view her as a "vagina dentata" with a partial plate. They are so terrified of "Mrs. Robinson" that they want to destroy her. Well, *White Palace* and *Tune in Tomorrow* view the "older" woman who dares to love a younger man much differently. Nora and Julia are warm, attractive, passionate women. They are rebels and romantic heroes. Max and Martin are lucky to be allowed into their lives and into their beds.

That's big change—and a hopeful one. But it's only a starting place. When a movie audience is encouraged to view a small-breasted and large-rumped woman as beautiful and sexy, and when we are allowed to see women of 60 or 70 as beautiful and sexually vital, then we will have made *real* progress.

A while back, *People Magazine* gave Sean Connery their yearly cover award, "The Sexiest Man Alive." He was just shy of 60. We're a long ways from the day when a woman of almost 60 could be called "The Sexiest Woman Alive," but films like *White Palace* and *Tune in Tomorrow* are a step in the right direction. As we baby-boomers become elders, who knows? The day may come when the Karen Stones of Hollywood will no longer look forward to having their throats slit in the night. Until that day comes, here's to *you*, Mrs. Robinson.

Isn't it romantic?
(If not, why not?)

· ·

Chances Are, See You in the Morning, and *Skin Deep*

I'm not quite sure when it happened, but at some point in the last twenty years the Romantic Comedy died. The ghost of its former self is still with us. There are still movies made and released that are labelled "romantic comedy," but these pale imitators are seldom either romantic or funny. And they rarely succeed as film entertainment either. It's no wonder that violent action films and sick schtick comedies are doing boffo box office when one of the mainstays of Hollywood formulas has fallen on such hard times.

In the old days, the lead characters in romantic comedies were fond and funny madcaps who loved life and each other. Think of Cary Grant, Katharine Hepburn, Irene Dunne, Jimmy Stewart, Carole Lombard, and all the other marvelous performers in their now-classic comedic roles. Whatever the pairing of stars, the result was the same. They always played a couple who were *Made for Each Other.* It didn't matter what ludicrous misunderstandings or familial obstacles were strewn in their path, we knew that nothing could really keep them apart. Both guy and gal were swell kids who were fated to find eternal bliss in one another's arms.

The exuberant energy and head-over-heels optimism of those classic romantic comedies was something the audience could count on. The formula might call for the boy to lose the girl, but such a loss could only be temporary. This is true of even those "sophisticated" romantic comedies like *The Philadelphia Story* and *The Awful Truth* in which the couple divorces in the first reel.

In the latter, lesser-known movie, Cary Grant and Irene

Dunne split in a pique of mutual distrust and jealousy, but we know their divorce won't last. All that's required to effect a reconciliation is for the two contrary lovebirds to get stuck in a country cabin together. Spontaneous combustion occurs. When they fall into bed together (off- screen, of course) at the very moment their divorce is supposed to become final, we know they'll be loving and true for the rest of their lives.

Today, even in a so-called comedy, audiences find it almost impossible to accept that kind of plot. We are too used to seeing couples splitting up and staying split. Divorces stick. Marriages (and other less formalized love partnerships) don't. Our romantic miseries are no longer a source of hilarious amusement because they are all too real and raw. We believe in hurt more than happiness, in most things, but especially in romance. And—this is the real clincher—we no longer think of men and women as natural allies ("You and me against the world, Babe!"), but rather as something closer to natural enemies.

It is not just feminists who see men in this adversarial light. Yet, somehow, it is the women's movement which has most often taken the rap for causing the rift between men and women, thus prompting societal disarray and all these messed-up movie formulas. Blaming feminism for it all is preposterous. Also true. Feminism, like a score of other social variables—the rising divorce rate, the public exposure (primarily by feminists) of domestic violence and child abuse, the "sexual revolution" of the sixties and seventies, the growing fears about sexually transmitted diseases—convinced us, in the years since we baby-boomers came of age, that relationships between the sexes are no laughing matter and they usually aren't even a close approximation of happily ever after.

How can contemporary romantic comedy do other than fail miserably? Realizing that they have a much harder sell, but hating to abandon a formula that worked so well for so long, filmmakers now know that for a romantic comedy to win over a cynical '80s audience it must fuel itself on emotions that have little to do with moons and June. While the most successful romantic comedies of the old days really were about the irresistible attraction between the male and female leads, the most effective romantic comedies of today aren't really about boy-girl romance at all.

Consider the romantic comedies of the last couple of years and you'll see what I mean. The Academy award-winning *Moonstruck* is really about the lure of a tightly-knit Italian family, not about the at-first-sight love of Cher for her one-handed baker brother-in-law-to-be. Similarly, Joan Micklin Silver's *Crossing Delancey* is about Amy Irving coming to love her Jewish heritage (symbolized by a pickle merchant from the old neighborhood) as much as she loves her dear bubbe.

Baby Boom and *Overboard* are about women falling in love, but it's motherhood they really fall for. The men are secondary attractions. In *Mystic Pizza* there are three boy-girl romances, but the focal relationship in the movie is that between the three female best-friend protagonists. And *Working Girl*, the most recent "hit romantic comedy," is really about women trying to make it in the business world (by tearing down other women). The romantic relationship between Melanie Griffith and Harrison Ford is given short shrift. A wise decision, since it makes even less sense than the rest of the film, and as a sexual chemistry experiment it doesn't sizzle, it fizzles.

When current romantic comedies attempt to span the emotional breach between men and women, they very often do so by fudging the humanity of at least one of the romantic partners. In *Date with an Angel*, Michael E. Knight drops his human fiance for Emmanuelle Beart, the angel sent to take him to heaven. In *Made in Heaven*, new soul Kelly McGillis and old soul Timothy Hutton fall in love up Above, and then have to try to find one another again on Earth. In Susan Seidelman's *Making Mr. Right*, Ann Magnuson finds the perfect man, only he's not a man, he's an android she can mold to her own romantic specifications. In *Big*, Elizabeth Perkins falls in love with a real, live, human male, Tom Hanks. But Tom is really only an eleven-year-old boy (hence his genuine sweetness and vulnerability) whose adult appearance is the product of a magic spell. A couple of years earlier, Mr. Hanks, then the grown and human one, found true love with a mermaid (Daryl Hannah) in *Splash*.

Modern movies which take a more traditional and completely human approach have the most problems. Like *Working Girl*, *Broadcast News* works well as a tale of yuppie ambitions, but its romantus interruptus approach to love (women and men still feel romantic about one another but can't seem to get it together long enough to go to bed, much less achieve a lasting relationship) makes it a less than satisfying romantic comedy. Films like *Casual Sex?* and *Cross My Heart* end happily, but they so faithfully enumerate the dangers and dishonesty of modern romance that you wonder why all the characters don't shake hands, wish one another luck (or, more likely, a speedy trip to Hades), and go off to lead solitary lives of celibate contemplation on a far-off mountaintop.

The three "romantic comedies" I've seen in the last three weeks try to breathe life into their dead formula in different ways. The most successful of the three is, as you might expect, the most old-fashioned. *Chances Are*, a comeback picture for the beauteous and talented Cybill Shepherd, is a throw-back of a movie from the opening credits signature song by Johnny Mathis onwards.

An example of the other-worldly romances mentioned earlier, *Chances Are* is the story of Corinne Jeffries (Shepherd), who watches Louie, the husband she adores, die in a traffic accident on their first anniversary. She never recovers romantically from her loss. Although in the 23 years that follow she leads a happy life as a mother and a museum curator at the Smithsonian, Corinne has never loved another man. She never even sleeps with the docile and completely devoted best friend of her dead husband (played by Ryan O'Neal), although he has

Is it better the second time around—when your dead husband returns in a new, younger body (Robert Downey, Jr.)? Corinne (Cybill Shepherd) looks eager to find out, in this shot from Chances Are.

patiently waited all these years for her to recognize his supportive friendship as true love.

The stalemate—we know, after all, that a woman cannot be
truly happy without a man—of Corinne's life is broken, not by
her own choices or actions, but by the return of her dead
husband in the body of a Yalie classmate of her grown daughter,
Amanda (Mary Stuart Masterson), named Alex (Robert Downey,
Jr.). Because hers is a love that has been frozen in time since the
mid-'60s, her romance with Alex/Louie suffers from none of
the bitter realities of an eighties relationship. By creating a
sentimental time-warp, sisters Randy and Perry Howze (*Mystic
Pizza*) managed to write a script that works as a romantic
comedy, even as it stretches our credulity to the bursting point.

See You in the Morning, another new romantic comedy, is
much more believable as a representation of modern love-
lives, but it is therefore not half as effective as escapist fun.
Writer/Director Alan J. Pakula is one of those brave souls who
tries to continue the tradition of the romantic comedy and still
explore some of the sticky issues of modern man-woman relations.

Although he is best known for *Klute* and *Sophie's Choice*,
Pakula also directed one of the better romantic comedies of the
last decade, *Starting Over*, in which Burt Reynolds dumped his
new love, Jill Clayburgh, for his old love, Candice Bergen, but
then changed his mind and won back the heartbroken Clayburgh
with a couch from Bloomie's.

See You in the Morning is described as "a romantic comedy
about renewed relationships." Like *Starting Over* it is about the
once-burned overcoming their shyness and beginning again
with new partners. Both parties bring with them a lot of
emotional baggage and two children each.

He is Larry (Jeff Bridges), a shrink who divorced his fickle,
high-fashion model wife (Farrah Fawcett). She is Beth (Alice
Krige), a homemaker and sometimes photographer whose
selfless dedication to her role of helpmate wasn't enough to
keep her first husband (David Dukes) from committing suicide.
She and her two children (Drew Barrymore, Lukas Haas) are
still trying to heal the guilt and grief when she meets Larry.

Pakula's film acknowledges that Dad/Man-loves-Mom/
Woman is a far more complicated romantic equation than boy-
loves-girl. He explores his theme of families getting married
with much more honesty and sensitivity than those cheery
sitcomish '60s films like *With Six You Get Eggroll* and *Yours, Mine
and Ours*. And Pakula's cast gives uniformly fine performances.

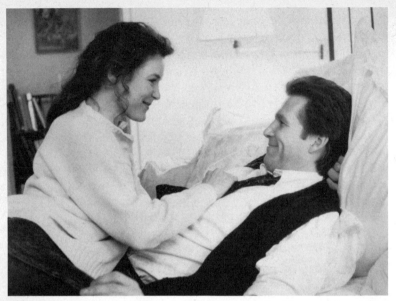

Taking a break from the hard work of blending a family, Mommy-woman Beth (Alice Krige) shares a loving moment with Larry (Jeff Bridges), the new Daddy-man in her life, in See You in the Morning.

If Mr. Pakula cheats his subject matter at all, and I fear that he does, it is in making his two leads a little too saintly. I can accept Beth as a self-sacrificing woman who has trouble acting on her own needs and desires. I've known plenty of women like her. But I have never known a man like Pakula's hero, Larry.

Larry is cheerful, gentle, understanding, and romantic. He pushes Beth to be more ambitious and independent and bends over backwards to build relationships with Beth's children. Talk about being in touch with your feelings—Larry not only knows exactly what *he's* feeling and why, he also recognizes, understands, and can analyze in the most sympathetic manner possible, all the secrets in everybody else's hearts and minds. I know he's supposed to be a psychiatrist, but this guy is still way too good to be true.

I think that Pakula originally meant to be more realistic in his representation of his hero than he ends up being in the final film. When Sidney (Linda Lavin), a mutual friend, first introduces Beth to Larry, she describes Beth as a "wonderful woman," and Larry as a "shit," and concludes that they'd be perfect for one another. There are occasional comments and scene snippets that imply that Larry did indulge in some macho lady-killing right after his divorce, and that he is having trouble committing himself to Beth, but we never see any of his negative traits. The Larry we see has no "shit" in him. He is saintly through and through.

Pakula should, I think, get points for showing men the way they should be rather than the way the dear creatures so often are. His efforts to be realistic and, at the same time, affirming, are worthy of praise. Although he expresses more admiration for his own sex than will seem necessary or believable to most women in the audience (while failing to fully develop the character of Beth), we gals have to make allowances in a semi-autobiographical screenplay by a man. Pakula's I'm-Okay-You're-Okay optimism sure beats the cynicism of much of what passes for romantic comedy.

For a while Pakula takes the high road in portraying relationships between the sexes (so high a road that the comedy half of his formula suffers), more directors take a lower road. So low it's subterranean! One of the kings of the low-road romantic comedy is Blake Edwards. His screenplays are, they say, also autobiographical. His movies certainly focus on his male leads, while wasting little time on the development of his female characters (who are usually only burlesque-style babes meant to be ogled and/or ridiculed). But Edwards also doesn't bother idealizing his male hero. On the contrary, he takes great joy in making his romantic male lead as big a sleazeball as possible.

Edwards isn't alone in this. It's possible, in fact, that his successes with films like *10* (about a man who dumps his beautiful, talented, and devoted lover—played by Edwards' real-life wife, Julie Andrews—to chase after a young girl he sees for the first time on the way to her wedding) and *Micki & Maude* (about a bigamist who marries and impregnates two women) is the major inspiration for what I call the Repulsive Romeo School of Romantic Comedy.

Increasingly, the men in romantic comedies are such jerks that it makes your skin crawl to think of any woman entering into, much less staying in, a relationship with them. *The Pick-Up Artist*, *Surrender*, and *Blind Date* (also by Edwards) are just a few recent examples. But Edwards' new movie, *Skin Deep*, brings the school to an all-time low.

Skin Deep is the story of Zach (John Ritter), an extremely successful author, currently suffering from writer's block, who bides his time waiting for his muse to return by drinking anything alcoholic and boinking anything with breasts. The film opens with the following scene: Zach's long-suffering wife walks into her bedroom only to find an attempted murder in progress. Zach's mistress is trying to shoot him to death for seducing their mutual hairdresser.

If that scene doesn't sound all that funny, you probably will want to skip the movie's most famous scene in which two naked men with erections wearing nothing but glow-in-the-dark condoms fight over a naked woman in a dark room. As I've said, this is not exactly sophisticated or cerebral humor. Nor is it romantic in the least. Nor will it appeal to any self-respecting woman.

I think Edwards enjoys making his hero as piggish as possible. It's as if he wants to tell women that they should love and accept men no matter how exploitive and uncaring they are. In *Skin Deep*, Zach gets to compulsively sleep around, drink like a fish, injure and maim people's pet dogs, and in every way

Would you buy a used marriage from this man? Skin Deep's *Alex (Alyson Reed) looks like she's buying every word issuing from the mouth of her alcoholic, sex-addict ex-hubby, Zach (John Ritter).*

act like a social menace. And he *still* gets a happy ending. This guy's on a roll, in more than hay. In the last reel, he cleans up his act (so he says) and writes a best-seller about it. He then invites all the women he seduced and abandoned to come to his book party. Since none of them hold a grudge, they all show up—including his ex-wife, who promptly takes him back.

Edwards has made the romantic comedy a tool of woman-hating backlash. As such, it doesn't work. But Edwards's more agreeable modern counterparts don't make movies that work much better. We women are in touch with our anger and disenchantment with man-loving. And men have never been out of touch with their anger towards women—especially the uppity variety. It's not a beneficial climate for romantic comedy.

As much as I love those wonderful old movies, and the rare modern film (e.g., *Roxanne*—based on a nineteenth-century source) that brings back the old warmth, I fear that romantic comedy will never be the workable, truly enjoyable movie formula it once was. For it to be the loving and funny entertainment we remember from days past, we will all have to buy back into that treacherous old romantic mythology lock, stock, and barrel. Or else women and men will, in real life, have to get to a new trusting place with one another where there's less anger and more love and respect. Backwards or forwards. Either is a tough journey. And I'm not holding my breath that we're going to get there any time soon.

The Lost Race of Hollywood

THIS BROKEN HOME, SOUTH AFRICA
A World Apart

Imagine that you are a daughter whose relationship with a dearly loved mother is the source of much conflict and pain as well as sustenance. (Chances are, you will have no trouble imagining that one.) Imagine too that as a child you often felt shut out and abandoned by your parents, but that you were stricken with guilt when you expressed your anger and resentment, because your parents were sainted soldiers in a righteous struggle, and time spent away from you was devoted to the greater good. Finally, imagine that just as you and your mother are beginning to work through the old hurts to find a loving peace with one another, the evil government she had resisted all of her life tracked her down in exile and killed her.

Heavy. This is *very* heavy emotional baggage we're talking about here. This is the personal history Shawn Slovo carries with her.

Slovo's mother was the South African activist and writer, Ruth First, the first white woman imprisoned under the "90-Day Law" (which allowed the South African regime, during the savage suppression campaign of the early '60s—detention laws have since worsened—to lock up any person for 90 days at a time without charge, trial, or legal counsel). Exiled with her three daughters to Britain in 1964, Ruth First continued her political work and writing against apartheid.

In 1979, she returned to Africa to work and teach at the Center for African Studies at Eduardo Mondlane University in Maputo, Mozambique. She was just completing a study of Mozambican migrant workers who by economic necessity are forced to work the gold and diamond mines of South Africa when a parcel bomb sent by the South African security police found her in her university office, and cut her down at the age of 57.

It was Shawn Slovo's need to come to terms with her relationship with her murdered mother that compelled her to writer her first screenplay, *A World Apart*. And what a screenplay it is! It is, at once, the best feature film Americans have yet seen about the horrors of apartheid, and one of the finest explications of the mother-daughter relationship I have ever witnessed on screen.

As the film opens, Gus Roth (Jeroen Krabbe), a handsome, smiling family man in a business suit, is leaving his comfortable middle-class suburban Johannesburg home on a "work" trip of which her can tell nothing to his inquisitive thirteen-year-old daughter, Molly (Jodhi May). As he drives away in the darkness, after a last kiss from his wife, Diana (Barbara Hershey), it is the last they and we will see of him for the course of the movie.

This is very much a *Little Women* kind of story. The male head of the household is off being noble elsewhere, leaving the

A World Apart, *a brilliant and poignant first screenplay by Shawn Slovo (right), also represents the auspicious feature film directorial debut of noted cinematographer Chris Menges (left).*

women of the clan to carry on. Of course, it has been said that Louisa May Alcott, in her autobiographical novel, sent her irresponsibly Transcendental daddy off to war because she couldn't (in her secret heart) stand the guy. Shawn Slovo's attitude towards her father appears to be more genuinely affectionate. The real-life Gus Roth, Joe Slovo, is an even more famous South African radical than Ruth First and has lived in semi-underground exile during much of his daughter's life. (Living in Zambia, high on South Africa's hit list, he is chair of the outlawed South African Communist Party, and for many years was chief of staff for the military wing of the African National Congress [ANC]. Still with the ANC, he is the only caucasian member of their executive committee.)

In *A World Apart*, Dad is a good guy who's just not there. That leaves Mom to keep the family together. But unlike the idealized, hearth-loving, self-sacrificing Marmee of Alcott, Diana Roth is no Super-Mom, and has little energy or interest in the domestic life. She is too busy writing exposes of government atrocities and reporting on black worker resistance to spend her time planning toddler birthday parties or coaching her eldest daughter for a flamenco contest.

Birthday parties and dance competitions are meaningless indulgences compared to the struggle for basic freedoms and survival native black Africans face under apartheid. But such frills *are* important symbols of well-being and normalcy for a white, middle-class girl. And that, despite the political activism of her leftist parents, is exactly what young Molly is.

Molly's life is filled with incongruities and contradictions, as are the lives of all whites pampered and protected under South Africa's haywire racist social system. Though Molly is taught (unlike her schoolmates) to treat blacks as equals, her household nevertheless includes (like those of her schoolmates) several black servants. Dependent on the family's black maid, Elsie (Linda Mvusi), for much of the mothering the politically active Diana is unable to provide, the sensitive Molly fully realizes Elsie's own maternal heartbreak at being forced, by law, to abandon her own children to a motherless life back in her "township" in order to work in isolation for a white family to earn the money to feed them.

It's a crazy world that keeps a child from her mother. And Molly's turn has arrived. Although occasionally indignant and spiteful over her mother's benign neglect, the lives of Molly and her sisters Jude (Merav Gruer) and Miriam (Carolyn

Diana Roth (Barbara Hershey, center) fights apartheid in print, and even in the streets. Here, she challenges South Africa's police with daughter Molly (Jodhi May) standing at her side.

Clayton-Cragg) are still relatively placid and happy, despite the absence of their father, until the day the South African police arrive to tear the house apart. They confiscate most of the books and papers within, and haul Diana to jail under the 90-Day Law. The brutality of apartheid has the power to tear mother from child, and to cut off a child—in this case, Molly—from her childhood.

With her mother not distant, but *gone*, Molly finds it much harder to hang on to any sense of normalcy or safety. Her parents are vilified in the press as traitors to the Afrikaner regime. Her classmates ostracize her, and her best friend forsakes her for more socially acceptable playmates. She becomes a 13-year-old outcast, orphaned by her parents' political dedication.

Meanwhile, Diana is also an outcast, isolated week after week in solitary confinement. She is allowed no contact with friends or other prisoners, no exercise, no writing materials, and no book but the bible. Her only respite from the cruel solitude comes when she is taken, at all hours of the night and day, for interrogation.

Muller (David Suchet) is her principal interrogator. The perfect inquisitor, he is a soft-spoken gentleman with no heart. He knows how to recognize weakness and how best to attack it. Diana's Achilles heel is not her political life, but her private one. It is as a mother and daughter that she feels most vulnerable. When Muller contemptuously dismisses her "Joan of Arc" political passion as "an excuse for being a terrible mother," he has accused her of the one "crime" she herself feels guilty of. Barbara Hershey shows us the pain of Diana's guilt, even as she struggles for exhausted composure in the face of her enemies.

Diana's sufferings are great, and the filmmakers give us the full impact of her pain and the bravery of her endurance. We hate apartheid for what it does to Molly and Diana. But they are not its only, or even its most important, victims. The thing I respect most about *A World Apart* is that the film does not try to equate the repression of whites with the oppression of blacks.

Diana's imprisonment is clearly a violation of her human rights. And her mother and daughters are heartsick and frightened when she is taken from them. But there are worse things. Interspersed with scenes of Diana's jail experiences are those of a black revolutionary, Solomon Mabusa (Albee Lesotho), a friend who is also Elsie's brother. His interrogations aren't conducted by gents in dapper suits. He is beaten and tortured by men in gestapo-like uniforms. Director Chris Menges doesn't show us his torture, but in a powerful and very frightening scene Menges brings us *in* to Solomon's prison experience in a way that cannot help but leave the audience shaken to the core. Solomon's eventual death in detention (although it occurs off-camera) and Elsie's inconsolable grief when she learns of it are events the viewer takes as personal losses.

This is what *Cry Freedom* should have done, but failed to do. Although Sir Richard Attenborough's film of last year should have represented the black struggle better, since it supposedly focuses on the life and death of South African Black Consciousness leader Steven Biko (Denzel Washington), it didn't. *Cry Freedom* spent almost all of its dramatic energy on the difficulties of Donald Woods (Kevin Kline), a white journalist who befriended Biko.

I have no doubt that Attenborough is a fervent foe of apartheid, but his liberal, white, impress-everyone-but-offend-no-one sensibilities seriously impair the power of his film. The oppression of South Africa's blacks is shown in epic wide-angle shots of bulldozed shanties and gunned-down demonstrators. Seeing this at a distance, the audience may be horrified but they also remain detached. Biko, who should be the movie's real hero, is established as a saintly, peace-loving young man and then, midway through the movie, he is killed off.

The emotional climax of *Cry Freedom* should be Biko's death. Instead it becomes the flight of Donald Woods and his family from South Africa. When Woods makes his escape, his peril and the suspense of his flight are milked to the point of excruciation. Along the way he is helped by several blacks who tell him that any friend of Steve Biko is a friend of theirs. Being a friend of Steve Biko is enough to keep Donald Woods safe, but *being* Steve Biko wasn't enough to keep Steve Biko *alive*. Attenborough does nothing with the tragic, horrible irony of that fact.

One gets no sense that *Cry Freedom* is being ironic in its juxtaposition of the sufferings of whites who survive and prosper with those of blacks who remain behind, dead, in mortal peril, or downtrodden to an early grave. Shawn Slovo and Chris Menges deal with their very similar subject matter much differently. Although they would have been completely justified in exploiting Diana as a martyred heroine (since that is exactly what Ruth First is), they tell the story of young Molly and her Mom in such a way as to always acknowledge that the primary struggle in South Africa is that of her native black majority.

Irony is everywhere in *A World Apart*, combined with an absurd and biting humor. The recurring use of Chubby Checker's 1961 hit, "Let's Twist Again," is a perfect example of this. The first time we hear it, it is Chubby himself singing, as Molly and her best friend test their hula-hoop skills to the beat of the record. The scene is warm and innocent, interchangeable with similar scenes (of white youth entertaining themselves with black culture) acted out in millions of prosperous American suburbs in the early '60s.

The second time we hear the song it is performed live, at Molly's request, by a black South African combo at a racially mixed party thrown by Diana Roth. Their lilting, funky interpretation of the tune is interrupted by a police raid: the storm of boots and the frenzied barks of German Shepherd attack dogs.

The last time we hear the song, it is being sung by white prison guards who taunt black prisoners with it as they force them to polish a prison floor at a feverish pace, propelling the cleaning rags with their bare feet. Even the most harmless and exuberant of pop songs is made cruel and ugly by a "twist"ed society.

Admirable politics, presented in a complex and sensitive manner, is certainly reason enough to recommend *A World Apart*. But much of the power of this film lies in the fact that it is visually stunning. Chris Menges, who makes his directorial debut with the film, started his career shooting documentaries and went on to become an award-winning (he won Oscars for *The Killing Fields* and *The Mission*) cinematographer. His twenty-five years of experience behind the camera show in his powerful use of natural light and a style of scene composition that is intensely realistic and, at the same time, beautifully intimate.

The performances in *A World Apart* have that same quality, and since much of the cast consists of children and untrained adult actors, a great deal of the credit must go to Menges. Barbara Hershey, the film's "star," gives a wonderfully honest performance, allowing her character a kind of steely valor that is not always sympathetic, especially in a Mommy. But then, this is a film brave enough to admit that good revolutionaries do not necessarily make good mothers. Even so, *A World Apart* is not about mother-blaming. As a woman of conscience, Diana Roth could have done no less in fighting apartheid. Her children pay the price for her politics, but as Molly begins to understand by the end of the film, it is a price worth paying. It is a necessary sacrifice by those too young to understand it.

At Cannes this year, Hershey shared "Best Actress" honors with Jodhi May and Linda Mvusi. And a wonderfully fair split decision it was. May, in her first professional (on-screen or off) acting job is exquisite. There is nary a dry eye in the house during her two major scenes with Hershey. Mvusi's performance in her supporting role is very powerful. So, too, is the performance of Albee Lesotho, as Solomon; in real life Lesotho was detained and tortured for eighteen months by South African police, and his performance in this film, as a black South African, is an act of courage is more ways than one.

A World Apart is an important film to see. But don't go see it, dutifully, because it is the politically correct movie of the moment. See it because it is beautiful and moving. An unforgettable film.

We are still waiting for films about South Africa that will tell the stories of black protagonists. We need feature films of leaders like PAC's Robert Sobukwe. And we *need* films about the Elsies of South Africa, and "major motion pictures" about women like Albertina Sisulu, Thenjiwe Mtintso, Frances Baard, Lilian Ngoyi, Thandi Modise, and Ellen Kuzwayo. If stories like their were told on the movie screens of London and Paris and Washington, perhaps the West would actually do something to end that particular atrocity known as apartheid. Ruth First lived and died doing her part and, in her cathartic love-hate tale of a daughter's remembrance and final forgiveness, Shawn Slovo carries on her mother's work.

1963, MADE SIMPLE

Shag

Nostalgia is a powerful element of American popular culture. It always has been. A wistful testimonial to the good old days can seem like a perfect relief from our present day troubles. And now that all of us baby boomers can look back at our "youth"—it is, after all, twenty years since Woodstock—nostalgia is likely to be an ever more prevalent aspect of Hollywood filmmaking. We'll be seeing more and more movies and TV shows that look back with yearning on the halcyon days of the sixties.

I deeply distrust every single one of them. Nostalgia is as a sweet remembrance also dishonest. It encourages a dangerously sentimental form of selective memory. Okay, I'll admit that I can get as sentimental about my past as the next person. But I also remember that there was nothing halcyon (Webster defined as "idyllically calm and peaceful . . . serene . . . happy . . . golden") about the sixties as we lived them. Anger and outrage and alienation were the order of the day. Those of us who weren't angry were usually stoned out of our gourds. And there was a lot of gut-gnawing anxiety for young and old alike.

The most exhilarating and angst-ridden times were, for most white, middle-class baby boomers, the late sixties. So far, few movies have looked back on those days. Those that have, like the excruciatingly sincere *1969*, have failed as entertainment and therefore bombed at the box office. The more successful '60s nostalgia flicks (hit movies, from *American Graffiti* to *Dirty Dancing*) have been about the early '60s, those days before the assassination of President Kennedy, often referred to as the "Camelot" years.

The early sixties are a much more fertile ground for nostalgia. A movie can call those times placid and carefree, or, in the words of the press-kit for the movie *Shag*, "a simpler time . . . . full of such total optimism and innocence," and get away with it. A movie can conveniently forget events of paralyzing fear like the "Russian Missile Crisis," during which common citizens of the globe watched the Superpower male leaders play their headgames with one another and wondered if our world was about to be vaporized. Early '60s nostalgia also gives white Americans permission to forget the years of struggle known as the Civil Rights Movement, and to even feel an unacknowledged longing for those days when racial superiority was an acknowledged belief.

Shag is just such movie. It is sweet and entertaining, but it gives us a tunnel view of its time period: the summer of 1963 in South Carolina. It is the story of four young women, best buddies, who have just graduated from high school. Pudge (Annabeth Gish) is bright and college-bound and attractive, but she still defines herself, with a little help from her parents, as a chubby and unattractive child. Luanne (Page Hannah) is a senator's daughter who has had to be a lady-like credit to her father for so long that she's in danger of becoming a permanent Miss Priss. Melaina (Bridget Fonda) is a blond beauty with a wild streak. She is the stereotypic preacher's daughter who longs to break out and break away—to Hollywood, if at all possible. And Carson (Phoebe Cates) is a girl of fine family and sterling reputation who is about to make her family the even prouder in-laws of a tobacco empire by marrying the dull but handsome scion (Tyrone Power, Jr.) of the family.

Since wedding bells are about to break up that old gang of theirs, the four decide to ditch the tour of Fort Sumter and Charleston's gracious homes sanctioned by their parents and instead have one last fling at Myrtle Beach. As you might expect, the weekend of fun turns out to be of pivotal importance in all of their lives. Romance blooms, longings and ambitions are fulfilled—all in a most predictable and winsome way.

Coming of Age films about teens in the late '50s and early '60s are a dime a dozen. There is nothing particularly special about *Shag*—except that it is a coming of age tale about four friends who are *women*. It makes a nice change from all those *Diner*'s and *American Graffiti*'s we've had to sit through, in which women are just the lure of sex and the threat of domesticity for male protagonists. Maturation movies that focus on women are still few and far between.

Shag has much in common with *Where the Boys Are*, a movie about four girlfriends who, during college spring break, go to Fort Lauderdale in search of fun and sun and boys. But *Where the Boys Are* wasn't meant as a nostalgia flick. It is set in the early

What, me *worry about civil rights? The young female leads of* Shag *(from left to right, Page Hannah, Annabeth Gish, and Phoebe Cates) have better things– fun, sun, and romance–on their minds.*

sixties because that's when (1960, to be exact) it was released. And its view of the sexual lives of young women is as simplistic and rigidly moralistic as you'd expect for that time period.

Despite the hedonistic image the film's title and setting suggest, and the now almost campy flavor of its humor and music, *Where the Boys Are* is really an exceedingly pious tract in support of the sexual double standard. Two of the four friends (Paula Prentiss and Connie Francis) know they are "good girls." Their virginity is never really at risk—especially since one is too tall and the other is too strong and athletic. But the two perfect blonds of the foursome (Delores Hart and Yvette Mimieux) must face a crucial chastity crisis.

Hart's character is a smart and rebellious young woman who spouts free love back on campus. She keeps her thighs firmly pressed together, however, when George Hamilton starts to romance her on the beach. Because she holds *out,* we know that she will hold *on* to her rich, suave suitor. She wins his respect for now, and soon she will win his wedding ring.

Poor Yvette, on the other hand, is so desperate to get engaged to an Ivy League man that she sleeps with the first guy who asks and ends up used and abandoned by a succession of partners who are all after *only one thing*. She is raped when she tries to say no (after once saying yes) and afterwards, in total catatonic despair, walks onto the highway where she is struck down by a car.

Shag tells a very different story of female sexual awakening. All four friends are preoccupied with their virginity, but more because it is a big step into adulthood not yet taken rather than because their value as marriageable women will be destroyed if they lose it. The demurest good girl of the bunch actually sleeps with a young man she has just met—whom she is greatly attracted to but not necessarily in love with—and is quite pleased with herself afterwards. With some wonderment she admits that such behavior is "wild," but concludes that she's been that way all along and "just didn't know it till now."

In its portrayal of good girls becoming sexually active and feeling good about it, *Shag* injects a dose of 1989 hindsight into its 1963 storyline. It is an example of the dishonesty of selective memory, but for those of us who view enforced chastity as a grand old tradition of male oppression we never want to see again it is also a welcome fib. In this case I was glad that screenwriters Lanier Laney and Terry Sweeney cheated history. But in another key area I found their selective memory very disturbing. And that is in the failure of the movie to acknowledge the racial turmoil of the time.

Keep in mind that this is the summer of 1963 we're talking about. This is the summer of the Birmingham "Children's Crusade." This is the summer George Wallace took his famous "Stand at the Schoolhouse Door" ("Segregation now, segregation tomorrow, segregation forever!"). This is the summer Medgar Evers was gunned down at his front door. This is the summer of "wade-ins" (to protest exclusion of blacks from public beaches) throughout the South. This is the summer 200,000 people would march on Washington to demand racial equality.

Since none of these events occurred in South Carolina, you could argue that the filmmakers were completely within their rights to ignore the civil rights struggles of that crucial year. But South Carolina was by no means immune. A massive sit-in campaign and demonstration siege occurred that summer in Charleston. Before a "truce" was reached, 700 blacks were arrested. Meanwhile Earl Warren's Supreme Court was voiding many of the earlier convictions of South Carolina sit-in protestors, like those imprisoned and fined for sitting down at the lunch counter of S.H. Kress in Greenville. While Clemson and the University of South Carolina desegregated "without incident" in 1963, desegregation of the state's lower schools went somewhat less smoothly. And the state of South Carolina closed its public parks in 1963 rather than abide by a Federal Court order to integrate them.

Yet the characters of *Shag* have nary a care in the world. Certainly none of the young privileged white leads makes any mention of the social turmoil around them. Their only concerns are romance and partying. And what of black characters? There aren't any to speak of, or for the leads to speak with. The only black presence is the black band who plays all the beach music the young whites love to shag (yes, it's a dance, not a haircut) to, and a black maid who rolls her eyes at the goings-on of the young white folks. They seem cheerful and unaware of any racial conflict. They sing and clean. They apparently know their place in that "simpler" world of "total optimism and innocence."

That's why I hate the kind of sweet nostalgia of movies like *Shag*. They leave out anything that would make a white, middle-class audience feel unhappy about the past. Instead they invite a reactionary longing for a time when it was our world and we knew it. And the audience doesn't have to feel guilty about those feelings either, when *Shag*'s screenplay ignores both the brutality of white resistance to civil rights and the less dramatic but equally damaging day-to-day hurts inflicted on non-WASPs living in a WASP world.

Racism is ignored. So are all the other prejudices. In *Shag*, when Chip (Scott Coffey) makes a casual joke about having to be Italian to get on American Bandstand, he uses the word "Italian" and not "wop" or "dago" as he probably would have. When Melaina confesses that she'd love to sleep with President Kennedy, her friends are shocked by her lust for a married President, but none rebuke her for lusting after a Roman Catholic who was (finally) moving forward on the demands of blacks for integration.

The racist social structure starts to look like the lost Eden when its image is scrubbed all fresh and clean. Forget about the hurtful language (the word "nigger" was not, according to *Shag*, in current usage in 1963 in the Carolinas). All the open prejudices are tactfully deleted along with visuals of the "colored" facilities of American apartheid. There isn't even an "Impeach Earl Warren" billboard along the highway in this peaceable lily-white world.

A (white) friend who grew up in South Carolina, but who was already away at college in 1963, thought I was really over-reacting when I expressed to him my feelings of outrage at *Shag*'s limited and far-too-comfortable view of 1963 South Carolina. He told me that things really were placid there. And that whites didn't throw around racial and ethnic slurs because they ignored the existence of people like Italians and Catholics, while blacks were just a part of daily life they ignored like the furniture.

Maybe so. But I remember traveling through the Atlantic Coast states of the South as a young (Italian, Catholic) girl, and that's not how I remember it. And even if the lives of privileged white South Carolinians were still that tranquil and oblivious in 1963, I still don't accept *Shag*'s picture of the good old days. If *Shag* doesn't completely cheat history, then the question still remains, why pick *this* history, *this* group of sheltered, self-satisfied whites to make a movie about? I think I know the answer. And that's why this sweet little movie makes me so bloody angry.

We know that it's possible to make a silly, completely entertaining dance movie about the early sixties that com-memorates all the past, the good and the bad. John Waters did it last year in *Hairspray*. Ricki Lake, as Tracy Turnblad, danced the Madison like a dream and found true love with her partner. She also helped to integrate the local teen dance show and amusement park. Even *Dirty Dancing*, hardly an enlightened movie when it comes to class issues, paid lip service to its liberal young heroine's resolve to change the world. Both of these movies more honestly render their time than *Shag* does. And both are better dance movies to boot.

Shag is, in many ways, a nice film. Zelda Barron's direction is light and assured, and the young ensemble cast works well together. But there is nothing nice about the way this kind of nostalgia censors our social history. I'm much more forgiving of those who can't take in the Big Picture while it's right in front of them, blown up, distorted, and larger than life. But looking back at our past, at a distance, is supposed to let us see things more clearly. Even a light-weight movie filled with dance and romance can give us that clearer vision if only the people who make it are honest enough.

Nostalgia is not exactly the ultimate right-wing conspiracy. *American Graffiti* can't be blamed for the election of Ronald

Reagan. And *Shag* certainly isn't responsible for the Webster v. Reproductive Health Services decision of the Supreme Court. But the way these and other nostalgia movies lull us into yearning for the good old days before African-Americans had basic social freedoms and before women had the right to control their own bodies, lends a tinge of threat to their cheerful sentimentality. They feed us a never-never-land that never was. The real world we worked so hard to change was much different. And it was no Camelot.

Rolling back the clock is something women and minorities have every reason to fear and to fight against. A spin on the dance floor isn't going to fool us. Hollywood can tell us "Go Back! Go Back!" as much as it wants. We ain't going.

FOR HOLLYWOOD, TOO, IT'S . . .

A Dry White Season

When Ben du Toit (Donald Sutherland) first meets the weary social justice lawyer Ian McKenzie (Marlon Brando) in *A Dry White Season*, the old barrister gives his prospective client a lesson in the realities of life in South Africa. Justice and law are, in most cases, McKenzie informs him, distant cousins. "Here in South Africa they are not on speaking terms at all." The same could be said of film and the struggle for positive social change. In most cases, they are distant cousins. In Hollywood, the power center of the American film industry, they aren't even on speaking terms.

That is why the making of *A Dry White Season*, a film about the tragedy of South African apartheid, is an accomplishment in and of itself. Euzhan Palcy, a Martiniquais (Martinican) woman filmmaker, and her producer Paula Weinstein, fought an uphill battle to bring this story to the screen. Dropped by its original studio, Warner Brothers, when Richard Attenborough's *Cry Freedom* didn't do boffo-enough box office, MGM eventually gave Weinstein and Palcy the green light, but made only a modest investment. To help keep within the nine million-dollar budget, the film's Hollywood stars—Sutherland, Brando, and Susan Sarandon—all took sizeable paycuts from their normal salaries. Brando, for example, variously cited as performing his support role for free or for scale ($4,000), could have literally gotten millions for returning to Hollywood in a star vehicle movie.

This, then, was a film made by people who care about social justice and who hope to wake up the film-viewing public to the atrocity of South Africa's oppression of its native peoples. I admire them all for their efforts. I only wish that *A Dry White Season* were a better film, the film that Euzhan Palcy is capable of making, the kind of movie she has, in fact, already made.

Palcy's first feature film, *Sugar Cane Alley* (1984), is a

treasure of a movie, adapted by herself, from the novel of countryman Joseph Zobel, *La Rue Cases-Negres*. Set in the 1930s, it is the coming of age story of a bright, sensitive boy, Jose (Garry Cadenat), whose one hope of escape from a life of back-breaking labor in the sugar-cane fields of Martinique is a good education away from his village. Despite the fact that the protagonist of the film is male, poorer, and of an earlier generation, the story reflects much of the experience of its screenwriter/director.

Palcy's father (a worker in a pineapple factory) and mother (born well-off, disowned upon her marriage, and later a shop worker), like Jose's grandmother, M'man Tine (Darling Legitimus), made many sacrifices to give their six children educations and a chance to achieve their ambitions. Palcy's ambition to make movies has driven her since the age of ten. She eventually studied at the Sorbonne in Paris and at the Vaugirard Film School and then started work on bringing *Sugar Cane Alley* to the screen. It was no small task for a young black woman from a small island with no film industry to make a feature film, but Palcy was determined and received help and encouragement from European directors Francois Truffaut (whom she called her "godfather" on the film) and Costa-Gavras.

Filmed on location on the island of her birth, *Sugar Cane Alley* is a wonderful movie because it is filled with emotion and rich in detail. It is not simply a sociological study of poverty in a cane workers' slum in a French colony. It is an intimate portrait of a small, close-knit community within a larger culture. Palcy exposes the evils of racism and imperialism by showing us life in the fields, in the schools, and in the barrio shacks these people call home. Wisely, she spends more time showing alley citizens preparing and eating their meals than she does the overseer taunting them in the fields or cheating them on payday.

Both are important, but had Palcy painted a picture of oppression alone, we would have seen the alley people only as victims. By showing them making do (as my grandmother used to call it) and taking care of one another, they become survivors, people whose humanity cannot be dismissed. When a character is fully human to an audience, their sympathies cannot help but be engaged.

Mixing the joys with the sorrows also makes for a more entertaining, as well as a more involving film. And in *Sugar Cane*

With A Dry White Season, *Euzhan Palcy became the first black woman to direct a feature film for a major Hollywood studio. In 1983, she made* Sugar Cane Alley *in her native Martinique.*

Alley Euzhan Palcy entertains as she instructs. She makes the invisible visible for the Martinquais themselves as well as for uninformed whites. The *Los Angeles Times* reported that in the first week *Sugar Cane Alley* played on Martinique, 150,000 people—over a quarter of the island's population—went to see it. (Only 40,000 went to see *E.T.*) Her people devoured these screen images of themselves again and again because, as many told Palcy, they finally felt they existed. Their lives had, at last, been made real for all to see.

Making the lives of people of color visible is precisely what Palcy set out to do when she resolved to become a filmmaker as a child. "It came out of anger," she told *Interview.* "I was very upset as a child at the portrayal of blacks in movies." She wanted to make positive movies about black peoples and their struggles. Thus, it is all the more frustrating that *A Dry White Season* be the film Euzhan Palcy should make on South Africa.

A Dry White Season is more black-identified than either *Cry Freedom* or *A World Apart*, the previous Hollywood features on apartheid, but it is still fundamentally the story of a white protagonist, played by Sutherland, and his reluctant awakening to the terrorist social structure that has provided him and his family with a good life.

Palcy had no illusions about what she was doing in the film. She knows this is a compromise. She has stated, oh so correctly, in various interviews, that the people in Hollywood don't care about apartheid. To the *Times* she said: "The people who have the money don't care about a film on black South Africans. They want to do films about blacks only if they are funny, or if they have star names like Eddie Murphy, Bill Cosby, Prince or Michael Jackson." She knew that to gain financing to make a film attacking South African apartheid, an issue she feels passionately about, the powers of Hollywood would have to perceive it as a white story which might appeal to a white audience.

A Dry White Season fit the bill. Written by a dissident Afrikaner named Andre Brink, the original novel details a white's consciousness-raising and eventual resistance to apartheid, and the subsequent disintegration of his life. The first screenplay, by *Chariots of Fire* scriptor Colin Welland, naturally reinforced the white focus and viewpoint. Palcy wanted something more, so she reworked the script so that it further emphasized the black family of Ben du Toit's gardener, Gordon Ngubene (Winston Ntshona), his wife, Emily (Thoko Ntshinga) and their children, and their family friend, a taxi driver named Stanley (Zakes Mokae).

Even so, our primary sympathies stay with Sutherland's du Toit because he is the only character the film lets us get close to. The Ngubene family are killed off, one by one, before they really come to life as complex characters the audience can care deeply about. While they fulfill their roles as victims, they never become the heroes of their own tragic story. The audience is horrified by the brutality and blood Palcy unflinchingly confronts us with, but we can too easily remain, at the same time, detached from it in the same way we distance ourselves from each fresh atrocity served up by the evening news in between come-ons for pizza pies and luxury sedans.

Palcy's relentless yet unemotional and almost documentary-like approach to her story does it a disservice. She needs to draw us into the lives of the Ngubenes and Stanley in the same way we are drawn into the lives of Jose and his M'Man in *Sugar Cane Alley*. She does not, possibly because she could not with Hollywood studio chiefs breathing down her neck. Yet even the white characters in *A Dry White Season* are types more than

She's comforting him now, but when Africaner wife Susan (Janet Suzman) has to choose between her husband, Ben (Donald Sutherland), and the powers that be, she sides with apartheid.

people.

I had no trouble accepting the archetypal evil of apartheid expressed in the person of Captain Stolz (Jurgen Prochnow) of the Special Branch. He is as chillingly cold and ugly as any camp commandant or SS officer in any WWII film I've ever seen. (And, ironically enough, Prochnow is a German actor.) I had more trouble stomaching the good/bad gender split within the du Toit family. Ben's golden young son Johan (Rowen Elmes) is portrayed as idealistic and eager to fight apartheid and support his "pa" when given the chance. The women of the clan refuse to be moved by the butchery in their midst. Ben's wife, Susan (the gifted Janet Suzman) remains rigidly aligned with white power and his daughter (Susannah Harker) is the Judas of the piece.

As with their right-wing sisters of the United States, I have no doubt that white women in South Africa often ferociously cling, in their own powerlessness, to white male power as a means of survival. But *A Dry White Season* doesn't show me enough of the motivation of these two women. Or maybe it's just that seeing Sutherland and an adorable son portrayed as brave and sensitive souls clinging to one another and their inherent goodness while their bitter and hard-hearted wife/mother is driven from their home brings back too many bad memories for me of the sexist, mother-bashing subtext of an earlier Sutherland film, *Ordinary People*.

The only sympathetic white female in *A Dry White Season* is a radical journalist, Melanie Bruwer, played by Susan Sarandon. But hers is a bit part that works well only as a plot device. And Emily Ngubene, the single black woman with a significant role, gets little more attention from the film. She silently suffers and in her own way courageously resists, but we never enter her grief or witness the wellspring of her bravery.

In *Sugar Cane Alley* there are many small, vivid scenes that make Palcy's story catch at our heart. Three come to mind. In one, Jose's best friend, a clever and headstrong girl named Tortilla, finds out that she will not be allowed to continue her schooling, and Jose comforts her by giving her his prized watch. In another, an elder called Mr. Medouze passes on to Jose the melancholy legend of the capture of his people into slavery. And, in the most touching, Jose lovingly bathes the feet of his grandmother.

These are the kind of incidental images that, if translated into the black South African experience, would have made *A Dry White Season* a brilliant, unforgettable, and deeply affecting film instead of the honorable but ordinary film that it is.

Any voice raised up against apartheid in South Africa or racism anywhere should be listened to with care, and heeded. In a country like ours, far too comfortable with our own racism, and disgustingly indulgent of the institutionalized racism of the South Africa's monstrous regime, *A Dry White Season* is a film that should be seen by everyone. I hope it's a hit. But it is not, I'm very sorry to say, the great film Euzhan Palcy could have made about South Africa if Hollywood would have invested its money in a story that was truly about black struggle and heroism. She had the creative power to do the job. But not, I fear, the creative freedom.

Palcy is quoted as saying: "My dream would've been to follow a black family in Soweto...but clearly nobody wanted to put any money into a black film maker making a movie about blacks in South Africa." *Why Not?* is the question we should be asking ourselves. And the answer, difficult as it is to know, should bring home to all of us a lesson about institutionalized racism. In Hollywood, as well as in South Africa, a change *must* come.

RACISM AT THE OASIS
Bagdad Cafe

It must be clear to anyone who ever knew me or read my writings that I make no pretensions of being an intellectual. So, maybe I can admit this now: I hate foreign movies. Not necessarily for their content. They are often better acted and directed, and much more humane and realistic than the products of Hollywood. I hate foreign films because they make me feel frustrated and inadequate.

Like a lot of moviegoers, I hate having to try to read and process the written messages at the bottom of the screen while trying to keep my attention on the top of the screen to pick up the action and the nuances of the performers' gestures and facial expressions. Dubbing is no help. It's so false, it's funny. Dubbed movies always remind me of that childhood game where you'd turn off the sound on your TV and make up your own goofy dialogue.

But most of all I hate foreign films because I know that no matter how carefully I pay attention, I'm still missing half of the film's content because I don't understand the finer points of the culture (or counter-culture) being presented or the language being spoken.

A co-worker told me about his experience watching the work of Juzo Itami. He greatly enjoyed both of Itami's recent films, *Tampopo* and *A Taxing Woman*, but while he was watching *Tampopo* in Brookline last year, he was frequently distracted by a Japanese couple sitting in the audience nearby. He noticed them because at times when neither the action nor the subtitles on the screen seemed to indicate that anything humorous was going on, those two folks were giggling and guffawing like all get out.

It's a nightmare I've experienced frequently at foreign films. I don't trust subtitles (how they put up five English words to every fifteen being spoken by the actors), and I know that there's no way subtitles can capture puns or topical or literary allusions in another mother tongue. And subtitles never translate the posters on the wall or the covers of the magazines on the coffee table or the ad copy on the back of the cereal box on the kitchen counter—all of which contribute to the texture and content of the film.

So why bother? Because international films are often wonderful creations which treat women in a (slightly) more serious and respectful manner than American films. They can give us a wider view of how other citizens of our world live. Of course, the great majority of foreign films (that make it to the U.S. art theaters) show us only the lives of the wealthy and upper-middle-class from Western European countries. They are elitist in the same way the majority of American films are elitist. But as limited as that view no doubt is, it is nonetheless often a valuable one. For example, Doris Dörrie's tweaking of male egos in *Men* showed us that yuppies are as obnoxious in Germany as they are in the U.S.

And, since Americans are so deeply ingrained with intense cultural jingoism, it's important for us to see "foreign" movies precisely so that we may feel some of that inadequacy and frustration. How salutary to be reminded that ours isn't *the* world culture or *the* world language or *the* world view. That's a hard lesson to learn and an even harder one to retain when you are constantly bombarded by the self-congratulation and xenophobia of American media. If we didn't see the *Tampopo*s and *Taxing Woman*s, we might think all Japanese are like the racist stereotypes we get from Hollywood films like *Gung Ho*.

So, okay, watching foreign films is good for my soul. They're still frustrating. But here's good news for sister sufferers. More and more European filmmakers are experimenting with English language and/or American locations in their movies, bless their hearts. If Americans still want to feel humbled, all they need do is realize that the reason European directors are making English language films is that they want to tap the massive U.S. market, and they know that Americans are such insular dolts that they won't watch a movie that's not in English, while the majority of the populace in *their* countries (e.g., France—as in Diane Kurys's *A Man in Love*) feel quite comfortable watching English-speaking films, and often feel no need to rely on translation devices.

Of course, some European directors would like to make their English-speaking films for (and in) Hollywood. But even when they do (e.g., Gillian Armstrong's *Mrs. Soffel*), their viewpoint and the way they express it on film is often a refreshing change from that of American-Hollywood.

Percy Adlon is a German director who was staying in Los Angeles, trying to break into Hollywood with a movie about his uncle (who was a member of Hollywood's fast set in the '20s), when he and his wife, co-producer, and writing collaborator, Eleonore, took a drive through Barstow and the Mojave desert. The way the story goes, the Adlons were captivated by the stark beauty of the place and the forlorn quality of the truck stops in that wasteland. To top off the barren magic of the Mojave, they had a vision of two "starbursts" of light, which they later found out were caused by the many mirrors of a nearby solar energy collection center. After their close-encounter-of-the-desert-kind, they immediately decided on a new project that would place a German woman in this American wilderness setting. They went back to Bavaria to complete their script, raise funds, line up their star, and collect the German part of their crew. Then they headed back to the Golden State.

The movie that resulted from their desert vision and their Bavarian writing sessions is *Bagdad Cafe*, and it is a well-intentioned, often enchanting comedy with some very serious problems. It stars Marianne Sägebrecht, who also starred in Adlon's earlier success, the German-language film, *Sugarbaby*. And much of the movie's enchantment flows from Sägebrecht and her central performance. The mere fact that she is allowed to shine as a star of a film is a dead giveaway that this is no Hollywood production.

You see, Marianne Sägebrecht is a forty-two-year-old woman. By American (Hollywood-and Madison Avenue-induced) standards for a leading lady, she is not only too old, she is also way too fat. You no doubt have noticed the women who play "fat" parts in Hollywood films. They are all size fourteen, tops, and filled with self-hatred, pitied by their friends, and rejected by potential lovers. They are also considered "character" actresses, support players for the size eight (six? four?) blondes who play the starring roles.

Well, Marianne Sägebrecht wears something considerably larger than a size fourteen, and she is a *star*. Percy Adlon was smart enough (and non-fatist enough) to recognize Sägebrecht's star quality, so he coaxed her from her career as "Mother of the Sub-culture" in Munich—she was a leading light in several experimental cabarets and coffee theatres which showcased both street performers and professionals—to star in his films.

In *Sugarbaby* (1985), Ms. Sägebrecht played a mortuary worker who, on her ride home one evening, is so attracted to the voice of a subway driver (who turns out to be thin, blonde, and more than ten years younger than she) that she goes on a campaign to seduce him. And her sugarbaby is delighted to be seduced by a woman as special as Marianne.

Around femininity issues, the film could be faulted (Marianne feels the need to put on 5-inch heels in order to look more alluring), but not around fat issues. Our heroine doesn't go on a crash starvation diet. She doesn't put herself down constantly. Although lonely when the movie opens, she is comfortable with who she is, and so is her new-found lover—who is, ironically enough, married to a woman with Hollywood beauty.

Sägebrecht is as zaftig as ever in *Bagdad Cafe*, and in the beginning you think she's going to be speaking German this time out, too. The film opens with a sternly clad German couple taking a rest stop on the side of a desert highway and having a hammer-and-tongs fight. Jasmin (Sägebrecht) stomps off, her shoes sinking in the sand. She doesn't care if she's stranded in the middle of nowhere, she's leaving her husband. She manages to haul her giant suitcase as far as a dilapidated way station called Bagdad. The Bagdad Cafe, with its fleabag hotel and gas station, is the whole town. And the entire populace of the town consists of an African-American family of five, a Native American man who works at the cafe, a dour white tattooist named Debbie (Christine Kaufmann), and an eccentric fellow of undetermined origin and occupation (Jack Palance).

The family, and its limited business interests, are headed by a shrewish matriarch named Brenda (CCH Pounder), who is so fed up with her shiftless, lazy husband, Sal (G. Smokey Campbell), that she drives him off the property, hurling empty oil cans at his head. That leaves Mom with her promiscuous teenaged daughter, Phyllis (Monica Calhoun), who will—temporarily, of course—run off with any male(s) with a motor vehicle, and her music-obsessed son, Sal, Jr. (Darron Flagg). Junior's infant son adds a third, less than cherished generation to the family circle. When he can't ditch his baby boy with his resentful mother, Junior ties him with a rope into a broken high chair.

They are an unhappy family, living in squalor in the middle of the desert. Then, in walks Jasmin with her giant suitcase. She decides to stay on in Bagdad. Maybe she wants to hide out in this hell hole so that she can find sufficient solitude to sort out her own life, but she *seems* more intent on sorting out the lives of Brenda and her family. With the heart of a German hausfrau, her first impulse is to clean. Next she reaches out to fill the emotional needs of the family. Jasmin is a miracle worker. She makes the cracked linoleum of the cafe gleam. And she instills the glow of love, hope and joy in Brenda and her kids. The hell hole soon becomes an oasis of delight in the California desert.

A truly sweet story about the magic of love, in which two women who dump their husbands transform themselves and each other and make a wonderful new life out of next to nothing, is what the Adlons *meant* to create. And this what they succeeded in concocting, in one sense. That's why *Bagdad Cafe* was recommended to me by several feminists and other fine folk as a wonderful movie experience.

If you keep an eye on the concept, and not on the execution of it, it's easy to applaud *Bagdad Cafe* without being deeply distressed by the racial stereotypes about black people that the

If we saw more joyful, loving embraces life this one between Brenda (CCH Pounder, left) and Jasmin (Marianne Sägebrecht), then Bagdad Cafe *might not seem so tainted with racist stereotyping.*

movie repeatedly reinforces. But, shouldn't we be distrustful of a movie that suggests that a strong, clean, loving white woman could march into town and, in a matter of weeks, straighten out the heretofore beaten-down lives of a family of weak, dirty, ill-tempered blacks? Absolutely!

The sad thing is that I think Percy and Eleonore Adlon genuinely meant well. Their sympathies are with the outsiders of life. And I think they have genuine affection for Brenda and her family and their Native-American neighbors. I think that their point was, in part, that we are all outsiders in some way and in some situations. A Bavarian white woman in the middle of the Mojave is the biggest outsider of all, and she therefore finds her kinship in this foreign land with American people of color.

But the Adlons of Bavaria no doubt learned most of what they know about American people of color from the parade of prejudices found in American movies and television. So, without *meaning* to be racist, they have created a very racist film—a film that perpetuates just about every cultural stereotype about African-Americans. And because *Bagdad* is a star vehicle for Marianne Sägebrecht, she is *always* the one who comes off looking heroic and intelligent—the displaced hausfrau as enchanting savior.

If the Adlons had portrayed the growing relationship between Brenda and Jasmin more as one of mutual support and love, those stereotypes would have seemed much less hurtful. If Brenda had been the stronger one sometimes, taking care of Jasmin when she couldn't cope; if she had been smarter or nicer or more resourceful than Jasmin from time to time, then their relationship would have seemed like more of a friendship between equals, and therefore more attractive and less offensive. But we see nothing of Jasmin's need for Brenda's smarts and strengths until the last line of the film. And that's too late.

Should you see *Bagdad Cafe*? On balance, yes, I think so. It is a mellow, absurd little human comedy in so many ways. To see Jack Palance as Rudi, the old Hollywood hippy turned desert-rat artiste, turn his tender and lusting gaze on Jasmin is a real treat. As he paints her, you know that he clearly recognizes her as a woman of great beauty. And he (and we) are able to appreciate Marianne Sägebrecht's beauty because Percy and Eleonore Adlon appreciated it first. That felt so good to me. Yet the bigotry, intentional or not, in the characterization of Brenda and her clan felt so *bad*, that I don't know if there's enough of a trade-off to warrant the investment of six bucks.

It seems like such a great idea for American audiences to get another view of our country and culture by watching foreign-made films that look at the United States. Movies like *Bagdad Cafe* could give us new insights into ourselves. Too bad Percy Adlon's optimism contains so little insight. With the kindliest of intentions, he has parroted the racist stereotypes of the American-made culture that informed his attitudes. That's not a new viewpoint. It's just more depressing proof of how far-reaching and damaging the old bigoted ways of Hollywood movies really are.

THE NEW "WOMAN'S FILM"

WOMAN TO WOMAN SCHMALTZ
Beaches

The first time I saw *Beaches*, I made the mistake of seeing it with a man. As the movie neared its end, my companion looked over to see me groping for the pocket pack of tissues in my bookbag, the tears streaming down my face. "Cut that out!" he said, digging me in the arm with a half-serious elbow. "This movie is pathetic!" I was too busy snuffling to reply.

The critics seem to agree with my gentleman friend. But that's not very surprising, since they are mostly gentlemen, too. The reviews have been positively scathing. Locally, the *Globe* labelled it "a whale of a failure." The *Herald*'s headline claimed that it "should've been buried." And topping them all, the *Phoenix* called it "hands down, the worst movie of 1988." (This, in a year that included the release of brilliant movies like *Hot to Trot*, *Hellbound: Hellraiser II*, *Rambo III*, and *Friday the 13th, Part VII*!)

Why such venom toward a gentle little movie about a 30-year friendship between two women? It's indeed a puzzlement. *Beaches* is by no means a great movie, but I found it genuinely entertaining. And an essential part of that entertainment is the tears the audience sheds in the film's closing moments. That I fear is the sticking point for the male viewer/critic. For regardless of their professed heightened sensitivity and emotional openness, men of the '80s do not find heavy emotional issues like physical death and undying love—especially between two women—entertaining. Crying in the dark isn't their idea of a good time. But that's part and parcel of the charms of a type of movie long-ago dubbed the "woman's film."

The "woman's film" is that exercise in schmaltz, also called "weepie" and "tearjerker," that focuses on a woman protagonist and her emotional life. It is a film about human relationships and the joys and heartbreaks they bring. People often die in these movies, but not of a bullet to the guts or a cleaver to the skull. They die of despair or disease. And their loss is felt by those around them, and by the audience, unlike the demise of countless humans mowed down in male "action" movies.

The woman's film has been around since the beginning of Hollywood, but hit its peak during the late '30s and early '40s when women made up a large percentage of the movie audience. We all have our favorite classic weepie. Perhaps it's Barbara Stanwyck's maternal sacrifice in *Stella Dallas*. More likely it's Bette Davis in any one of a dozen movies including *Now, Voyager* and *Dark Victory*.

Dark Victory is the ultimate classic of the *Camille* (dying heroine) school of woman's film. Bette plays the spirited socialite Judith Traherne, who fritters away her life of privilege in drunken parties (an inebriated Ronnie Reagan is one of her frustrated suitors) and horsey-set riding events until she is diagnosed with a terminal brain tumor. Then she must find the meaning of her life even as she faces down the grim reaper. I still cry every time I watch it.

To get a feeling for the critical response to the old tearjerker, I pulled out a 1939 microfilm of the *New York Times* to see what Frank S. Nugent had to say about *Dark Victory*. Mr. Nugent made a few good-natured cracks about how "the mascara was running" at the showing he attended, and conceded that "a completely cynical appraisal would dismiss [*Dark Victory*] as emotional flim-flam." But his review was also full of praise and concludes with the declaration that he was willing to "run the risk of being called a softy: we won't dismiss 'Dark Victory' with a self-defensive sneer."

Bless your heart, Frank. If only your male critical descendants could keep their self-defensive sneers to themselves, it would be a lot more pleasant for us women (daughters as we are of those mascara-wearing ladies of the 1939 movie palaces) who would like to be left alone to enjoy our tears at a modern-day weepie.

And that's what *Beaches* is. I wouldn't want to hide the truth from you. This is an '80s tearjerker with all the trimmings. It is the story of an ambitious working-class singer and actress named CC Bloom (Bette Midler), and her life-long friendship to a owning-class heiress named Hillary Whitney (Barbara Hershey). They meet as eleven-year-old girls on the beach at Atlantic City (hence the title), and through a childhood as pen-pals and a young adulthood as roommates in New York City, they cement a friendship that survives separation, jealousy, failed marriages, and even death as the central, sustaining relationship in both their lives.

To see devoted friendship between women portrayed in a positive light is so unusual in a modern-day Hollywood movie that I can't help but recommend *Beaches* to other women. (My recommendation isn't really necessary. Despite its critical lambasting, women are indeed flocking to it.) But there are other reasons to see this film. Number one among these is Bette Midler in her first dramatic starring role since *The Rose*. This is definitely Midler's film, filled with her singing and her divine, brassy presence. All five-foot-one of her so dominates the screen, even in her quietest scenes, that she dwarfs the performances of her co-stars, including Barbara Hershey.

Sad to say, the most interesting thing about Hershey's performance in *Beaches* is her bizarre looks. When I first saw the trailers for the film, I wondered why Hershey looked so unlike herself. I noticed that she had straightened her hair but felt sure that there was some other difference I couldn't pin down. The media pinned it down for me. Or perhaps I should say needled. It seems that Ms. Hershey had a "lip lift" done before she

Don't get too distracted by Barbara Hershey's lip-job, with its supposedly sexy, bee-stung look. Beaches, *a wonderful, weepy salute to women's friendships, is really Bette Midler's movie.*

started filming. The surgical injection of collagen, fat, or silicone is supposed to give the recipient a sexy pout and a more alluring mouth. But Hershey doesn't look more beautiful; she looks puffy. Her normally very mobile features seem bland and rigid. Perhaps she thought her new stiff upper lip would enhance her portrayal of a rather repressed upper-crust female. More likely the decision was a more personal one.

Commentary on the lip-lift hasn't been kind, and my initial impulse is to defend Hershey from this particular batch of sneers. Whatever cosmetic procedures she has had done have also been done by hundreds of other women, many of them actresses and models. Why shouldn't poor Barbara do what she likes with her own body if it makes her happy?

And, yet, I too am horrified that *Barbara Hershey*, a woman known for her risk-taking and far-from-glamorous roles, should resort to what the knee-jerk, hard-line feminist in me must lament as an act of self-mutilation in the name of male-defined beauty. But Hershey's new pout is distressing for aesthetic and artistic as well as political reasons. To me, she is actually less beautiful here than in *A World Apart* and *Shy People*. In *Beaches*, she looks like a woman wearing a mask, not the vibrant actress who could communicate so much with the slightest changes in her facial expression.

Barbara Hershey is, alas, not the only stiff performer in *Beaches*. None of the men do themselves particularly proud although James Read, as Hillary's snake of a lawyer husband, does what he can with the handful of lines allotted him. John Heard appeared to give his slightly more sizeable part less effort. Heard can be an impressive actor, but he's a mess as CC's husband and theatrical mentor. A man who should be a charismatic and sexually compelling man of the theatre is played like he's a distracted, bored schlump. In his key love scenes with Bette, Heard appears to be staring off into space as if he wished he were anywhere but in this movie. (Something tells me that he shares that contempt for the tearjerker with the other men of his age group and just took the part for the paycheck.) Spalding Gray, as Hillary's obstetrician and CC's lover, plays his part with such a gaga expression on his face that you feel sure that he's one of those doctors who swipes drugs from the hospital medicine cabinet.

There is a practical reason why the male performances in *Beaches* are weak that has nothing to do with the skill or dedication of the actors. The male roles in this movie were written weak. Men are incidental accessories in *Beaches* the way women are unimportant set decorations in films too numerous to mention. Screenwriter Mary Agnes Donoghue knows that this movie should be what Hershey is quoted as calling "a love story between two women." And that, no doubt, is one of the other reasons male critics have been so strident in their attacks.

Donoghue's script falls down here and there, as does just about every script that ever attempted to span thirty years in two hours. I wanted more intimate details of CC and Hillary's relationship. I needed to know more about what their relationship was like when they weren't facing crisis or conflict. But I can't criticize Donoghue too sternly when she's done such a miraculous job of adding substance and dumping so much of the emotional flotsam of the less-than-scintillating original material she was adapting for the screen.

Beaches (the filmmakers didn't not invent the unfortunate title) was originally a novel by Iris Rainer Dart. It is a novel some people would call a beach book, some people would call an airport book, and other people would call something rude. It is written like a TV movie of the week. (Which isn't surprising, because Dart used to be a TV writer.) There is a crisis in every chapter, strategically placed, as if to bring people back after commercials. And that's a lot of crisis.

If one of the women finally finds a good man, you may rest assured that he will die in a plane crash as he rushes home to consummate their love. Dart was so intent on peppering her prose with mini-cliffhangers that she didn't build a sufficient foundation for her heroines' devotion to one another. Donoghue makes her best-friends roommates. Dart's characters never live together, or even near one another for more a than a week or so, until the time when one nurses the other in her final illness.

All things considered, then, Donoghue does an admirable job of creating day-to-day familiarity where none existed in the book. Dart, however, handles at least one aspect of the story better. And that is the final illness of Hillary, whom she calls Bertie. In the novel, Bertie is dying of ovarian cancer. Death is painful and messy. And CC, not the most responsible or domestic person in the world, is exhausted and frightened by the role of care-giver. At one point, as she empties a portable commode, she fears that she can't continue.

Hollywood, with its belief in keeping everything as photogenic as possible, is far less honest on this score. The movie Hillary slowly dies of viral cardiomyopathy, which is a real illness. But the way they play it on the screen, it is clearly a case of "movie disease." Just as Greta Garbo, in *Camille*, looked too good to be a woman dying of tuberculosis, and Bette Davis looked as healthy as her favorite horse right up until she died of her brain tumor, so Hershey, as Hillary, has a death that is far too tidy and poetic.

But, what can I say? I still loved this movie. (And I'm not ashamed to admit that!) *Beaches* celebrates our friendships. And it's not afraid to be schmaltzy. If you hate everything about soap operas, you will undoubtedly hate this film. But if, like me, a good soap or woman's film satisfies you on some level, despite their manipulative emotionalism, then run, do not walk, to see *Beaches*.

Just when I'm ready to sneer at a soap or a tearjerker movie, it breaks through my skepticism and grabs hold. Today, as I took a break from writing this review to fix a sandwich, I switched on the television to catch some of "All My Children," a daytime serial I never see anymore. Cindy had finally lost her battle with AIDS, and I watched a moving memorial service in which her family and friends put the finishing touches on her panel for the Names Project memorial quilt. I refuse to dismiss that scene with a self-defensive sneer. Yes, it was hokey. No, it wasn't completely realistic. But it was moving and satisfying entertainment that honored people caring for one another. *Beaches* provided me with that same kind of satisfaction.

As you can imagine, when they coined the term "woman's film" it wasn't exactly a compliment. And the male view of such heartfelt dramas has become increasingly contemptuous since then. But I'm glad to know that Bette Midler isn't afraid of a little critical contempt. She's seen plenty of it over the years.

Beaches is the first production of Midler's "All Girl Productions," a company she runs with Bonnie Bruckheimer-Martell and Margaret Jennings South. Their next project? Another weepie, a remake of *Stella Dallas*. Finally, women giving women a chance to cry in the dark once more. Bless you, girls.

BIMBOS AND BITCHES
IN BIG BUSINESS
· ·
Working Girl

Some omens are too powerful to be ignored. Like the ones that told me that I would hate Mike Nichols's new hit comedy, *Working Girl*. The first warning was, of course, the title. The girl referred to, Tess McGill, is thirty years old but not yet, in the eyes of Hollywood, a woman. (And we thought we'd won that battle years ago!) The second omen was the ad, plastered everywhere, which succinctly described the three leads as "The Charming Bachelor," "The Boss from Hell," and "The Secretary." As expected, the charming bachelor (Jack Trainer played by Harrison Ford) is a man, and the secretary (Tess, played by Melanie Griffith) is a woman. But if we all took a moment, shut our eyes, and tried to envision an evil taskmaster, how many of us would picture someone strong and handsome—and female? Nichols's version of the beelzebubish boss is a woman we have long admired for her working-woman heroism, as the space-warrior Ripley, and most recently as the dedicated primatologist and environmentalist, Dian Fossey. The boss from hell is Sigourney Weaver.

So, okay, maybe Nichols was casting, and Weaver was playing, against type. Nope. Weaver's role of Katharine Parker is the same tough career woman she usually plays. Except this time her strength and espoused feminism are depicted as phoney baloney that exploit and undercut another woman.

Likewise Griffith, best known for her many undressed-for-success nymphet parts in films like *Body Double* and *Something Wild*, has been much ballyhooed for playing against type, too, for this "breakthrough" role as an up-from-the-ranks business whiz. But Melanie is also playing the same old part. Except this time her sex-kitten lingerie is sometimes (but not always) covered up by more sensible attire.

But I don't want to forget my omen number three (auguries should *always* come in threes), which was the real clincher. A male co-worker was describing the movie, just open, to a female co-worker (who, appropriately enough, comes closest to having a "secretary" job description of anyone in our library). He had liked the film a lot and believed that it was very pro-careerwoman and, as such, would be a movie she would really relate to. But the more he described of the storyline, the more outraged his listener became. "That sounds terrible!" she said. She then called me over and suggested in no uncertain terms that I review *Working Girl* and "tear it apart." Okay, Laura. This one's for you.

Yet I can understand my male co-worker's liking for the film. It is shared, after all, by the majority of critics—also male. This is a modern Cinderella story, better told than most. There's no violence or gratuitous sex. (There is gratuitous sexism, but that's another matter.) The tone is spritely—although the pace drags a bit here and there—and the look is stylish. During this Christmas movie season so filled with mindless and mean comedies (*The Naked Gun, Twins, Dirty Rotten Scoundrels*, etc.,) a relatively classy amusement like *Working Girl* can seem a blessed relief.

But, in its own sophisticated way, Mike Nichols has created a movie every bit as mean and mindless as the rest. Suave technique cannot mask this film's hateful and divisive representation of women in the business world as bimbo or bitch cutthroats who compete for career advancement and male bed-partners. And, let me tell you, that's not my idea of a pro-careerwoman movie.

Working Girl opens with Tess commuting to Manhattan on the Staten Island ferry, past the benevolent presence of the Statue of Liberty. The men she works with at a large investment firm also smile on her benignly, but they have a wolfish glint in their eyes. These fresh-faced finance grads aren't that much higher on the dog-eat-dog food chain than Tess, but they buy and sell all day, and they view a lowly secretary as just another commodity to trade. They try to exploit Tess for her blonde baby-doll good looks even as they rip off her business savvy. They don't want to put her on a pedestal. She is the pedestal; an essential stepping stone in their own rise to power. That's why they refuse to sponsor her for the company's executive entrée program.

Remember the collective spirit and sisterly affection of 9 to 5? *Well, forget it. Today, movies like* Working Girl *reduce our careers to woman-vs.-woman competition in boardroom and bedroom.*

The first few minutes of *Working Girl*, which show Tess trying to be cooperative and at the same time self-respecting, are fine. Her revenge on a boss who sets her up as a party favor for a coke-snorting buddy in arbitrage is, in fact, the best scene of the movie. It also lands her in hot water. Personnel officer Olympia Dukakis, wasted in a minuscule cameo role, assigns Tess to a new boss, but first lectures her: "You don't get ahead by calling your boss a pimp."

In some advance promo clips of the film shown on a variety of television shows, Olympia also delivers a big-sisterish speech to Tess counseling her not to aim too high because working-class women like themselves are never allowed to live out their career ambitions. Interestingly, this speech is nowhere to be found in the final movie. The tenor of the scene therefore completely changes. Instead of coming off as a sympathetic figure who cares about Tess and who fought some of the same battles before she accepted a dead-end career, Dukakis comes off as a stern corporate bureaucrat who makes it clear that on her next "strike" Tess will be "out."

But Tess thinks that with this new job placement she's lucked out, not struck out. This time her boss is a woman.

Katharine Parker is a cool and very professional upper-class mergers and acquisitions analyst whose first order of business is to tell Tess know how she likes her coffee. ("I'm light, no sugar.") The next thing Katharine does is insure Tess's fealty with promises of respect and mutual support. She tells Tess that they are a "team," and offers to teach Tess about everything from power-dressing to the fine art of finessing a deal.

Of course, even before her crucial double-cross of the trusting Tess, we know that Katharine is no mentor. She is playing her assistant for a sucker. This barracuda doesn't care about anyone but herself and is apparently even more eager to steal Tess's ideas than her male bosses were.

Katharine's contempt for other women, especially Tess, is so obvious that the supposedly intelligent Tess must be a nitwit not to see it. When Katharine hosts an elegant cocktail do, she makes Tess do all the serving and excuses her exploitive behavior with the snide justification that "you can't busy the quarterback passing out the Gatorade."

A woman this selfish and career-minded is, of course, devoid of proper feminine emotion in the romance department, as well. She looks forward to a ski weekend with her current beau because she's "indicated that [she's] receptive to an offer," and fully expects his proposal of marriage. Her willingness to "merge" with Mr. Right isn't love. She later links it to the loud "tick tock" of her biological clock.

Katharine's ski trip results in a badly broken leg that gives Tess a chance to discover her boss's treachery, and to avenge herself in the bedroom as well as the boardroom. Tess impersonates, in Katharine's absence, the affluent executive she so wants to be. In a few days time she puts together a highly profitable deal with the help of Harrison Ford, the charming bachelor—who just happens to be that lover Katharine is tocking her clock for.

Tess proves her business acumen and she puts her night-school degree and all those emerging market seminars to use in a way that would impress a seasoned player and which seems about as plausible as a pumpkin turning into a carriage. Maybe I could have accepted the coincidences and spectacular improbabilities of Kevin Wade's screenplay if I'd been able to accept Melanie Griffith as Tess. I never could.

Griffith is the daughter of Alfred Hitchcock's last tortured ice-maiden protege, Tippi Hedren (whom Hitch ruined as an actor when he could not possess her). Melanie can give an excellent performance in the right vehicle. She has the cuddly, kittenish sex-appeal of a post-punk Marilyn Monroe. She bats her large, lovely eyes and purrs at the lens and the camera adores her. She was perfect for Jonathan Demme's *Something Wild*, in which she played a flaky rebel with kinky sexual tastes who careened down the road of destruction with the careless air of a child in a bumper car. Her image has developed into that of a bombshell who is wise in the ways of the world and the bedroom but who just a sweet, easily hurt kid (non-threatening to the male ego) at heart. Very Monroe.

That is not, however, the image best suited to the part of Tess, the ambitious working-class woman who has worked and studied long and hard in a determined struggle to build a career in finance. Tippi Hedren: now *there's* a woman who could have played this part and made me believe it. Remember her as *Marnie*? She was as serious and smart as she was beautiful. Embezzling all those lust-filled bosses was child's play for her (until she met her waterloo in that sleek monster, Sean Connery). It's possible that Melanie Griffith could have made me believe in Tess, too. But Nichols and Wade didn't give her a chance to stretch herself. They purposefully traded on Griffith's type-cast image as the sexpot of the '80s in a role that demanded something totally different.

The scene where Tess first meets Jack Trainer, the man she will need if she's going to pull off her impossible big-money deal, is moderately amusing. Moreover, it's completely ridiculous. Tess steals an invitation meant for Katharine and borrows a $6,000 dress from Katharine's closet and a couple of valium from Katharine's medicine chest. Thus armed, she crashes a high-powered cocktail party filled with the movers and shakers of Manhattan's business community. All the other women are dressed in their pseudo-male business uniforms (as Jack observes with considerable disgust). Tess walks in wearing an off-the-shoulder black cocktail dress with sequin sparkles, black silk stockings, and four-inch black heels. She then flirts with Jack (not knowing, of course, who he is), willingly drinks Tequila cocktails with him (knowing that she's already pumped full of tranquilizers), leans into his face and murmurs seductively that she has "a head for business and a bod for sin." She leaves with him but is so stoned that she can't remember where she lives. Then she passes out.

How can we take this creature seriously as an ambitious careerwoman? How can Jack? Yet he does. When they meet officially the next day, he still eagerly enters into the business deal with her that is as crucial to his career as it is to hers. And when it starts to gel, he promptly falls in love with her, too. I was less easily won over. Even upwardly-mobile working-class women know the importance of proper business dress. And we know that tranks and booze don't mix. (After waiting all her life for this chance, would a smart cookie risk blowing it by getting bombed out of her gourd at an influential gathering?) And we working-class working girls hardly ever vacuum our rugs, as Griffith's Tess does, wearing nothing but a pair of french-cut bikini panties.

I hear tell that some of those male critics who liked *Working Girl* saw it as a throwback to the career-women comedies of the '40s. Which comedies are those? *Working Girl* is nothing like any of the classics I remember. Try to picture Katherine Hepburn or Rosalind Russell playing one of their career parts as this kind of bimbo. Maybe you can. I can't. They had more respect for themselves and the women they played.

I don't blame Melanie Griffith for this mortified character. She read the lines and performed the actions written for her as she was directed to do. The black garter-belt shots were probably not her idea. Neither do I blame Sigourney Weaver for the woman-hating monster she plays. Weaver, in fact, manages to suffuse her villainy with such irony and playfulness that she dilutes much of her role's misogynist sting.

Likewise Joan Cusack, as Tess's best friend from the old neighborhood, overplays her part to the point of hilarity, without crossing over into the ludicrous and insulting. Cusack has played quite a few female best-buddy support roles in her short career, and she's wonderful at it. She, if not the movie itself, really is a marvelous throwback to the '40s comedies. She may well be the Eve Arden of the '80s and '90s. And *that's* a real compliment in my book.

As for Mike Nichols, if he was trying to create a screwball comedy or a farce, he forgot to tell half of his cast. Certainly neither Melanie Griffith nor Harrison Ford got the message. Mr. Nichols is true, at least, to his fairy tale concept. In *Working Girl* the evil step-sister is banished. And, since this is a male-written fable, it is the charming prince and the noble king (Philip Bosco as tycoon Oren Trask) who champion our poor little (sexy) princess. Through their noble, masculine love and sponsorship the princess is insured a golden new life.

Some would call that a happy ending. I'm not one of them.

A RECIPE FOR SUCCESS

································

Mystic Pizza

To say that a film is "formula-ridden" or "by the book" is not exactly a compliment. Critics usually employ such phrases when they are feeling particularly snide. And yet, there's nothing really wrong with a formula. Chemists and mathematicians swear by them. Of course, they're looking to achieve the same results time after time. And so is Hollywood. The preferred result is always big box office. So anytime a film hits it big, you can expect to see countless pale imitations of it in a year or so.

And that's enough to make anyone feel snide. Familiarity breeds contempt among movie-goers. We aren't as dumb as we look, sitting in the dark with our mouths filled with popcorn. We know when we've been had. We know when we've seen the same movie done better before, and we don't like it. That's why sequels and imitators rarely do as well commercially as the original hit.

On the other hand, they rarely belly-flop, either. Familiarity is also a comfort. We are drawn to formula fiction like mystery stories, and formula films (be they slasher flicks or buddy movies), because they are old friends. Old shoes. At the very least, they're a known quantity. Not quite as much of a cultural crap-shoot as the movies the critics hail as "groundbreaking" or "visionary." (Those are the ones that can really send you out of the theatre shaking your head in disgust.)

The key to a good formula book or movie isn't all that different from the key to a meal cooked well with the aid of a recipe. You use the best ingredients you can get. You follow the cookbook fairly closely, but you add just a pinch of this and a touch of that. With a great deal of care, you try to transform somebody else's concoction into your own. If you do it right, people will recognize the dish as one they've eaten before, but never better. And they'll eagerly come back for seconds.

Believe it or not, extended cooking analogies do not come

naturally to me. (I may be a woman, but I'm *not*—heaven forfend—the family chef.) But somehow it seemed an appropriate comparison as I sit down to write about one of the tastiest formula movies I've seen in a long time, *Mystic Pizza*.

You could say that *Mystic Pizza* is a buddy picture. But in this case the three friends are all women. That alone makes it a refreshing variation on the formula, since shockingly few buddy pictures are made about us gals. And, here's a switch, this is a buddy picture in which there are no punches thrown, guns fired, cars demolished, or cities leveled. This one is about relationships. You might, therefore, prefer to think of it in terms of another formula—the "woman's picture." But this is no weepie. No one dies. And hearts may be broken, but only temporarily.

Mystic Pizza may well straddle two formulas because it was written by committee. Writer and director Amy Jones (*Slumber Party Massacre*, *Love Letters*) came up with the story while on holiday in Connecticut, and she produced the screenplay with the sister-writing team of Perry and Randy Howze, and with recent Pulitzer-winning playwright Alfred Uhry (*Driving Miss Daisy*). But despite the many hands, and the two formulas, *Mystic Pizza* somehow works.

From the opening title sequence of childhood photos (some of which employ that ridiculous *National Enquirer* technique of phony photography, superimposing one person's head on another's body) to the sappy closing theme song ("I know that we'll be friends for life . . . ."), *Mystic Pizza* makes clear its focus. In contradiction to the ads that claim that this is a story about "six people . . . searching for the perfect romance," this movie is really about three women maintaining the perfect friendship—so that they can survive their far-from-perfect romances.

Kat Araujo (Annabeth Gish) and her sister, Daisy (Julia Roberts), work with their childhood pal, JoJo Barboza (Lili Taylor) waiting tables at the title pizza parlor owned by Leona (Conchata Ferrell). High school is over. Each young woman must now face the growing demands of adulthood. Working out relationships with the opposite sex is a major part of that process.

And that's not just Hollywood's obsession with romantic love talking. Working-class women like JoJo and Daisy and Kat are expected to leap directly from high school into marriage and child-rearing. Kat, the brainiest and most ambitious of the

Shoulder to shoulder (left to right): Julia Roberts, Lili Taylor, and Annabeth Gish serve up a heavenly little formula flick in a 1988 release that women made a "sleeper hit," Mystic Pizza.

three, has won a partial scholarship to Yale. Her mother and friends aren't surprised that she's "got no time for boys." But sister Daisy, wild and fun-loving, is expected to settle down now. And JoJo, who already has a steady boyfriend, is expected to immediately marry, be fruitful and multiply.

The thing is, JoJo isn't ready to sign her life away. As the film opens, she is walking down the aisle, her face as white as her gown. The magnitude of what she is about to do has her in a blind panic. She passes out as a way of getting out of her wedding.

She loves her long-time boyfriend, Bill (Vincent Phillip D'Onofrio), but when the priest starts intoning about the "binding and permanent union" of marriage, it's more than JoJo can take. She fears that she'll soon be trapped at home with lots of kids, "picking fish scales out of Bill's boot." She wants Bill. She just doesn't want the kind of marriage she sees around her in her Portuguese-American community.

It is a flight from commitment coming from the woman, not the man. Bill thinks the marriages around him look great. (Who wouldn't want to have someone to pick the fish scales out of their work boots?) He is humiliated when JoJo backs out of the marriage and morally outraged that she still wants to sleep with him. The movie plays JoJo's resistance to marriage for its gender-switch comedy value, but the thing I liked best about the treatment of JoJo's fear of losing her/Self in marriage is that a very common female phobia was, against tradition, actually being shown on screen.

And Lili Taylor, a little dynamo, brings all the intricate emotions needed to the part of JoJo. She is a comedy natural with a quirky beauty that may never allow her to become a star, but that makes her a joy to watch. A more conventional beauty, with almost as much sass as Taylor's, is Eric's little sister, Julia Roberts.

Roberts's Daisy is the wildest of the three young women. Like JoJo, she is sexually active. Unlike her friend, she has little interest in a man who smells of fish. Permanent relationships of any kind hold little interest for her. There is only one reason to marry, according to Daisy, and that's "to get the Hell out of Mystic." Her best prospect for an escape-route lover is a "preppy with a Porche" who flirts with her over a pool table while slumming at her neighborhood bar.

But Charles Gordon Winsor (Adam Storke) may not be as good a catch as his automobile would indicate. It's a test of Daisy's romantic smarts and more specifically of her self-respect to see what she'll do to maintain the relationship. But, at least her lover is single. Her perfect sister Kat has a crush on the married man she baby-sits for.

Kat works hard at four jobs to raise enough of the green stuff to make use of her scholarship to Yale. Her new boss, architect Tim Travers (William R. Moses), is a Yalie, too. He is the kind of gentle, creative, well-educated man most likely to stir the heartstrings of a sexually-inexperienced egg-head like Kat. But the audience can tell, even if Kat can't, that Tim is also one of Hollywood's white, soft, marshmallow-yuppies.

Annabeth Gish has the thankless task of playing Kat. Brainy goody-goody types are death to portray, but Gish never lets her character slip into angelic nerdiness. Kat is fallible without being foolish. And she's such a sweetheart that when her heart breaks, it'll almost break yours.

The nice thing about *Mystic Pizza*, compared to formula precursors like *Three Coins in the Fountain* (1954), is that the filmmakers felt no need to pair everyone up in marriageable sets by the end of the film. Only one couple gets married at the end of *Mystic Pizza*, and you can view their wedding as a happy ending, or not—the filmmakers acknowledge a certain ambivalence even on the part of the bride.

The lack of complete romantic resolution, in triplicate, never really matters because the key relationships here aren't boy-girl, but girl-girl. That's why the final clinch in this movie is among the three women. The audience is given an upbeat ending, but the all the sentimental surety of the story rests in the undying friendship of JoJo and Daisy and Kat, not in their marriages to Misters Right. It's an ever-after of a different sort, this sweet little film that tells us that love is a crap-shoot, but sisterhood is a sure thing.

Part buddy-picture, part-woman's picture, *Mystic Pizza* is a formula movie that justifies the existence of formula movies. It follows the recipe but adds just a pinch of the *je nes sais quoi* that makes a movie worth watching. It's kind of like Leona's pizza. Her secret combination of herbs and spices makes hers "a slice of heaven." The movie first-time director Donald Petrie and his writing committee and talented cast put together may not be heaven, but it'll make you glad you went to the movies. And these days, that's high praise, indeed.

ARTIFICIAL FLOWERS

Steel Magnolias

In 1939, that golden year of classic Hollywood, George Cukor directed a very fine film from a sharp, funny script by Anita Loos and Jane Murfin featuring a matched set of sterling performances by an all-star, all-female cast. It was called *The Women*, and it was a fairly faithful adaptation of Clare Boothe's hit Broadway play of the same name. *The Women* is a fascinating piece of both literature and filmmaking. Seldom have women been given so much attention. Seldom have we been portrayed in such a uniformly negative manner. Long before she married the king of the Time-Life empire, Henry Luce, and turned Catholic and passionately Republican, Boothe had flirted with the first wave of feminism. But there is nothing feminist about her first hit play (produced a year after she snagged her mogul second husband) in which Clare exposes her sex as shallow, vindictive, and consumed by greed.

The Loos/Murfin adaptation allowed the film cast, including Norma Shearer, Joan Crawford, Rosalind Russell, and Paulette Goddard, to show a little more compassion and friendship for one another than their stage counterparts. For that reason, and its tighter construction, the movie is an improvement over the play, even though Boothe's version was, surprisingly enough, more critical of its own snobbishness. Unlike her adaptors, Boothe associated some of the women's empty-headed nastiness with their owning-class status. Servants, beauticians, and nurses are shown to have a slightly more acceptable value system. However, none of the just-plain-gals had more than a few lines.

Minor differences exist between stage and screen versions, but Cukor and the film's writers had the good sense not to alter the most essential aspect of the play, its all-female cast of characters. Absolutely no men appear in *The Women*, although their importance as a means of wealth and security for pampered (but powerless) women is a matter of obsessive concern. Men are a subject of constant discussion. They are sometimes ridiculed, but more often fought over and pined for. But they are never seen. *The Women* proclaims what it is about in the title, and neither Boothe nor Loos and Murfin wish to allow their attention to wander from their study of women's relationships with one another.

What a pity over-producer Ray Stark and I'd-rather-be-dancing-director Herbert Ross weren't as focused. They talked fledgling screenwriter Robert Harling into diluting his perfectly good stage play, *Steel Magnolias*, by adding scores of characters (most of them men), a smattering of low-humor sight gags (like a bird relieving itself on Shirley MacLaine's face), and a variety of sentimental and tacky locales. Bobby Harling's two-act love letter to the strength and sisterhood of Louisiana women ends up, in the hands of Stark and Ross, looking more like a Mardi Gras parade.

Harling wrote his play as therapy a few years back. He needed to work through his feelings about his older sister, Susan, a pediatric nurse, and her fight to live life, as a diabetic,

Passing on a few secrets of southern femininity, M'Lynn Eatenton (Sally Field) has a heart-to-heart with daughter Shelby (Julia Roberts) on her very pink wedding day in Steel Magnolias.

on her own terms. The play's central relationship was based of that of his sister and his mother. And it represents two generations of fierce maternal instinct and self-sacrifice.

More generally, *Steel Magnolias* is about the friendships of small-town women. The sole setting of the play is a home-based beauty parlor in Chinquapin, Louisiana, where six women gather regularly. While not a great play, it provided the audience, as well as the six characters, with the release of "laughter through tears," a favorite emotion of us all.

The movie isn't half as good, although most of Harling's one-liners are still there, and the tragic touches of the plot are milked for everything they're worth. The overall effect of the movie is manipulative instead of heartfelt. Stark and Ross didn't open up their story, they flattened it. With Ross's restless camera zipping from Christmas carnivals to Easter egg hunts on flower-drenched green hillsides, there is little chance for quiet intimacy at Truvy's Beauty Spot. The relationships of the women are likewise belittled when the screen is constantly full of men shooting off guns, throwing footballs, making moon-eyes, growling and scowling, and otherwise making a nuisance of themselves by drawing attention to their presence.

It's not that I think men shouldn't been seen or heard at the movies. (Well, maybe I *do* sometimes feel that way when I've seen a particularly nasty male-bonding-from-hell flick, but that's another story . . . .) It's that they had no business in this particular story. They're extraneousness is obvious in every scene. And it's not as though even one of the male characters is developed in a meaningful way. Tom Skerritt, as Drum, is an eccentric in search of some mannerisms. And Sam Shepard, as Truvy's husband, Spud, doesn't even try to play the Southern red-neck he's supposed to be. He plays himself, a sullen, sophisticated big-shot, doing an indifferent impersonation of the sullen, unsophisticated Camel-smoking cowboy he likes to write about.

Shepard spoils every scene he's in, which is even more of a shame than it should be because his scenes are played with Dolly Parton, who gives the movie's best performance. The pink-clawed and puffy-wigged Ms. Parton is delightful as "glamour technician" Truvy Jones. When she says a line like "there is no such thing as natural beauty," you're sure that no one else could say it with such sincerity and humor. Her Tennessee twang sounds exactly like what it is. But if she never sounds like she's from Louisiana, she still comes several states

Removed from its hair salon setting, Robert Harling's play ends up fudging class realities. Would a beautician (Dolly Parton) hobnob with a rich, socially-prominent widow (Olympia Dukakis)?

closer than anyone else in the cast.

The rest of the bayou belles, when they can hold an accent at all, sound like escapees from *Gone with the Wind*. The authenticity of the women's accents wouldn't have mattered as much if they'd been given a chance to develop their characters and their relationships more. But Ross is too busy pushing pink roses and plastic reindeers at us.

The all-star cast of *Steel Magnolias* is, if anything, even more impressive than that of *The Women*. But they are sorely under-utilized here. Next to Parton's beautician, Shirley MacLaine as the rich and crusty matron, Ouiser Boudreaux, comes the closest to capturing her character. Sally Field as M'Lynn Eatenton and Julia Roberts as her daughter are certainly capable of delivering the pathos of the storyline, but they are given precious little to build it upon. Daryl Hannah's fundamentalist geek, Annelle, exists primarily as an arbiter of bad taste. And Olympia Dukakis looks, I must say, like the proud Greek-American that she is. She neither looks nor sounds like a woman named Clairee Belcher.

The problem with *Steel Magnolias* is not, however, bad

casting. These actors are some of the best working in Hollywood today. Their rapport appears excellent. And all seem to be mature and generous enough to set aside stardom for a good stretch of ensemble acting. Ross just refuses to let them come to rest together in Truvy's salon (or M'Lynn's living room) for more than a moment.

The best scenes are the quietest ones, but we are allowed far too few of them. The scene in which Shelby (Roberts) tells her mother that she is pregnant is refreshingly uncluttered and honest, but I wanted more of it, and more scenes like it in this movie. When, later, the women gather together to comfort each other, it is the climax and conclusion of Harling's stage play. But the film cheapens the honest emotion of what should be the film's finale with a tacked-on scene pairing the women off with their men. The last shots are of slapstick and speeding vehicles, complete with a wave-your-hankie leave-taking crowd scene. It's an ending that glorifies the continuation of the nuclear family instead of commemorating the solace of women's friendships.

Harling, voluntarily, one assumes, allowed the intimacy of his little world of women to be shattered. It's sad, really. Because I think Robert Harling likes women more than Clare Boothe Luce ever did. (She was one of those so-called feminists interested in change only so she could get her own piece of the pie. When Henry Luce bought her her own dessert cart, she showed what she really thought of the rest of us.) *The Women* liked women less, but enjoyed the pleasure of our (nasty) company more. Rosalind Russell was able to milk the physical comedy of her malicious bitch role to the hilt. Norma Shearer was radiant as the proud and naive wife and mother. Joan Crawford's predator was allowed a few touches of sympathy, as were the rest of the silly, selfish and weak women of the extensive cast.

The marvelous cast of *Steel Magnolias*, even though their characters are uniformly sympathetic, never come together with as much intensity as *The Women*. Mrs. Luce knew that a rich man's wealth and power can dominate a woman from hundreds of miles away. In her own twisted way, she ably made that point. Harling knows another truth—that as long as women are there for each other, to share the giggles and the tears, we can get through anything. Unfortunately, Ross and Stark never allow him to really prove his point. They fill the screen with gewgaws and male mushheads. The women gather, on cue, for group shots, but they never become the family Bobby Harling meant them to be.

What's the world coming to? Women used to be able to find refuge from the world of men in the beauty parlor, at least. In Tinsel Town, they'll strip us of even that sanctuary. It is easy to be entertained by the Rastar Production of *Steel Magnolias*. And it's nice that Hollywood is making laugh-filled weepies for women leads again. It would be a lot better if they'd learn to do it right. They could start by giving the female stars enough time and attention to develop their juicy characters and caring relationships.

Hot-house flowers may have big blooms, but they seldom smell as sweet as the real thing. So it is with these six artificial steel magnolias. They never prove their metal, and they never completely win our hearts.

A HARD WOMAN IS
GOOD TO FIND

• •

Blue Steel and *Impulse*

Women are hungry for our own forceful, resolute "action" heroes. It's never been easy to find them. And the hardest place to find them is on the silver screen, where the ultra-sexist, pumped-up-on-steroids action picture is still the dominant formula. Most popular written fiction formulas have, since the '70s and the mainstreaming of the women's movement, more readily reflected a change. Even science fiction, long considered a man's domain, has experienced a real feminist flowering since writers like Joanna Russ and Vonda N. McIntyre forced critics and readers to see the exciting possibilities of a fictional world where women matter.

Mystery fiction has always included women in the first rank of authors. And if Harriet Vane always played second-sleuth to Peter Wimsey, there have been other (albeit infrequent) examples of intelligent woman investigators in starring roles since the nineteenth century. Yet, for the first century or so of the genre, about the best we could hope for were Miss Marple types who were smart and determined, but physically non-threatening, frail and prim ladies who packed their knitting, never a rod.

And maybe it's a good thing women detectives relied on wits instead of firearms. Because the kind of thriller heroine who'd carry a gun was usually much less appealing to women than those old-fashioned spinster masterminds. Created with male audiences in mind, heroines with names like Modesty Blaise (or the countless minor *Playboy*-style Mata Haris with monikers like Pussy Galore) all had the killer instinct and a body to die for. These were boys' fantasies, these bombshells who enjoyed lobbing bombs and spraying rooms with Uzi fire. This purposely titillating melding of sex with violence held little appeal for most women.

For women who wanted female heroes who were both brave and believable, who sometimes carried a gun but never enjoyed using it, well-read mystery readers began to take heart in the late seventies. But it wasn't until 1982, with the first cases of Sara Paretsky's V. I. Warshawski and Sue Grafton's Kinsey Millhone, that the woman-created, woman-affirming "hard-boiled" mystery really took off. I was one of the mystery critics who hailed these tough new women heroes. And yet, I remember how those women private eye novels of ten and fifteen years ago sometimes troubled me.

For example, in Paretsky's first book, *Indemnity Only*, her Chicago-based p.i. sometimes slid into machisma, a reckless bravery and wilful violence which, for me, didn't quite ring true in a woman hero. V.I. was no male fantasy. Ironically, because of that, her best role models weren't those girlish sexpot spies that came before her, but instead the male hard-boiled detectives of the '20s and '30s and beyond. It only makes sense, then, that V.I. at times acted more like a man (or the pop. cult. representation thereof) than a woman.

That's no longer true. Vic Warshawski is now *all* woman, and a real feminist hero. The fact that Sara Paretsky was able to create and maintain a really tough, real woman goes beyond her own personal literary achievement. It means that the authors who create hard-boiled women after her—already, there have been dozens—will have an easier time of it. They have a tradition to follow, and their female heroes have a role model that works.

If mystery fiction could make such tremendous progress in its portrayal of women in ten years, one wonders why Hollywood is still floundering so badly. The success of *Alien* (1979) and *Aliens* (1986) with both critics and audiences should have insured a real blossoming of the female action hero. Such was not the case.

The few women's action films that did follow tried to feverishly link feminine attributes to the explosive extermination of bad guys. Like the newly maternal Ripley of *Aliens*, Amy Madigan in *Nowhere to Hide* (1987) is ruled more by her identity as a loving mom than she is as a blood-thirsty social avenger. She retains our sympathies because for most of the movie she is the hunted, not the hunter. And she has us believing the predictable fireworks of the film's climax because of the sheer power of her understated performance.

No one saw *Nowhere to Hide*, and since its release, women adventure heroes have generally been nowhere to be found. Whether it's in a low-budget post-apocalyptic science fiction film like *Cyborg* or in a big-budget high-concept cop buddy flick like the two *Lethal Weapon* movies, women's roles have remained shockingly, schlockingly retrograde.

The female cyborg may be the hope of all civilization, but she couldn't make it ten feet without the flying feet of martial arts hero Jean-Claude Van Damme. And those lethal, wise-cracking good guys Mel Gibson and Danny Glover define women by their roles as wives and daughters and bed-partners. In those two blockbuster hits, and in the countless male adventure movies like them, women are still important only as victims to be rescued or avenged.

Two new films, both directed and co-written by women, cop thrillers with women in the starring roles, try to do better by us. But both seem to suffer, like the women private eye novels of a decade back, from the lack of a workable model. They want to be ground-breaking, but they only scratch the surface of rich possibilities hidden in their storylines. And their female heroes just can't hold on to their credibility. Long before their final scenes, their characters slide into male impersonation or male fantasy.

The better of the two is *Blue Steel*, the first major-studio feature from director Kathryn Bigelow. It stars Jamie Lee Curtis as a New York rookie cop by the name of Megan Turner, who (on her first night on patrol) is forced to shoot a robber, quickly tarnishing a badge she's worked long and hard to attain.

When no weapon is found on the man Megan blows away—spectacularly through a plate-glass window—at a neighborhood grocery store, Megan's captain has no choice but to suspend her. This is unbelievable plot device #1. Not only does the movie audience witness the robbery and killing, but so do the store's cashier and half a dozen customers. According to the screenplay by Bigelow and co-scripter Eric Red, not *one* of those witnesses actually *saw* the wild-eyed robber waving around that .44. In addition, we are asked to believe that one of the store's frightened customers managed to swipe the fallen robber's gun and slip away with it without giving it (or a statement) to the police.

And, wouldn't you know, the witness who palms the weapon just happens to be a high-paid commodities trader waiting for a trauma to turn him into a schizophrenic psychotic.

Wounded, exhausted, and dressed in a uniform stolen from another cop, Megan Turner (Jamie Lee Curtis) proves she can out-macho any male hero as she chases her psychopath dream-date in Blue Steel.

Eugene Hunt (Ron Silver) falls in love with the thrill of death and with the beautiful cop who introduces him to the thrill. He carves Megan's name onto his bullets and starts popping off citizens of Manhattan.

When the police big-wigs realize that this new series of killings is somehow linked to their suspended rookie, they immediately bring Megan back onto the force. Her key-witness status gets her promoted to detective, where she'll work on the case with a seasoned, cynical and seriously handsome veteran, Lt. Nick Mann (Clancy Brown). Those on the alert for predictable plot developments might assume that Megan will take a tumble for Nick. She does, but that comes later. First comes her budding romance with the serial killer she's searching for, Eugene.

The preposterousness of the plot of *Blue Steel* left me gasping at times, and giggling at others. (And I wasn't the only one in my audience snickering at the screen by the monster-that-would-not-die climax.) But I can't deny the skill of Kathryn Bigelow's direction. Some of the visuals she works up with cinematographer Amir Mokri are absolutely stunning. And she helps Ms. Curtis give a compelling and appealing performance in the lead. There is so much to recommend in this movie, but so very little of it is related to the main plot.

Repeatedly throughout the film, men ask Megan why she became a cop, and it's the real answer to that question that is most fascinating. Like the men in mystery novels who find detection, as P.D. James termed it in 1972, *An Unsuitable Job for a Woman*, *Blue Steel*'s menfolk are appalled that a good-looking woman like Megan should want to become an androgyne in blue. She tells the nice-looking accountant introduced to her by her best buddy, Tracy (Elizabeth Pena), that she likes "to slam people's heads up against walls." (Needless to say, the fellow shies away, never to call her for a date.) When her new patrol partner asks her why she joined the force, her deadpan reply is that "ever since I was a kid, I've wanted to shoot people."

Both men are uncomfortable with Megan's humorous rejoinders for a very natural reason: she's serious. Her ambition to become a cop was fueled by a real yearning for power and a suppressed wrath, not against "people," but against *men*.

When, later in the movie, in the middle of a nighttime stake-out, Nick asks her the same question, Megan's answer is succinct and completely honest: "Him." You can believe that she's referring to Eugene, the maddog in the pin-striped suit, if you like. I don't think she is. She's thinking about her father when she says that. And she's thinking of papa, too, when she talks about shooting people and slamming their heads against walls.

Megan's father, Frank (Philip Bosco), is a batterer with a long history of abuse against his timorous wife, Shirley (Louise Fletcher). We are never told whether Frank abused Megan herself. Regardless, Megan has always wanted to humiliate her brutal father and protect her "mommy." Now she can. Megan's real triumph isn't in her final confrontation with her dream-date-from-hell, Eugene. Her finest moment comes when she finally clamps down on the first sicko who ever claimed to love her, her "daddy."

The sub-plot that provides Megan with her motivation is so much more interesting, and infinitely more believable than the primary cop plot, that I really wish Bigelow and Red had had the grit to see it through instead of falling back on an inane stalk-counterstalk two-step between Megan and Eugene. Did Megan's first big case have to be *about* Megan? (Couldn't it have

Trained as a painter, writer-director Kathryn Bigelow fills her movies with stunning visuals. Style seems to triumph over substance, however, in a violent thriller like Blue Steel.

been a mystery involving domestic violence, which Megan would passionately care about?) Make your female cop hero the primary target, and she is liable to come off looking like a just another damsel-in-distress.

Bigelow and Curtis don't want that. To convince us that Megan is no frail flower, they feel they must model her after the male stereotype of the crackpot vigilante with a personal score to settle. When they socialized little girls to work cooperatively, Megan must have been off watching a Charles Bronson festival. She thinks nothing of injuring or endangering other cops, or blowing a guaranteed capture of a known killer, if it means that she, alone, will get the chance to decimate her one-time dinner date.

"I, The Jury" vendettas are moronic, but they make even less sense on a so-called professional than they do coming from a distraught civilian. On women, whom the movie-going public is not trained to associate with mindless machismo, such antics are even more likely to appear ludicrous.

Megan isn't even very good at vigilantism. While Mel, the Lethal Weapon, can kill the majority of people he meets in a day with no difficulty whatsoever, Megan can't seem to kill her single yuppie target no matter how hard she tries. Over a period of several hours, Megan has to shoot Eugene several times *and* run him down with a car before she can finally empty a revolver into his heart, presumably killing him.

By milking the big, bloody showdown, Bigelow allows Megan to look like a total screw-up. And when, in the last shot, our hero collapses, a wounded and thoroughly vanquished-looking victor, Bigelow even denies Megan her final triumph. Jamie Lee Curtis ends up playing a part no more heroic—less heroic, it could easily be argued—than the plucky scream-queens she played in those horror films early in her career.

Considering that Bigelow's only prior solo directing gig was a vampire movie called *Near Dark*, her bloodthirstiness is no great surprise. But I would have at least hoped that a woman director wouldn't exploit her lead actor's body. Kathryn bailed on that one, too. (And considering the voluptuous beauty of Jamie Lee Curtis's physique, I should have seen the obligatory sex scene coming, from that moment in the title sequence when we're given a thrill peek at Megan's lace bra, as she buttons up her blue uniform.)

There are plenty of "B" directors who would have had Curtis stripping down, like some Immodesty Blaze, in every other scene. Bigelow is more considerate of her character (and her female audience) than that. The love scene Bigelow inserts into her story is nonetheless a stock situation that doesn't really make sense for her characters. By making Megan bed down with the wrong man at the wrong time, Bigelow betrays her again. All the tasteful low-lighting in the world can't make that scene anything but exploitive. Follow it immediately with an attempted rape by the maimed killer and you have a movie that deserves to fail.

I was less disappointed by Sondra Locke's second film *Impulse* only because I expected far less from it. I knew that much provocative use would be made of star Theresa Russell's lovely bod, but at least all the slinky outfits she's forced to parade around in fit (and how!) her character. Russell plays a vice cop named Lottie Mason.

Compared to Jamie Lee Curtis's sturdy patrol officer in blue serge and steel-tipped oxfords, a cop hero who's constantly dolled up as a hooker for solicitation sweeps would seem a much

Sondra Locke acted in action films with her onetime significant other, Clint ("Make my day") Eastwood, before directing one herself. Impulse *follows her deservedly little-seen debut,* Ratboy.

more exploitive image. It is, and is recognized and criticized as such by screenwriters John DeMarco and Leigh Chapman. That's what makes their convoluted cop thriller almost worth watching.

As with *Blue Steel*, the most interesting aspect of *Impulse* is the intersection between the hero's private and professional life. Unlike Megan, who is new to the force and eager to feel the power of the uniform, Lottie has been on her detail too long. She's spent so many of her days and nights treating men like tricks that she's lost all respect for the opposite sex. As for self-respect, the dishonesty of her daily work life has played havoc with that, too.

A good vice cop, Lottie tells her police-appointed shrink, Dr. Gardner (Lynne Thigpen), can't be a completely normal person. Judging from Lottie's supervisor, Morgan (George Dzundza), that must be true. He is a bigger dirtbag than what you'd find on an industrial Hoover. He tries to coerce sex from Lottie, first with promises of a promotion, and then with threats of losing her job. She refuses. He retaliates, making her already difficult work situations as painful and as dangerous as possible. On one drug bust, with Lottie as the wired buyer, Morgan maliciously roughs her up and then dumps her in a holding cell for hours. He claims he's only protecting her cover, but she knows differently.

The straight-arrow assistant D.A., Stan Harris (Jeff Fahey), sees what's going on, too. He doesn't like it, but demonstrates his disapproval by hassling the victim instead of the perp. Lottie stoically dismisses Morgan's harassment as "part of the job." Stan remonstrates that "it's not right." But Lottie sees too much of what's "not right" to be surprised at her boss's hatred of her for not putting out.

For all of his high-mindedness, Stan never offers Lottie any practical way for ending Morgan's harassment without scuttling her career. But then nice-guy Stan isn't completely comfortable with what Lottie does for a living. He has his own romantic agenda where she's concerned, and would probably prefer it if the woman he's falling for didn't play a fallen woman every evening.

Impulse could have said some truly challenging and subversive things about how little difference there is between good girls and bad girls—and between nice guys and bad guys. It almost does, before it gets hopelessly lost in the mire of its own plot. Lottie tells Dr. Gardner that she feels drawn to the life she mimics day in and day out. She likes to "feel the power over" the male "strangers" she entraps. She enjoys the fact that she can "make them pay."

It's all a harmless fantasy until, after one rough night of kill-or-be-killed undercover action, Lottie stops in a bar. Still in her slutty work clothes, she attracts the attention of a man with a roll of bills. He offers to buy—and not just her tequila shooter.

Dressed like a hooker, treated like one by her brother officers, Lottie has the impulse to just live out the fantasy, for once. She even goes home with the guy. In his bathroom, she throws water on her face and gets a grip on reality. But before Lottie can back out, her "date" is executed by a hitman. This is when the larger crime plot of *Impulse* really kicks in, and this is when a promising movie kicks the bucket.

For a story as riddled with coincidence as with bullets, consider that the anonymous fellow who propositions Lottie

She may look demure here, but—out of frame—vice cop Lottie Mason (Theresa Russell) is actually checking her gun. She relies on it more than on lover, Stan (Jeff Fahey), for protection.

(and then is promptly eliminated) is none other than the murdering drug dealer Stan has been searching for as a key witness in the same case Lottie has been working on for the D.A.'s office. If I've lost you already, you probably won't want to see *Impulse*. It gets worse. Much worse.

"I can never rely on anybody but myself," Lottie tells Stan. And in the violent situations of the film, that's even true. Lottie can wipe out an enemy with an efficiency Megan Turner would envy. But on the emotional front, even with her dates with murderers and trysts with partners, Megan has a strength Lottie is never allowed by her creators.

As a means of forcing a romantic solution, Chapman and DeMarco give their hero a moral cliffhanger of the lady-or-tiger variety that calls for her to choose between big money or her honey. Knowing what she knows of men, which would she really choose? Knowing what you know of Hollywood, what choice do you think the filmmakers *really* give her?

Blue Steel and *Impulse* are both the kind of failures that make you realize how good they might have been. *Blue Steel* tells us why a woman might become a cop. *Impulse* tells us why she might want to quit. They bring up emotional issues related to domestic violence and sexual harassment that their screenwriters couldn't reconcile with a conventional, male-oriented cop thriller. And so they abandoned their richest thematic material, and with it their heroes.

It's not enough to superimpose a woman character on a male formula. Action doesn't have to mean continuous violence. And just because the hero is a woman doesn't mean romance is her only means of redemption. Mystery writers like Sara Paretsky have shown us that women can be authentically hard-boiled and that a feminist hero can appeal to men as well as women. Now some brave filmmaker, maybe even Kathryn Bigelow or Sondra Locke, needs to prove that Hollywood can do it, too.

LOSING OUT AND GETTING EVEN

BAD GIRLS ON TRIAL

The Good Mother and *The Accused*

There are certain doctrines of patriarchy that run so deep, that are reinforced in our society so many times, in so many ways, that we may never get free of them. One such tenet relates to female sexuality. It claims, in fact, that female sexuality is an oxymoron. For virtuous women, at least. The deadly loop of patriarchal logic holds that good women are not sexual, that bad women deserve to suffer, and that, therefore, women who are sexual deserve pain and misery.

This is a belief that Hollywood has always embraced whole-heartedly, the so-called Sexual Revolution notwith-standing. Back in 1977, Diane Keaton taught us bad girls a lesson by being stabbed to death by her one-night-stand, Tom Berenger, in *Looking for Mr. Goodbar*. (Interestingly, this was a film that reinforced homophobic as well as a misogynist atti-tudes, since the sexual woman who dies for her sins is murdered by a psychotic who just happens to be a gay man filled with self-loathing.) More than ten years later, Ms. Keaton is still suffering for being unpure, as she goes on trial as *The Good Mother*.

Sue Miller's first novel of two years back was a phenomenal success, and could almost have been predicted as such. It was an exquisitely written story that had it all: believable characters, searing courtroom conflict, tender motherlove, *and* graphic sex. The mix was magic. And the message, that women are never really the captains of our fates, and that wanting it all is an act of female hubris begging for tragic consequences, was just what a backlashing American public wanted to read. Feminists read it too, of course. And loved and hated it. For burned-out feminists, Miller's novel was like a Stephen King horror story. It vividly expressed our nightmares about real-life in the '80s. Reading *The Good Mother* is enough to make you want to trade in your "Sisterhood is Powerful" tee-shirt for one that reads

"Life's a Bitch—And Then You Die."

It is no wonder that *this* is a novel Hollywood rushed to exploit. Producer Arnold Glimcher optioned Miller's novel long before it hit the *New York Times* best-seller list. Before it was even *published,* in fact. And what Glimcher, screenwriter Michael Bortman, and director Leonard Nimoy have done with Miller's novel is pure Hollywood. They have deflated the characters, diluted the sexuality, and amplified, instead, the backlash pessimism and beaten-down passivity of the title character.

Diane Keaton plays Anna Dunlap, the good mother. Divorced from an uptight workaholic lawyer named Brian (James Naughton), our heroine supports her young daughter, Molly (Asia Vieira), by working in a laboratory washing test-tubes— in the book she has a less housewifely science job testing lab rats—and teaching piano. Anna seems to want little from life except for Molly. Molly *is* her life—until she meets an attractive artist, Leo Cutter (Liam Neeson), at the laundromat. But there is, it appears, no room for romance in the life of a madonna with child. In Anna's case, becoming sexually active directly leads to

These two belong together, but in The Good Mother, *Anna Dunlap (Diane Keaton) loses the daughter she dotes on, Molly (Asia Vieira), for daring to discover the joys of her own sexuality.*

113

her "losing" the lodestar of her universe, Molly.

The biggest structural problem in the movie of *The Good Mother* is that the filmmakers are too embarrassed to really explore female sexuality, the subject they build their entire storyline upon. Part of their prudery was to be expected. In the book, Anna's sexual awakening is a process initiated by herself (in discussions of sexuality with other women, and time spent masturbating before her day begins), but not in the movie. Phallocentric to the last, the male filmmakers want Anna's awaking from her "frigid" life to be a direct result of the kiss (and other physical attentions) of her prince, Leo. But if that's what they wanted, they should have turned up the heat in the sex scene department.

Neeson, who is surprisingly good in the part, plays Leo as a cuddly, laidback Irish gent, not as the novel's abrasive and magnetic sexual force. And Keaton's Anna is hardly a woman undone by passion. The only time she doesn't seem in total control is when she indulges in those Annie Hall mutters and twitches that bring a regrettable sameness to every part she plays. These mannerisms can work quite well is lighter roles, like J.C. Wiatt in *Baby Boom*, but they don't belong here. Keaton's tongue-tied ineffectual air doesn't suit the role of Anna. And, I'll admit this, it generally annoys me. If she wants to play everything like a ditz, she should stick to ditzy roles, and leave the intelligent parts to the countless other women actors who can handle them better. Keaton, the screen personality, was especially jarring during Anna's seduction scene, where she comes off like an "aw-shucks," bashful schoolgirl instead of a repressed, full-grown adult. Her Anna never does let loose— until her climactic (and far too predictable) scene of maternal grief with all its screaming and crying and breaking things.

Letting loose is, however, the crucial action of this char- acter. For the audience to endorse the filmmakers' homily that sex is a woman's downfall, we must first be convinced that the ruinous relationship we are watching is one of passionate abandon. We must believe that a thoroughly sensible Anna becomes, temporarily at least, too horny to think straight. Keaton is never completely convincing as either the "before" or "after" Anna. Nimoy is, no doubt, also culpable in the matter. His direction of the lovers is the epitome of Vulcan restraint. Keaton and Neeson achieve a friendly tenderness with one another but the earth never moves beneath their bed. Theirs is so much a mom and pop kind of passion (even during the controversial scene wherein Molly climbs into bed with them while they are making love) that it's hard to believe that anyone could seriously question their morals.

Since we don't see Anna and Leo as *overly* passionate, and Leo's crucial episode with Molly is never shown nor even discussed as frankly as it should have been (the word "erection" is never uttered), the decision of the court isn't tragic and misguided, it's stupid. Yet Keaton's Anna responds to the decision much more passively than Miller's Anna does. Compared to Miller's heroine, Keaton suffers more for doing less. And the overall message of the movie is therefore even harsher towards women.

Sue Miller's heroine is kicked in the teeth by the patriarchy for daring to discover sexual passion. She is a lonely, hurting woman when the book ends, but she hasn't given up. She has her friends and she has herself to keep her going. She tries to actively salvage her life and her relationship with Molly in her own limited way. She begins again.

Hollywood's Anna is KO'ed by the court's decision, and is down for the count. Yet she is shockingly placid about her losses, as if she believes that the decision of the court *really is just*. She has even fewer resources. (Ursula is a close, supportive friend in the book. She is merely a jolly piano student in the movie.) Keaton isn't a woman painfully beginning again. She is a woman whose life is over. And what a nasty, reactionary statement that is: that a woman's life is so utterly maternal-obsessive that not living every day of the year with her child is enough to render her entire existence meaningless and void.

Keaton's kinship with her aunt (Tracy Griffith), who gave away her child and later destroyed herself, and with her grandmother (beautifully played by Teresa Wright), who spent half of her adult life wishing she were dead, seems absolute and poetically correct when seen through Nimoy's viewpoint of sun-dappled devastation. Nimoy has said that the essence of this story is summed up in three words: "It's about loss." So perhaps his movie isn't a failure. That's what The Good Mother is about to me, too. Women losing.

Also playing at theaters nationwide is another story of a woman up against the legal system for being less than pure-as-the-driven snow. But here the woman, and her champion, another woman, can be seen as winners at the end of the movie. And that makes for a very different movie experience.

The Accused is the story of Sarah Tobias (Jodie Foster), a waitress who likes to "smooth out the edges" of her life, of which she has many sharp and pointy ones, by smoking a little dope, and having few drinks. One night, not significantly different from many others, as she kicks back at a bar where a girlfriend works, she is viciously gang-raped on a pinball machine by three men, while several of the other bar denizens goad and cheer on the rapists to continued brutality.

The film's storyline cannot help but remind us of the 1983 gang rape of 21 year-old Cheryl Araujo of New Bedford, who stopped at Big Dan's tavern for cigarettes and a drink and was gang-raped on a pool table. Four men were eventually convicted of "aggravated rape," two more tried but acquitted. As we all remember, the attack took place in a public area of the open bar. While attackers repeatedly assaulted Ms. Araujo, several male witnesses laughed and cheered and watched while the victim "begg[ed] for help."

But it is *not* Cheryl's story, which is far too tragic for movie audiences to believe, that is told here by screenwriter Tom Topor. The names, and a great deal more, have been changed. Topor's story is set in Washington state among rigorously non-ethnic characters. The external story elements may be different, but the key issue is the same in both cases. Is the person who witnesses a crime and doesn't intercede for the victim in some way responsible for what happens? Are they guilty? And, if so, should that guilt be punishable by law?

The men and women who made this film answer a resounding yes to all three questions. They argue that witnesses should be held accountable for their sins of omission. And the filmmakers themselves might have some sins they want to expiate by making this movie. I can't help but wonder whether producer Sherry Lansing got behind this project at least in part to prove to women that she is the feminist she claims to be. You see, Lansing and her partner Stanley R. Jaffe were the producers of last year's blockbuster woman-hating hit, *Fatal Attraction*.

Much as I'd like to think it, I know that guilt doesn't fire Hollywood producers. Making money does. But even if monetary gain was her main concern, Lansing is talking a good game with *The Accused*. The press packet agitates for changes in our laws, citing rape statistics and making a pointed reminder of the Kitty Genovese murder. And in a short profile in *Premiere* magazine, Lansing said that she wanted to "make it impossible to hear about another rape without feeling outraged." She hoped the movie would "inspire Good Samaritan laws,

No rape victim "asks for it." Sarah (Jodie Foster), hero of The Accused, *is a drunken flirt in a mini-skirt and revealing blouse, but she neither wants nor deserves the violence about to befall her.*

making it a felony not to stop or report a crime unless doing so puts you at risk."

It is doubtful that *The Accused* will have such far-reaching beneficial effects, but I do believe that this movie, despite its faults, is on the side of women, while *The Good Mother* is not. *The Accused* shows women being victimized by male violence and victimized again by a male-identified "justice" system. But it also shows women as survivors who can band together to fight back in some way instead of passively accepting injustice and torment as their due. For its good intentions, I am willing to forgive such a film its various sins of commission. Then again, I don't need to ignore them.

Many women will be exceedingly troubled by Topor's use of a worse-case-scenario heroine-victim. We might well ask ourselves why the woman gang-banged had to be drunk and doped-up, and wearing a revealing blouse, a mini-skirt and heels, and a come-hither look. Foster even performs a sexy dance (first by herself, and later with a partner she voluntarily kisses) immediately before the attack. Doesn't the use of such a situation somehow imply that *this* is precisely the type of woman who gets gang-raped? And doesn't this invite the audience to think that such horrors only happen, after all, to bad girls, and not to them, or their wives and daughters?

Such a message is, I fear, an unfortunate by-product of telling this story in this way. Yet I can't completely condemn the filmmakers for utilizing a bad girl heroine because there is clearly a positive message as well as a negative one operating here. *The Accused* says to us, "Here is a classic situation you would dismiss, if you read about it in a newspaper, as a case of stupid woman who should have known better. You would have called her a tease who was asking for it. Well, take a closer look at this woman and what happens to her. See? *NO* woman asks for *this*. Get it through your thick skulls—this is ugly, horrible, violence."

Yet a dilemma still exists. How do you deliver the positive message without slipping a negative one in at the same time? Maybe you shouldn't show the rape at all? But if you don't, how do you expose the gang-rape as a social rite between men (instead of a sexual act between a man and a woman). By shooting the rape scene the way he did, director Jonathan Kaplan (*Heart Like a Wheel*) shows that Sarah was merely the target, the object of the violence. It wasn't about her. It was about male enjoyment of violent ritual together. As shot, the witnesses are clearly active perpetrators even though their pants stay zipped the entire time. And that is the point this movie sets out to make.

Is the rape titillating? I don't know. It certainly wasn't for me. And won't be for any woman. We see it late in the movie, after we have come to know and respect Sarah as a brave and worthwhile person. That helps keep the audience from enjoying the violence, but it doesn't guarantee horrified outrage. At the showing I attended, several young boys, aged from approximately ten to thirteen, snuck into the theatre expressly to watch the rape—which they vocally enjoyed. It's scary to think how early these male rituals start. And how unfortunate it might be for a woman to meet these same boys in a parking garage one night soon.

If the exact same story with the exact same scenes had been filmed by a feminist female director like Lizzie Borden, it would have no doubt looked and felt totally different. A feminist, for example, wouldn't have indulged in the kind of isolation games male filmmakers love to play with their heroines. Sarah has no close female friends (the only female friend we see [Ann

Hearn] was actually at the bar when she was raped and did nothing—although this *is* explained away, more or less, late in the film). Nor does Sarah have any family support. And her lover is worse than useless. This sets her up her relationship with her legal champion as the primary relationship in the film.

It's hogwash, of course. But at least the D.A. is a woman. (In Topor's bad-girl-on-trial screenplay of last year, *Nuts*, the savior lawyer was Richard Dreyfuss.) Kelly McGillis plays Assistant District Attorney Katheryn Murphy with an icy professionalism I found quite convincing. But did the rest of the women in Sarah's world have to seem so uncaring? Feminists are sure to see red when a rape crisis center worker makes a brief appearance in the film and is portrayed as even less sympathetic to Sarah's plight than the male cop who accompanies her back to the bar.

There are plenty of aspects to *The Accused* that are handled badly. I could carp for pages. But there are, on balance, even more to recommend it. Chief among these is Jodie Foster's stirring performance as Sarah. She plays her character tough, and not in a mawkish, slut-with-a-heart-of-gold way. You feel

How nice that a woman, Katheryn Murphy (Kelly McGillis), is Sarah's courtroom champion, but why is the film's male cop (Terry David Mulligan, left) more empathetic than its rape crisis worker?

119

her pain. And you also feel her anger, which springs from inner-strength and self-respect. She is, at all times, a survivor. She wants to fight back. And she forces the system, represented by Katheryn, to help her fight.

Class, lifestyle, and personality differences are great between Sarah and Katheryn. The filmmakers aren't so stupid as to imply that these two women will now be life-long best friends. But even if they never meet again, they have come together in a way that makes a positive difference in both their lives, and very possibly in the lives of other women. That's something you see precious little of in Hollywood movies. And it compares very favorably with movies like *The Good Mother*, in which bad girls/sexual women make their bed, of nails, and are then told they better bloody well lie in it. And smile at their suffering.

MALE MYTH, FEMALE REALITY
Shame

The movie hero enters. He is a mysterious loner brought by chance—and his trusty horse or motorcycle or spaceship—to this place, this time. The place could be anywhere. The time is one of crisis. Good (represented by old-west homesteaders, modern day hardworking stiffs, space-age goody-goodies) is locked in battle against Evil (open-range ranchers, violent street gangs, monstrous aliens). The good guys are losing.

The stranger, who wants nothing more than to be left to his own demons, at first seems both cynical and uncaring. But knight-errant nobility cannot be denied. Soon he is standing tall on the side of truth and justice. His altruistic championing of the besieged innocents tips the scales of power. Good triumphs. Evil is destroyed or driven out.

Whether you wanted to or not, chances are you've seen such movies more than once. Hollywood has always embraced such macho mythology. George Stevens' *Shane* is arguably the best rendering of that myth. Now Australians, known for their own frontier folklore, have created a fresh variation on the age-old theme. The film is *Shame*, and the pun of the title is, no doubt, intended.

This re-telling of a classic male myth is significant in its attempt to transform it into something female, even feminist. The loner/hero of *Shame* is a woman. The good guys at peril are also female. And the evil they must band together to resist is misogynist violence.

The film opens in the bucolic countryside of New South Wales. A helmeted figure in black leather roars along on a mud-spattered motorcycle. A road mishap forces the androgynous biker to backtrack to a town called Ginborak to seek repairs. As the biker pulls up in front of the local saloon, the town's young men take notice of the expensive and powerful machine and its leather-clad rider. Their expressions register envy, respect, apprehension. When the helmet is removed and the heavy leather jacket unzipped, their faces undergo a complete transformation. The arriving stranger is no longer a virile figure, a symbol of strength and freedom and a possible threat. She is now merely a woman. (Or so they think.) Their looks of uneasy admiration change to a sneering flirtation.

Asta Cadell (Deborra-Lee Furness) gives them a half-smile that recognizes both attitudes and dismisses them. She isn't at all flustered by or interested in the male posturing she evokes. All she wants is a drink and information. She gets the drink. But when she asks for a place to stay while she fixes her Suzuki Katana, the local sheriff, all sweaty armpits and greasy smile, tries to jolly her out of town.

Asta is not a woman to be jollied. She goes as far as the local garage owned by a taciturn fellow named Tim Curtis (Tony Barry) hoping he'll fix the motorcycle. He's uninterested in the repair job, but allows her the use of his tools and orders the part she needs to complete the job. The snag is that the part has to be shipped from the big city. Asta is stuck in a tense and unwelcoming town.

Curtis, a reluctant host, allows Asta to camp out in a shed behind his garage, annoying his mother, Norma (Margaret Ford). The Curtises seem, at first, unfriendly. But Asta soon sees and overhears enough to tell her that this is nice family at a time of crisis and pain.

Tim's teenaged daughter, Lizzie (Simone Buchanan) is brought home from the hospital that same night, the victim of a gang rape. And she is only the most recent in a long list of Ginborak women assaulted by bands of the town's young men. The women of the town live in fear, and the men either see no harm in the recreational activities of their "fun-loving boys," or feel powerless, like the women, to stop it. The sheriff is one of the complacent accessories, and even good men like Tim (and Ross, the husband of another victim) see the "shame" as falling somehow on their soiled womenfolk, and on themselves for not keeping them clean.

In keeping with her loner image, Asta isn't immediately filled with a fervor to stop the male rampage. Sympathetic though she is to young Lizzie, Asta would like nothing better than to get her part and get out of town. When her repairs are completed and her leather donned once more, she does not, however, make her escape. Norma entreats her to stay one more day and look after Lizzie. She'll lose her job at the pet food plant (where most of the town's women toil) if she doesn't get back to work. For Norma, a day means the difference between making a living or not. "What's a day to you?" asks Norma of Asta.

In truth, Asta does seem a different breed of woman than her sisters in Ginborak. Her motorcycle is the outward symbol of her rugged, independent spirit. She is an educated professional (while browbeating the sheriff to do his duty, she admits that she is a barrister) who is neither feminine in her attire or attitudes, nor easily frightened by machismo. The men perceive her as unwomanly. They call her "Butch" and "Dyke." To Lizzie the difference is less one of sexual identity than class identity. "You must be rich" she tells Asta. "You're not careful."

The difference is also a political one. Asta is a feminist, at least in the sense that she no longer denies her own rights and powers as a human being. And although she does little in the way preaching to the women around her, her example alone is

Director Steve Jodrell consults with his star, Deborra-Lee Furness, about her role as Asta, brave hero of Shame. *Asta's trusty steed—a motorcycle—awaits their next adventure, nearby.*

empowering. Lizzie decides to "lay charges" against her attackers. Since the one woman who tried it before her had been broken by her failed fight for justice, Tim and his womanfriend, Tina (Gillian Jones), advise her to "leave it to somebody else to be brave." Lizzie's stoical Gran, Norma, thinks otherwise. As a token of her support, she irons a dress for Lizzie to wear to the police station.

Now if this were one of those classic, ultimately upbeat old westerns, there would be a final, violent confrontation (with six-shooters on all sides) between the white hats and the black hats that would leave the black hats eating dust. But director Steve Jodrell and writers Beverly Blankenship and Michael Brindley take more realistic approach to the old myth. And their approach makes perfect sense.

After all, if you're a white male farmer up against a white male rancher who has a ruthless quick-on-the-draw hired-gun in his employ, evening up the showdown might be as simple as recruiting Alan Ladd, a good-guy gunfighter, for your side. It's not so easy for a woman against the patriarchy. I respect the fact that Deborra-Lee Furness doesn't play (despite what some reviewers claim) Asta like some Dirty Harriet. If made in the U.S., I'm sure that *Shame* would have included a gunfight, even if the old six-shooters were upgraded to .38's and .45's. No guns are fired in this movie. But there is violence. All of it played with enough authenticity to make the viewer wince and turn away from the pain and ugliness of it.

In realism's name, the filmmakers did something else, too. They allowed innocent people we have learned to care about to suffer horribly, and in one case, to die. And Asta, our strong and brave hero, is powerless to stop the suffering and death. In the final scene she seems as dumbfounded by grief and guilt as the rest of the Ginborak townsfolk. And that's a problem, even if it is much closer to the uncomfortable truth of women's lives.

Women sitting in movie theaters don't need any help in feeling powerless to stop male violence. That's the way we feel every time we open up a newspaper or walk an empty street after dark. What we need is positive cultural reinforcement of our efforts to take back the night. We need the Asta Cadells of the movies to triumph, along with the women they try to help. If there are any dead at the end of such movies, we need for them to be the men who perpetrated the violence in the first place. That's simple frontier justice. That's the tradition of the stranger/hero in Hollywood myth-making. It's the kind of storybook ending men take for granted, the kind of triumphant closure women are (almost) always denied. In that sense, *Shame* is just the same old story for us.

Shame is an admirable low-budget "action" movie. Jodrell's direction is honest and sensitive. He can take an action sequence and make it tense and interesting without falling in love with the violence of it, or taking on the viewpoint of the brutal male. That's an unusual talent in a male director. Furness and the rest of the cast give totally believable performances, aided by a solid script. But that ending! It left me feeling cheated and depressed.

I hate to say this, but for sheer catharsis and entertainment, the American revenge thriller is much more satisfying. This male formula took off with Clint Eastwood's exterminator-cop, *Dirty Harry* (1971), and Charles Bronson's civilian vigilante in *Death Wish* (1974). In the Death Wish series, Bronson, formerly a liberal pacifist kinda fellow, learns to enjoy blowing bad guys away after his wife is murdered and daughter brutalized. In the second movie his daughter is killed, causing his relapse into violence. By *Death Wish 4: The Crackdown*, Bronson has no women family members left to avenge (he is clearly a very dangerous man to be related to!) and must resort to avenging the daughter of his new girlfriend, who has been killed by tainted crack.

These are potent fantasies for men who equate violence with self-esteem. To avenge the destruction of a woman who belongs to you is to re-affirm your manhood. But there have also been movies of women avenging themselves and other women. There was the high-fashion victim-blaming of *Lipstick* (1976), which accorded Margaux Hemingway no justice for her own rape, but let her get off for murder when avenging the traumatizing of her little sister, Mariel.

Ms. 45 (1981) told the story of a young woman, twice-raped, who murders and disposes of one of her attackers and then goes on rampage against hetero-sexist men throughout New York. She takes out at least 17 before she is stopped.

Even Dirty Harry, in *Sudden Impact* (1983), meets up with an avenging angel in the form of Sondra Locke, who hunts down the men (and one woman!) who gang-raped her sister and herself. She gives the men a "38 caliber vasectomy" before killing them. She is so much a soul-mate of Harry's that he doesn't have the heart to take her in at movie's end. He lets her off scot-free.

Some recent films are, or at first appear to be, more earnest and less flamboyantly brutal in their contemplation of women fighting back. *Extremities* (1986) is an ethical debate of a movie, and it has the dull, talking-head scenes to prove it. Arguments are heard on the topic of a woman's right to deadly force against rape and male violence. But it's what we see in this movie, and how we see it, that's always worried me. Director Robert M. Young didn't even try, by the looks of it, to keep prurience out of his "male gaze." The viewer experiences the power-hunger and sexual excitement of James Russo's rapist much more intensely than the emotions and actions of the film's remote heroine, Farrah Fawcett.

More successful, but less well-known, is a low-budget sleeper from last year called *Positive I.D.* which presents a Texas homemaker and real estate agent (Stephanie Rascoe) plotting vengeance as part of her process of recovery from torture and rape. The film affirms that a woman must reclaim her life, re-create her Self, after the shattering violence. If reprisal can be a meaningful part of that reclamation, so be it, the film seems to say. Yet there is nothing glamorous about the violence in this movie. And there are no magic bullets to aid in Julie Kenner's recovery—so she gets off a few ordinary, deadly rounds instead.

Probably the most radical statement on female vengeance came from the Dutch feminist Marleen Gorris. In *A Question of Silence* (1984), three women beat, kick, and stab a boutique owner to death, not for his overt violence against them (his greatest sin seems to be a condescending disapproval of shop-lifting in his store), but for his symbolic representation of everything oppressive to women in a patriarchal society. That's a message that could leave even Dirty Harry feeling queasy.

Vengeance is everywhere in movies. And it's there because it makes the audience feel good. Cheap movie highs are not necessarily a sign of high art in filmmaking, of course. Nor are they uplifting for the audience. And a film full of bloody reprisal may call itself "realistic," but the ease with which screen vigilantes kill again and again without mortal injury or major legal ramifications is just about as believable as Dumbo taking flight.

If Asta Cadell had grabbed an Uzi and mowed down large quantities of Ginborak men, it wouldn't have made *Shame* a bet-ter movie. If the townswomen had turned the tables and started roving Ginborak in packs to victimize men who dared to walk the streets alone at night, *Shame* wouldn't have seemed more realistic. Woman-instigated violence wouldn't have made

Shame a better movie. And it certainly wouldn't have made it more truthful.

What we need here is a middle ground, a region for movie women to inhabit that falls somewhere between that moral high ground where good girls die young, in terror and agony, far too often, and that knee-deep-in-blood sewer we know as the male vigilante film. Such a place may exist, but Asta Cadell and her creators are unable to take us there.

In *Shame*, a woman who dares to fight back is destroyed as a direct result of her act of justifiable resistance. Truthful as such a storyline may be to the real "facts of life," it is not a truth I can bear to hear and see anymore.

I can't help wondering how different the story would have turned out if, when the helmet and black leather had been stripped off, the film's biker hero really had been a man. Perhaps then the innocents would have triumphed on Ginborak's dusty main street. Or at least in its court room. Instead, our strong and active female hero learns that standing up to the bad guys takes more strength and action than she and the mostly female good guys can muster.

In the long run, the crisis Asta helps ignite might make Ginborak a safer, happier place for women. But the short-term result, which is as much as the filmmakers share with us, is tragic and dispiriting. Asta's helping hand only makes a very bad situation ten times worse. When the knight-errant undergoes a gender-switch she comes off looking suspiciously like an interfering and incompetent biddy.

In movieland, the men can heroically play "eye for an eye." Women are still left hoping that the meek shall inherit the earth someday. I don't want female movie heroes to become macha vigilantes. I just want our side to win once in a while. Often enough to allow us to believe that winning is possible.

ROSEANNE'S REVENGE

She-Devil

Roseanne Barr is fat and loud and female. She is also a star. Consider, for a moment, just how seldom those two statements have been paired together. Can you name another woman who comes close to her body image and personality, who has achieved her level of popularity in this country? There have been other fat and funny women, but their jokes were fueled by self-hatred and a hatred of all women. There have also been maternal character actresses who were large of girth and big of heart. These women were almost always portrayed as kindly and quiet. They were packaged to provide as much wholesome comfort as a breakfast of Aunt Jemima pancakes topped with Mrs. Butterworth syrup.

Not so Roseanne Barr. While she may be, in her own no-nonsense way, maternal, she is never the self-effacing wife and mom. She is a presence that cannot be ignored. She dominates any stage or screen she appears on. And not just because she weighs 200+ pounds. It is more that she proudly represents everything a good girl is not. Her sarcasm knows no taboos. She talks about sex and bodily functions openly, while she cracks gum or munches on Cheetos.

Barr was born for rebellion. She grew up Jewish and female in that stronghold of Mormon patriarchy, Salt Lake City. Struck down by a car when she was a teenager, her physical wounds healed much more quickly than the mental and emotional ones. She "went nuts" and was committed to the Utah State Hospital for close to a year. Released, she was no longer able to pretend to be either a nice Jewish girl or a wholesome Mormon. For a time she led a "hippie" lifestyle. Later she lived the life of a trailer park homemaker with three small children. Through it all, rebellion was in her heart. It was this subversiveness that she tapped to produce her comedy.

The anger and the craziness is still there in her. That is her power as a performer. But I don't sense the self-hatred endemic to most of the women who have made a success of comedy. Roseanne Barr appears confident. She even seems proud of her round body, which she wouldn't mind baring in a film "as a political statement."

The pride she takes in her body is, if you'll excuse the phrase, no small thing. I remember when she was interviewed last year by Oprah Winfrey. Oprah, who had just Optifasted herself into a daintier dress size, seemed genuinely taken with Barr's uppity attitude and smart mouth. She nonetheless felt compelled, as a convert to the "control" of ultra-dieting, to sympathetically ask Roseanne whether she didn't think there was a thin woman inside of her crying to get out. No, said Roseanne. On the contrary. When she had been thin, she felt there was a fat woman inside crying to get out. And she went on to inform Oprah that women's need to be thin was a male invention for a world where women were supposed to be quiet and not take up too much space. Her Fat Liberation stance was by no means original. But she was saying it on national television with the authority of a celebrity—to a woman of equal celebrity who was aching for her to reject her fat self. I loved it. And I loved her.

Now Roseanne Barr is breaking into the movies. Her first film is *She-Devil*, directed by Susan Seidelman and co-starring Meryl Streep. And it would have been a much more successful movie if Rosie had been allowed to play a character closer to her own personality and to the image she projects in her stand-up act and in her weekly sit-com. *She-Devil* is mildly enjoyable, but could have been hilarious if Roseanne Barr had been allowed the same comic license as Meryl Streep (who shows that physical farce is yet another of her many talents). Instead, the filmmakers hold Barr in check, cleaning up her natural image even though the part of Ruth, the She-Devil, seems tailor-made for my favorite profane Domestic Goddess.

Barr has often called herself a "Domestic Goddess," re-claiming a term from the rightist best-seller *Fascinating Womanhood* that was originally used to describe a woman who slavishly served her man, and by so doing, honored God. Roseanne uses it "as a term of self-definition, rebellion, truth-telling." Her Domestic Goddess is a Nemesis, goddess of retribution, she has proudly claimed. And when you see the way she can puncture male self-importance with a sarcastic barb, you know she isn't *just* kidding.

Ruth Patchett (Roseanne Barr) is as pleased as punch to meet romance writer Mary Fisher (Meryl Streep). But when husband Bob (Ed Begley, Jr.) leaves her for Mary, Ruth becomes a She-Devil.

How appropriate that Barr should break into film playing just such a goddess of retribution. Feminist novelist Fay Weldon wrote *The Life and Loves of a She-Devil* in 1983. Her title character is big and homely and clumsy and has suffered for it all of her life. Without beauty or the saving grace of wealth she receives only contempt from others, especially her husband. When he falls in love with a romance novelist who embodies the feminine ideal, Ruth snaps. She becomes the Kali of suburbia, answering marital betrayal with wide-scale destruction of all her accountant husband and his glamorous and beautiful lover hold dear.

Weldon's Ruth is, in fact, ruth-less. She doesn't want to teach her husband a lesson. She wants to rip him apart. And she wants Mary Fisher, the gorgeous Queen of Romance, completely obliterated. Seidelman and her screenwriters, Barry Strugatz and Mark R. Burns (*Married to the Mob*) aren't willing to take revenge that far. They want everyone to like their *She-Devil*. But they end up making too nice-nice with a character who should be a Fury.

This is the film's major flaw. By neutralizing the intensity of Ruth's anger, the filmmakers blow their entire plot. Ruth's elaborate plan to deprive her husband of his four big "assets" (home, family, career, and freedom), makes no sense coming from their mild-mannered Ruth. Such conniving only makes sense coming from a woman who's consumed by fury and the need to get even. Ruth's revenge could have been very funny and very powerful. But Seidelman and her writers are so concerned with keeping Ruth sympathetic that they allow her to become boring. And film novice Roseanne Barr will inevitably take the heat for this.

It is surprising as well as disappointing that Seidelman didn't play Ruth closer to Roseanne considering that Seidelman picked Barr for the role specifically because of her image as a hilarious Nemesis. Like Madonna in Seidelman's first feature hit, *Desperately Seeking Susan* (1985), Barr was selected for the part because it was "an extension of her persona." Seidelman realized that any husband who would treat Roseanne Barr like dirt had better be prepared to eat some dirt shortly.

Bob Patchett (Ed Begley, Jr.), in Seidelman's *She-Devil*, gets his comeuppance, but in the end of the movie he is eating

Director Susan Seidelman (left) said she was drawn to the novel The Life and Loves of a She-Devil *by Fay Weldon (right) because of its insights into "the politics of beauty and femininity."*

cookies (he baked himself), not dirt. I didn't mind that. But I did mind the implied reconciliation between Ruth and Bob. Such forgiveness is appropriate for saints, not she-devils. The new Ruth is a woman who humbled her husband and his lover, and built a new life for herself, helping other women who've been "thrown away," through her Vesta Rose Employment Agency. She doesn't need Bob (or even her kids) to validate her existence any more. By suggesting that she might go back to a husband who clearly doesn't deserve her, the filmmakers negate all of their heroine's new-found strength and independence.

It's easy enough to point a finger at Strugatz and Burns and claim that they were trying to expunge Weldon's feminism from their screen adaptation of her novel. But, the fact is, I prefer their version of the story in many of its aspects over both Weldon's original and the BBC production of the novel produced a few years back.

The movie Ruth remains chaste after she is dumped by Bob. This fits her good-girl status, and means that Strugatz and Burns need not admit that Ruth and her friend and business partner, Hooper (Linda Hunt), ever had a sexual relationship. Call it a homophobic cop-out if you like. But I can't really see it that way, since Strugatz and Burns also leave out the fictional Ruth's several pathetic affairs with men. And Weldon's Ruth had each of her affairs (whether that with Hooper or a sexual sadist judge) for practical, completely calculated reasons that had nothing to do with love or sexual attraction. Similarly, Strugatz and Burns do, perhaps, show too much mercy for Bob. But since they show an equal amount of compassion for Mary Fisher and Ruth, I'm willing to forgive them.

Fay Weldon is just as ruthless as her heroine. In her novel, she breaks the other woman's heart and bank account. Mary Fisher is so desolate at the end of the book that she wishes to be dead. Cancer finishes her off. Weldon's she-devil is alive and prosperous at the end of her novel, but hers is a life that is a complete denial of self. Ruth becomes Mary Fisher. She spends millions of dollars and years of her life going through an excruciatingly painful surgical transformation that leaves her the dainty duplicate of her rival. She is thin and pretty and blonde. She even has six inches sawed out of her legs so that she will no longer be tall.

I thank Seidelman and her scriptors for rejecting this scenario. Their solution is, by my standards, a much more feminist one. Ruth's well-laid plans allow both her and Mary to take control of their lives. Ruth teaches Mary a lesson about the limits of Romance and then forgives her. Ruth herself changes a great deal, but not externally. Ruth avenges herself in a way that allows her to live happily ever after as her own proud, fat self. For that I am especially grateful. For as much as I like Meryl Streep, I wouldn't want Ruth to end the film looking like her. I like Roseanne Barr too much exactly as she is. And I would have liked Ruth, the She-Devil, a great deal more if she had come closer to the sarcastic Domestic Goddess we all know and love.

Well, not everyone loves Roseanne. Many critics who have reviewed the television show *Roseanne* and the film *She-Devil* have observed, acidly, that Roseanne Barr is no actress. So what? It may be true that Roseanne does not, at this point in her career, have the character range that an experienced technician like Ms. Streep has. She doesn't need it. Like Mae West, she is more a presence than a performer. But what a presence!

She's too much for some people to take. My mother, for example, will leave a room rather than watch Roseanne Barr on a television screen. There are rumblings that despite (or possibly because) of her popularity, America is beginning to turn against Roseanne. Attacks in the tabloids as well as backlash from quasi-lefty papers like the *Village Voice* are becoming more frequent. And columnist Diane White recently decided, in print, that she never wants to see Barr, hear about her, or read another word about her as long as she lives.

I wish White a long and happy life. But I hope that she's frustrated by constant reminders of the large, unrelenting presence of Roseanne Barr. And I think she may be. In *People* magazine's New Year's poll, Roseanne was voted Americans' "favorite female TV star." (Followed, not very closely, by another of TV's tough cookies, Candice Bergen.) And when asked to name which of several currently hot performers was "most likely to have a flourishing career in the year 2000," they again placed Rosie on top.

Is it silly of me to find this very encouraging? No matter. I can't help but be happy when someone loud and fat and female, like Roseanne, becomes a star. In a world where women are still expected to be quiet and not take up a lot of space, it's important to have women like Roseanne Barr around to break the rules in her highly visible way. When moviemakers discover how to effectively bring her powerful presence to the big screen, I'll be happier still.

GIRLS JUST WANNA HAVE POWER

Heathers

Life is so much simpler when you accept things just the way they are. That's true for teen movie heroines like Veronica Sawyer (Winona Ryder) in *Heathers*, and it's most definitely true for middle-aged movie reviewers like me. In trying to maintain a feminist/humanist sensibility, you always have to be on guard for the obvious and hidden -isms on the screen. But who wants to be constantly watchful when you're watching a movie? Eternal vigilance totally blows a movie's "mindless entertainment" value for you.

Beyond the movie itself, even the language with which movies are reviewed and analyzed by traditional critics can set your teeth on edge. Let me unclench my jaw and explain. I have the new, independent feature, the aforementioned *Heathers*, to talk about. The descriptor of choice for this movie and its ilk is "Black Comedy." Even the filmmakers, in their own press-kit, call this movie a black comedy. I, on the other hand, feel the need to reject that term.

"Black Comedy" is, it is true, an old and time-honored term for any novel, play or film that invites us to laugh at serious subjects like death and pain—the very things we mortals fear most. My problem with this bit of accepted critical jargon (in case it isn't obvious) stems from the fact that the word "black," a word we associate with a race of people, is in this case synonymous with the words "nasty," "perverted," "morbid," "grotesque," "absurd," and "sick." Our white power-culture has always defined black in negative terms, equating it with evil. (All those black hats Jack Palance wore were certainly no accident.) And this needs to change just as surely as the pernicious imagery surrounding women needs to be eliminated.

Black comedy isn't the only piece of film lingo I've worried over for this reason. I went through the same internal debate over using the term "Film Noir" to describe a certain school of cinematic suspense. Film noir may also segue on some insidious level into our racism, but I decided that "noir" was borderline acceptable because it describes the powerful black and white cinematography of those films as much as it characterizes their vision of the "darker" (ouch!) side of humanity. Moreover, noir is, for most Americans, undoubtedly a neutral word, *not* associated with people of color—or anything in the English tongue.

"Black Comedy" is a more obvious call, although I know that there are those who find semantic anxieties such as these trivial and silly. But anyone who has ever studied the portrayal of women and non-WASPs in cultural media knows what a minefield words and visual images can be. Something which appears simple and harmless can, in fact, communicate a message that is both complex and harmful. Even so, you could reasonably wonder why, if I don't like the term, I don't just ignore it. Because ignoring a thing not only doesn't work—you can grit your teeth so hard that you break a filling over something you *think* you're ignoring—it also fails to actively reject it. If a term has a racist connotation, I want to stop using it and find a workable alternative.

But what? For now, I'll settle on "Shock Comedy," because that's what these movies try to do. (I considered Sick Comedy in honor of the "sick joke" humor these movies use to lampoon the sickness of society at large, but I feared that even that term could be an quagmire—of the ableist variety. I tell you, it's rough for a writer when words are the enemy!)

Shock comedy may be cheerfully bizarre like the classic *Arsenic and Old Lace*, or it may be a gut-wrenching gross-out like the modern cannibalism tales, *Eating Raoul*, and this year's *Parents*. On the shock continuum, *Heathers* falls somewhere in the middle. In the film's key action, a teenaged girl kills herself (with a lot of help from two classmates) by chug-a-lugging a cup of liquid drain cleaner. Director Michael Lehmann and screenwriter Daniel Waters encourage us to laugh out loud as her body shatters a glass coffee table. This is *not* the kind of film content you would expect to please a feminist viewer like myself. Here's another shock: I actually liked *Heathers*.

My positive reaction surprises even me, since *Heathers* is one of those movies I went to expecting to hate. But it is, in its own warped way, a wicked little comedy with a virtuous heart.

Westerburg High in Sherwood, Ohio, is an affluent, middle-American high-school filled with trendy teens whose love of power politics far outweighs their interest in book-learning. One such teen is our heroine, Veronica. Which makes her an unusual protagonist in a teen flick.

In most teen movies, from *Footloose* to *Carrie*, the hero is an outsider who would like (at least part of the time) to fit in better. In this movie, our hero Veronica is an insider, "a member of the most powerful clique in school." She is an outsider only in a nominal sense of being the only female member of the inner circle who is not named Heather. Veronica has achieved a position of power among the school's star jocks and fashion-plate harpies, but she has reluctantly concluded that "popular" is not a good thing to be.

Power corrupts, even in high school. And the Heathers, Veronica's three "best friends," are cafeteria fascists. They have it all: looks, intelligence, wealth, and the admiration of their peers, but rather than rejoice in their good fortune, they seem to only take joy in bringing misfortune upon others. Their favorite sport, next to croquet on a well-manicured lawn, is insulting and humiliating less popular classmates. And while Veronica has come to abhor the reign of terror of the campus hotshots, she remains a collaborator because to rebel against them is to jeopardize her own social standing.

So Veronica rebels passively (or so she thinks) in a way women have passively rebelled throughout the ages. She attaches herself to a new boyfriend—one her sophisticated friends and zoned-out parents are sure to disapprove of. He is Jason Deane, known as J.D. (Christian Slater), a new kid at school who revels in being on the outs with the in-crowd. J.D. (James Dean? Juvenile Delinquent?) rides a motorcycle and wears black leather. He is unruffled by the abusive welcome he receives from the school's two most popular jocks. They initiate him into Westerburg's social strata (J.D. has instantly been relegated to unclean and uncool pariah status) by hurling homophobic insults at him. When the conflict escalates, J.D. simply pulls out a large caliber pistol and plugs them both. With blanks. This time.

Veronica admires J.D.'s independence and his contempt for the self-proclaimed elite of Westerburg High. Veronica is fed up enough to want to bring her so-called pals down a few pegs. Little does she know that J.D.'s intentions are to bring them down so far that they are six feet under. Before she knows

Veronica (Winona Ryder), expert forger and avid diarist, knows all about the power of the pen. By the end of Heathers, *she also knows the power of the sword— poison, guns, explosives....*

it, Veronica's "teen angst bullshit has a bodycount."

First, she helps J.D. mask, as a suicide, the death of the meanest Heather, she who drinks the "wake-up cup of liquid drainer." Heather Chandler (Kim Walker) becomes, posthumously, even more cool and admired than before. Classmates and teachers alike are amazed at her depth and sensitivity (she correctly used the word myriad in her "suicide" note). And the entire school is soon mesmerized by the mystique of teen suicide.

Veronica hopes that the death will make Westerburg a kinder and gentler school. No such luck. Heather Chandler's despotic rule may be over, but there's always a Heather to take her place. The once insecure and bulimic Heather Duke (Shannen Doherty) eagerly takes up the scepter as the school's malicious head honchette. And J.D. isn't ready to end his fun, either. The macho jocks are his next target for "suicide."

As with most shock comedies, *Heathers* makes light of some of the heaviest issues of modern life, in this case violent death and the false romanticism of teen suicide. If you take this movie as seriously as most of us take these issues, if you see it as a literal statement, you are sure to be outraged by it. But like the best shock comedies (e.g., *Dr. Strangelove* on nuclear war), *Heathers* isn't making fun of teen suicide or murder. It is ridiculing society's response to it. And it does that very well. Waters's script is clever, tightly constructed, and genuinely funny.

Still, there is something in this film to offend everyone who wants to be offended. When J.D. decides to do away with the two most sexist and homophobic BMOC's, he stages it, with ironic glee, as a "double-suicide" between two lovers, complete with "homosexual artifact" props. And then watches Sherwood react. These are scenes that can be perceived as homophobic, anti-homophobic, or possibly both at the same time. I let you chart your own response.

For J.D. there is no remorse. The two had "nothing to offer the school but date rapes and AIDS jokes," so what's the problem?

But, for me, the saving grace of this particular shock comedy is that Veronica *does* see the killings as a problem. Although she is often dismayed and angered by her snobbish pals (the two dead neanderthals had been spreading lies around school about her promiscuous, kinky activities), she doesn't think killing is the best way to resolve conflict. J.D. is dangerous and exciting, and she finds it "hard to control [herself]" when she's around him. But when she finally completely realizes that he is a "psychopath, not a rebel," she breaks from him.

It is at this point that the nasty satire of the first two-thirds of the film transforms itself into something more melodramatic. Those who like their shock comedies to be one nasty snicker after another right up until the closing credits will undoubtedly conclude that the movie runs out of gas. Those viewers who are shocked by *Heathers'* initial humor will probably not be mollified by Veronica's turnaround. They will see the ending as too little too late. But for me, Veronica's resolution of the mess she helped to create was just what I wanted from this wacky film. And Winona Ryder was just who I wanted to see in the starring role.

Ryder, who is all of seventeen, has never given a bad performance, although she has been in several atrocious films. In her second role, as the pubescent heroine of *Square Dance*, she gave the only believable performance in the entire movie, putting veterans like Jane Alexander and Jason Robards to shame. Her Veronica is even better. Ryder brings such honesty to her high-camp role that you actually believe a kid like this could exist. And, astoundingly, you think you *might* actually like to meet her.

Heathers is not for everyone. But I went to it expecting a deeply sexist film that trivialized the killing of young women, and found something else. I found a movie about one young woman's process of empowerment in which she first looks for strength as a member of a group she has no respect for, and later looks for power in a lover she fears. But finally, Veronica, spoiled brat and murderer, realizes that the fire has to come from within. She finds her power, and creates positive change with it. That's a shock I can live with.

MOTHERHOOD IN PATRIARCHY

LIFE WITHOUT FATHER

Men Don't Leave

True story: Two women, strangers sitting directly behind me at our local cineplex, discussed the movie *Men Don't Leave* as they put on their coats: "I don't get it," said one. "What's to get?" said the other, adding, "It was about death and grief and getting your life back together." "Well, yeah, I got *that!*" said the first woman. "Then you got it," replied her friend. "Yeah, I guess I got it. I just didn't like it."

While I don't agree with the woman who didn't "get" or like *Men Don't Leave*, I can certainly sympathize with her. Jessica Lange's new film turns out to be quite different from the movie the audience is expecting. We think we're in for a very traditional starting-over romantic comedy, and what we get is something a little closer to life. And that something else will either delight or disappoint you, according to how hooked you are on Hollywood's pre-mixed solutions to life's little challenges.

Our movie rituals are important to us. We expect an American film to portray people in a certain way. And we expect the movie to solve their problems according to a playbook we all know by heart. In an adventure film the good guy solves his problems by snuffing his enemies. (He never really *wants* to kill anyone, of course. If he did, he wouldn't be a good guy. But we have no doubt when we walk into a theater to see a male adventure movie that the body count will be high and the good guy is likely to be one of the few characters left standing.)

Likewise, we have pre-conceived notions galore about romantic "starting over" movies, especially those with a female hero. The heroine is supposed to be incredibly brave and resourceful, and yet still be unable to make it on her own. Just when life gets to be too much for her, a man is supposed to show up to provide her with solutions to all her woes. Scratch that. He *is* the solution to all her woes. Their final embrace (or family tableau, in the case of a *really* wholesome flick) leaves both lovers, and their audience, secure in the knowledge that love conquers all.

For the macho men of movie land, laying hands on a semi-automatic rifle is all the luck needed. For the ladies, a handsome man laying his healing hands upon *them* is their Nick of Time (et tu, Bonnie Raitt?) salvation. We know, deep down, that such easy solutions are not only simplistic, but actually dangerous. It's easier, however, to see the danger in films preaching that young men should solve their problems with an AK-47 than it is to see the danger in the countless films, over the years, that have suggested that women could find personal happiness only through an emotionally-dependent relationship with a man.

The romantic solution is still fervently embraced by most of us. That's why a marvelous film like Paul Brickman's *Men Don't Leave* is liable to leave folks like that nice woman sitting behind me in the theater feeling cheated. This is a movie that has a (tentative, awkward) romance, but it's never *about* that romance. This deeply-felt comedy is indeed about "death and grief and getting your life back together." It is also a subtle but very evocative exploration of the impotence of motherhood in patriarchy.

Beth Macauley (Jessica Lange) married relatively young and produced two sons. As the film begins, she is living the life of the full-time, middle-American homemaker. It's a good life that revolves around her husband and boys. Their lives never revolve around her. Chris (Chris O'Donnell), a high-schooler, and 10-year-old Matt (Charlie Korsmo) count on their Mom for cooking and care, but they look to their Dad to really manage family life. Beth and Chris and Matt are all, in a sense, satellites to the man of the house.

John Macauley (Tom Mason) is a building contractor who is also a true family man: the kind who makes everything right for his family, just the way Hollywood men are supposed to. He has the kind of magical, masculine touch that can instantly stop a refrigerator from rattling, open the tightest jar lid, or make a favorite battery-operated toy come to life. His sons enjoy tagging along to his latest construction site to watch their dad oversee a crew of other men transform an empty lot into a house.

Beth is locked out from the father-son rituals that make up much of her family's life. There is one poignant moment, early in the film, when Beth stands outside her home watching her husband take a business call and, at the same time, rough-house

When Beth Macauley (Jessica Lange) squares off with her new neighbor in Men Don't Leave, *she sees her as the evil seductress of her son. But Jody (Joan Cusack) turns out to be a friend in need.*

with Matty. She stands in her darkened yard and watches through the window, and we feel with her both the tenderness of her love for father and son, and her sadness at their self-absorbed male-bonding. Her exclusion is a kind of rejection that wounds deep, if only for a split-second.

Dad's power as a parent and a provider is such a given, and the love of his family is so unconditional, that John Macauley can be careless with it all. Or so he thinks. He spends all of his time building someone else's houses, and lets the renovation of his own home slide. (Beth's workspace, her kitchen, is covered by a wooden frame and plastic tarp.) He leaves Beth home alone, waiting dinner, wondering where they are, and thoughtlessly takes his sons to a movie—a sex comedy "about guys" and their "prostitutes"—he knows his wife wouldn't want them to see.

Macauley is a good man, a good husband, and a good father. It's just that his reckless confidence in his own life makes him, at times, less than considerate of his family. When he dies, suddenly, he leaves his dazed wife with $63,000 worth of debts and no life insurance. With so much depending on him, it was foolish and irresponsible of John Macauley to show such disregard for his family's future. But you'd never know it to listen to Beth and the kids.

In death, Macauley still inspires absolute family fealty. Even after she realizes how dire her financial situation is, his wife remains determined, almost desperate, to maintain her husband's heroic stature in his son's eyes. At the same moment that she informs the boys that they are too broke to keep their house, she repeats to them their family credo, that John Macauley "took real good care of us, and he was a good father." She will allow no criticism of the fallen head of their family to pass her own lips or those of her sons.

Beth, whose role had always been a subordinate one in the family, now is fully responsible for that family. It's a responsibility she never expected or prepared for, and it's a role her sons never wanted her to play. She has never worked outside the home, but now she must find a job that can support three. When her house is sold, Beth packs up the boys and moves to Baltimore, where friends have lined up a job for her.

Beth's new position is as "assistant manager" (read: gofer and all-around whipping-girl) at a gourmet grocery and deli run by an irascible entrepreneur named Lisa (Kathy Bates). The job pays the bills—barely—but does nothing for Beth's self-confidence. One of Lisa's few joys in life appears to be the humiliation of her employees, and the tentative Beth suffers Lisa's scorn constantly.

Beth's sons, too, show little confidence in their mother. They've lost their father, and with him their comfortable home and middle-class standard of living. They are hurt and angry about that. Since they can't take their fury out on Fate, they take it out on Beth. (When Beth tries to set some limits for her rebellious teenager, reminding him that "Dad isn't here and I'm making the rules now," Chris caustically replies that he wishes "it were the other way around.")

As much as they may wound and worry their beleaguered mother, Chris and Matt are both good kids. They just don't know how to make a family without a father—and without the money a man can bring to a family. Young Matty finds a new friend with delinquent tendencies and becomes his partner in crime. He pines after his friend's father-headed family, and labors to make his own family whole (and solvent) again. Chris backs away from his mother and into the arms and well-ordered domesticity of a flaky x-ray technician several years his senior.

Joan Cusack is hilarious and touching as Chris's older woman, Jody. Beth is understandably outraged when she thinks this woman is trifling with her teen-aged son. But Jody is no trifler. She is drawn to Chris not (just) as a sexual conquest. Their relationship *is* supposed to be sexual, and is problematic for that reason. Brickman and co-screenwriter Barbara Benedek realized this, so they soft-pedaled the sex so much that we never even see the pair kiss or hug. This lack of frankness allows the audience to see Jody for what she really is, which is a help-freak, not a seductress.

"I'm pretty good at helping people," Jody tells Beth when they first meet. And she is. So much so that when Beth finally succumbs to the stress and grief and depression of her widowhood, when starting over gets to be too much for her, it is *Jody* who gives her the needed push towards recovery.

What? Another *woman* helps Beth? Where's the new heart-throb who makes everything right again? He's there, in the form of a sweet, sexy musician named Charles (Arliss Howard). This guy is living proof that not all the good ones are taken. Seriously cute, he's the kind of affectionate and supportive suitor who is also, clearly, a terrific dad.

No doubt about it, this is a guy Alex Forrest in *Fatal Attraction* would have gladly died/killed for. Better, even—Michael Douglas can't hold a candle to Arliss. When Charles serenades Beth with his laid-back but ardent rendition of "Bella Notte" (from *Lady and the Tramp*), we *know* that our melancholy heroine will immediately fall into his arms, her heart melted like a stick of butter over a bunsen burner. Only she doesn't. Defying Hollywood tradition, Beth's heart remains hard with sorrow. She won't be ready for an affair—even with Mr. Perfect —until she comes to terms with a few other relationships. Namely, those with her sons and with own self.

In many ways, *Men Don't Leave* is closer to a coming-of-age comedy than it is a starting-over comedy. As long as Beth stood in her husband's shadow, she was never able to come into her full power as a parent and person. Widowhood is a frightening liberation. It forces her to leave home and make a life for herself (and for her sons). It's not easy at 18. It's even harder at 40. The process will allow her to grow in stature, as long as she survives it.

But with Jessica Lange playing Beth, there can be no doubt that she is a survivor. Lange proves once again in this movie that she is that rarest of performers, a star who is also a character actor. Lange is equally brilliant and totally different in her lead role in Costa-Gavras's *The Music Box*, also in theaters now. Both characters have equal strength and determination, but unlike Beth Macauley, Ann Talbot, the lawyer hero of *The Music Box*, is in touch with her capability from the start.

Ann Talbot's good life is destroyed by a different kind of death: the death of her trust in, and respect for, her father. When she is informed that her father is a WWII war criminal of the most vicious sort, she is devastated. If true, the atrocities her father once committed will make his generous, hard-working immigrant's life—and hence the life of her entire family—a horrible lie. The treachery of patriarchy is even more literal in this film. Ann's entire value system is based on her belief in her benevolent bear of a papa. When the sins of that father are visited upon her, Ann is forced to redefine her life for herself, as herself, and no longer as her father's daughter.

In a much more light-hearted and light-handed manner, Lange explores similar territory in *Men Don't Leave*. Beth rebuilds her identity as a woman and mother when she is no longer John Macauley's wife. At least, by the end of the film, we assume she has. Unfortunately, although Paul Brickman is meticulous about recording the tragicomedy of Beth's devastation, he is less observant about her recovery. This is my only complaint with the film. I don't know whether Brickman ran out of steam or time, but he certainly short-changes his protagonist's hard-won victories over her many tribulations.

You know it's a bad sign when costuming has to do too many of the expository chores. J. Allen Highfill abandons Beth's girlish dresses for a more tailored look as the movie nears its end. In the last scenes, Beth is literally wearing the pants in her family. And she looks mighty good in them, too. All the same, I can't help but wish we had a little emotional content to go with the visuals.

Rather than share with us the widow's progress, the filmmakers give her different clothes and a more confident expression to wear. And rather than show Beth and her sons really rebuild their lives, Brickman and Benedek force the Macauley family towards a reconciliation with a rather contrived crisis that allows Beth to show off her parenting wisdom.

I won't complain too bitterly about this particular descent into sitcom because the majority of movies would have done worse. They would have hastened a happy ending by having Beth fall gratefully into Charles's arms. "Why get a life, when you can get laid?" most films seem to ask. *Men Don't Leave* has more respect for its hero than that. The romantic aspect of Brickman and Benedek's resolution is highly ambiguous. Charles is still around in the final scene, but his exact relationship to the Macauley family is really left up to us.

If you are so inclined—and most of us are—you can dream up your own love scenes as you drive home from the theater. Benedek and Brickman couldn't be bothered to play them out up on the screen. They knew it was more important to show Beth take to her bed with depression than for us to see her take to her bed with a new lover. And when she rises again from (mourning) the dead, it is her sons she is most concerned about, not Charles, her winsome heartthrob-in-waiting.

Beth's life had once been filled by her husband. Faced with the vacuum left by his death, Jessica Lange's Beth refuses to fill it with a new man. Frankly, I was surprised that Beth turned out to be—was *allowed* to be—such a mensch. I love it when my worst expectations are proved wrong about a film and the people who make it. And I must admit that I didn't have high hopes for Paul Brickman and Barbara Benedek.

Brickman's prior film, Tom Cruise's big break, *Risky Business* (1983), was (like the movie Beth didn't want her sons to see) a lamentable film about a boy and his prostitutes. It was an All-American adolescent male fantasy filled with easy sex and the entrepreneurial spirit. I was far from impressed by it, although it was both a critical and box-office hit. As for Benedek's screenwriting for *The Big Chill* and the very recent *Immediate Family*, it impressed me, negatively, as coming from a woman who had little understanding for her sex or her generation.

Men Don't Leave, despite a lopped-off ending that doesn't *quite* have the courage to say what it clearly wants to say, is a warm, funny movie about very serious issues. Patriarchy has a way of constantly reminding us about the Importance of Being Father. And, therefore, the importance of having one. But what is the impact of this cultural imperative on the millions of children growing up in families without fathers, and the mothers raising those children?

"Boy, they sure do love their daddies, don't they?" Beth wistfully observes to Charles's ex-, as the two women watch him frolic with his toddler son. She feels the loss for her own sons and could have easily opted to co-opt Charles as a new father for her boys. If she wanted to. Beth makes a better choice: To empower herself as a woman and mother.

Charles may be a part of Beth's life, but he will never *be* Beth's life. Men *do* leave, or die, after all. Beth knows that. Now she also understands that she can be happy and strong and productive with or without a man around. That's not the romantic solution that woman at the movie theater was hoping for, but it's something we need to see in movies a lot more often.

FATHERHOOD AND THE NEW BABY CULT

Look Who's Talking and *Immediate Family*

Webster was the Supreme Court's wake-up call to women that our tenuous right to control our own biological lives was at peril. We have heeded the call. We are up and fighting once more, and that's mighty good to see. Yet I was surprised at how surprised so many women were by the high court's decision. Some were women too young to remember those hard-won victories, and others were women who, having struggled to achieve such basic rights, actually thought they had changed society permanently for the better. There was no question in their minds that their daughters and their daughters' daughters would be assured that legacy of Choice.

The antichoice backlash should have been no surprise to anyone. It didn't surprise reproductive rights activists who knew that terrorist zealots who attack clinics are less of a threat than the reactionary judicial and legislative meddlers that have chipped away at our freedom these past ten years. It was also no surprise to anyone who carefully watches mainstream popular culture.

Take, for example, daytime dramas. Abortions are out, babies are in, as one soap magazine recently stated. Soap writers and producers have, in fact, been so scared to touch abortion that even rape victims haven't been allowed to terminate unwanted pregnancies of late. Instead, on shows like *One Life to Live*, involuntarily pregnant characters had to fall out of lighthouse towers or have restaurant wine racks fall on them so that they could miscarry. No one could get upset by an Act of God. It was the possibility of a conscious Act of Woman that scared everyone silly.

On nighttime TV, reproductive choice has been even less

of an option. Maude had a mid-'70s abortion, but few other shows or TV movies would touch that particular taboo. And the nuclear family has always been the king of TV. And I do mean king. Increasingly, TV shows are celebrating the New Daddyhood in the program's basic "concept." Some shows, like *The Cosby Show*, are just slightly hipper throwbacks to the days when Robert Young dispensed wisdom but never changed out of his sensible gray worsted suit. Others portray a slightly less traditional family structure. But in almost all cases, father knows best.

In a clear reversal of census statistics, TV's single-parent families are headed by male householders with no wife present. Sometimes it's a young dashing dad with young kids (*Paradise*) and sometimes it's an older dashing dad with grown kids (*Empty Nest*). Other times a surfeit of sexy dads (*My Two Dads, Full House*) father and flirt all day long. Even the servant-as-everybody's-parent shows have replaced *Hazel* with *Mr. Belvedere*.

Those few shows that have represented the fastest-growing real-life home configuration, the single mom and her kids, have usually been yanked in less than a season. TV's *Baby Boom* allowed the new single mom to stay unattached and professionally committed even as she embraced the joys of motherhood. Needless to say, it didn't do half as well as the more sexist movie that sent our New York career gal off to the sticks to learn how to be a real woman.

Pronatalist propaganda is at an all-time high in Hollywood movies, too. The message seems to be that men need and want fatherhood and that for that reason, rather than their own desire for motherhood, women should start popping out those babies again.

Movies may advertise that they are about *Parenthood* for both sexes, but even these are almost exclusively about dads. Did you notice that in that particular hit movie, even the "shitty" father, patriarch Jason Robards, had a lot to say about parenting while his wife, who should have been the matriarch of the clan, had nothing to say about anything throughout the entire film? Her job was to have all those children who are now dealing with their own parenting issues. Having done that, the movie wanted nothing more to do with her. So she was told to stand around looking worried and keep her mouth shut. (Which she did.)

Motherhood is everywhere in movies these days, which is not to say that mothers are being treated well or fairly. Women who are not mothers are portrayed even more viciously, as we all know. So it's no wonder that career women who are not totally mad or evil usually get themselves baby-boomed in film these days. Selfish non-moms may have to be bludgeoned into submission (i.e., into wanting to take care of a man's children) in a film like *Overboard*, but most women go more willingly into motherhood, whether it's their real choice or not. Two new films show two very different women coping with accidental pregnancies. Both women come to term, but neither ever comes into her own power as a mother.

The first out, *Look Who's Talking*, is a film written and directed by female schlockmeister Amy Heckerling. Heckerling, who has directed successful movies (*National Lampoon's European Vacation*) before, is in clover these days. She has created this year's *Three Men and a Baby*. While it may not make quite as much money as its predecessor, this film is one of the surprise hits of the fall season. Originally assigned the more appropriate title, *Daddy's Home*, *Look Who's Talking* is the story of a boy baby named Mikey and his search for the perfect dad.

Motherhood is not a conscious decision for Mollie (Kirstie Alley). A CPA stuck in a dead-end affair with one of her rich clients, Albert (George Segal), poor Mollie has obviously never heard of birth control. The animated title sequence shows hundreds of sperm racing along through her vagina and uterus completely unobstructed. Their male voices root one another on to the finish line until one (with the voice of Bruce Willis) invades the egg—which, like old Mom in *Parenthood*, has no voice at all.

Remember that famous Ladies Against Women placard slogan, "Sperm are People, too!"? Well, *Look Who's Talking* is that slogan brought to life. But this time there is no hint of sarcasm. Heckerling, although I'm sure she'd deny the intention, has created the most outrageous piece of "Right-to-Life" propaganda you are likely to see on your neighborhood screen. This cutesy gimmick flick actually goes a step beyond the standard right-wing diatribe. Operation Rescue and friends would have you believe that a zygote is a baby. Amy Heckerling encourages you to identify the sperm as a baby. What else are we to think when the voice of the ringleader sperm (Willis) has the same voice as the fetus, and later on, the same voice as the preverbal, postbirth baby boy?

To emphasize her antichoice point, Heckerling has what appears to be a nine-week (clearly a first trimester) fetus verbally express highly developed thoughts and feelings to the audience. Later, his accidental mom explains to his aghast dad that she won't terminate her pregnancy because the doctor told her her biological clock is ticking and besides, "this baby is you and me and I'm not going to get an abortion."

The fetus is not, however, a little Mollie'n'Albert. He is a much more witty, sensible, and sensitive human being than either of his parents. Mollie, while a nice woman, is never the protagonist of this film. It would certainly be a nice change to see a modern single mom as a film hero, but Mikey, even before birth, is the hero of *Look Who's Talking*. Second billing would have to go (again not to Mom but) to the man he picks to be his daddy, a taxi-driver named James, played by John Travolta.

For Mikey, having a dad is an imperative. And Mom agrees even though she seems to have a surprisingly easy time of single motherhood. Isolation, overwork, and a scarcity of suitable day care never appear to be a problem for her even though she lives alone with her infant son, and apparently receives no help from the biological father. She can make it alone, and she seems to believe that all men are self-centered idiots, yet she still agrees with her tyke that a father is essential to their family unit.

Mollie promises to find Mikey a "daddy." But, once again, the baby is way ahead of his mother. The audience knows that James is perfect father material because Mikey says so. But what does a baby know? Nothing about husband material, that's for sure. But that's okay. We aren't supposed to care about the relationship of Mollie and James. The one between Mikey and James is the only one that matters.

James is more than willing to pass along his sexist wisdom to his would-be son. Of men's relationships with women James marvels with Mikey that "you spend nine months trying to get out, and the rest of your life trying to get back in." Such philosophical insight is only surpassed by James's commitment to fatherhood, which he informs the baby always consists of "keeping the mother happy so she doesn't drive the kids crazy."

By the end of the movie, James is playing the role he and Mikey wanted for him. And Mollie? Well, she's still around, a woman letting a baby and a taxi-driver make her decisions for her. She still hasn't learned a thing about birth control, either. The first time she sleeps with James she gets pregnant again. The vocal sperm race through her once more and the film's final scene is another birth day. Motherhood is still not a conscious choice for Mollie, but we're not supposed to worry. She's playing the role James and Mikey want for her, and that's *all* that's wanted of her.

Look Who's Talking's *James (John Travolta) doesn't really view fatherhood as a big headache. How could he, when Mikey (Jason Schaller) constantly shows "daddy" just how cool he thinks he is?*

Surrogacy and much of the adoption industry is an even more blatant example of the diminishment of motherhood to the ability of a woman to carry a fetus for nine months for someone else. The movie *Immediate Family* addresses itself, half-heartedly, to the problem of infertility and the challenges of adoption. Written by Barbara Benedek (*The Big Chill*), and directed by Jonathan Kaplan (*Heart Like a Wheel, The Accused*), this is a movie that means to be serious and compassionate. And it is, in a way. It is also one of the most dangerously elitist films about parenting that I've seen in a long time.

Linda Spector (Glenn Close) is a successful real estate agent. Her husband Michael (James Woods), is—like the perfect dad/hubby material of *Baby Boom*—a veterinarian. They have the beautiful Seattle waterfront home. They have two cars any yuppie would die for (a turbo Saab convertible and a powder blue Jeep with four-wheel drive) outside it. What they don't have is a child.

Sick of medical therapies that don't seem to work, Linda and Michael go to a private adoption lawyer who advertises for, and finds, a pregnant girl in Ohio. Lucy Moore (Mary Stuart Masterson) is a sweet, frightened teen in need of a mother herself. Instead, she is about to become one. She seems to know that motherhood isn't right for her right now. But Benedek never tells us why Lucy is giving up her baby or why she didn't get an abortion. It must have been kismet. The Spectors want a child, and Lucy obligingly offers to give them hers. The well-to-do couple will be the parents she never had—for her baby.

It seems like a good match. Linda and Michael begin to love this girl who will give them a child. Bonding goes on right and left. But then the very bonding that's not supposed to happen, of course, does. Lucy falls in love with her baby and decides to keep him. The Spectors are bereft, and they show just how conditional their love for Lucy is. If the baby can't belong to them completely, they apparently want nothing to do with the infant or his mother. This, of course, is not the end of the film. I only wish it were.

Lucy takes her son home to Ohio, where she lives with her stepfather and her two younger step-siblings. Benedek and Kaplan show us a working-class life that is supposed to convince us that Lucy is abusing her child by keeping it. But what do they really show us? We see the stepfather's 18-wheeler parked in front of his modest little house. (Presumably we are supposed to shudder with horror that a child should grow up in a small house with a truck-driver for a bread-winner.)

We then see Lucy try to cook breakfast while she balances the baby on her hip. As we all know, cooking breakfast with a baby on your hip is a hard thing to do, but it doesn't make you a bad mother if you can't manage it. Most of us, including most teen-mothers, would face this crisis by putting the baby in his high-chair, rocker-seat, playpen or crib. And if we had none of those, we'd put him on a blanket on the floor and keep cooking. Not so Lucy. And when she accidently drops and spills her child's bottle she views this as her Waterloo.

Since dropped bottles occur thousands of times in a baby's life, it makes a poor argument for giving up a child. This is especially true for a girl like Lucy who no doubt has been caretaking her step-sibs for years. There are many reasons for placing a baby up for adoption. Lucy could have had many good ones. But the filmmakers can't be bothered to share them with us. For them, it doesn't matter why she gives it up as long as she does. Before you can say Similac she's delivering her son to a couple who don't have to cook their own breakfast (or any one else's) if they don't want to.

Benedek knows that there is something to be uneasy about

Baby makes five for adoption's menage à quatre. *Adoptive parents Glenn Close and James Woods want the baby of natural parents Mary Stuart Masterson and Kevin Dillon, in* Immediate Family.

with this story. She has the Spector grandmother-to-be state, with some apprehension, the shift in emphasis in today's adoption climate. It used to happen when a "child needed a home," and now the process is about "a parent needing a child." There's a big, ethical difference there and Benedek should have had the courage to explore it. She didn't.

No one, including Lucy, questions that babies should go where the bucks are. No one questions that babies are going, not necessarily to the people who would love and nurture them the most, but rather to those rich enough to pay the $20,000 price tag. And Benedek won't even touch the most important issue of all, that we live in a society that refuses women the social programs that would allow them to raise their children with dignity themselves.

My grandmother was, like Lucy, a teen-aged single mom. She worked as a chambermaid and laundress, and at one point was offered a large amount of money to hand over her daughter to rich hotel guests who had taken a shining to the child. My grandmother didn't sell. She and her daughter instead lived a life of grinding poverty until that daughter herself married at seventeen and became a mother. With my father's mechanic's pay and the easing of the depression, life got better. But even if it never had, neither my grandmother nor my mother would have ever regretted that decision to stay together.

To this day, my family is filled with Lucys—working-class women with few resources to sustain them when they become teen mothers. In the view of *Immediate Family*, these women have no business keeping their young. Those babies should go to homes where each has their own room filled with toys.

It would be nice if every child had a talking teddie bear, but the way to make that happen is not to take children from their poor mothers in Ohio or Honduras or Korea and sell them to Americans who own Saabs (and view a child as a life accessory of equal value). The way to give each child a decent life is keep that child in its community and to make that community a place fit for children.

Oops. The film critic is getting angry again. But her anger isn't really at people who adopt babies. And it is most certainly not at women who give them up. My anger is at a society that takes choice away from women, whether that choice be to terminate a pregnancy or to keep and feed and proudly nurture the babies they have.

In *Parenthood*, the hero of the movie, a caring dad played by Steve Martin, complains to his accidentally pregnant-again wife that "women have choices, men have responsibilities." It's the kind of catchy slogan "men's rights" groups will probably put on a bumper sticker, but ask the divorced mom trying to feed, clothe, and shelter three kids on a grocery checker's salary how true it is.

The glorification of fatherhood in today's films combined with the portrayal of women in the same movies as little more than breeding machines (at the end of *Parenthood*, every woman in the cast of child-bearing age, spanning from 17 to 45, has a baby of under a year old) is a treason against active motherhood and an attack on women who choose not to have children. It's another wake-up call for women. I hope we're listening.

CHILD-DEVOURING MOTHERS TAKE HOLLYWOOD

• •

Postcards from the Edge

A drunken and angry Doris Mann (Shirley MacLaine) tries to convince her sober and angry daughter, Suzanne Vale (Meryl Streep) that she isn't the worst mother on earth—or even in their Beverly Hills neighborhood. "What if Lana Turner had been your mother?" she asks Suzanne. "Or Joan Crawford?" "*These* are the choices?" counters Suzanne (getting a big laugh from the audience).

But these *are* the choices when you look at the best-seller and box-office images of movieland mothers. Add to the list B.D. Hyman's mom, Bette Davis, if you like. And now that *Postcards from the Edge* (the movie) has appeared, middle-America will surely be adding poor Debbie Reynolds to that list of legendary child-devouring Hollywood Moms. As I left the theater after seeing *Postcards*, I overheard one woman explaining to another who the film's writer, Carrie Fisher, was, and that MacLaine was actually playing Fisher's real-life mom, Debbie Reynolds.

That may not be true, but who could blame those women for believing that it is? By now, everyone's heard that Carrie Fisher's *Postcards from the Edge* (the book) is an autobiographical novel by Tammy's little girl, Princess Leia. And we've all been informed that *Postcards* is a true story about a young actress who almost loses her career and her life to her drug addictions. We're convinced that the novel's hero, Suzanne Vale, is really Carrie Fisher. And the reason we're convinced is that every article and television squib promoting the current movie adaptation has told us so, repeatedly. And if Suzanne is Carrie, then Doris must be Debbie.

In Fisher's novel, Doris probably *is* a close approximation of her real-life celebrity mom. But what the movie flacksters fail to mention is just how far from the novel the movie really is. We're talking lightyears.

One major difference has to do with the novel's central theme of recovery from addiction. The book focuses on Suzanne and secondarily on a male coke addict named Alex. Unlike the movie, it does of good job of showing how very difficult it is for a substance abuser to make that great leap of negatives from denial to saying no.

The movie of *Postcards* has very little *Edge* left on it. One minute Suzanne is OD'ing, the next she is in recovery. The process never seems that difficult because we see precious little of it. AA meetings are mentioned a couple of times, but we are never shown one. Nor do we get more than a passing glance at Suzanne's life in detox and rehab. In fact, the movie almost makes Suzanne's drug habit seem like an anomaly, as if the majority of film biz folk (and most of the rest of us) didn't fit in to one of two categories: those who take drugs, and those who take One Day At A Time.

The shift is purposeful, I'm sure. The filmmakers would probably claim that they spent little time on the drugs theme since they were trying to make a comedy, and the topic of drug-abuse is such a downer. But that doesn't wash. Fisher's novel is all about drug problems, romantic failure, and Hollywood career headaches, and it's *at least* as funny as the movie.

No, the shift away from a drug recovery theme was towards something else. And that something else is mother-blaming. In the movie, it's no longer the temptations of Sodom and Gomorrah that almost wrecked Suzanne, it's her mommy. It's Doris who gave her only daughter a model for substance abuse (with her dependence on late night bottles of wine and mid-morning yogurt-fruit frappes spiked with vodka), and it's Doris who strains her daughter's fragile sobriety with her constant nagging.

What a transformation from book to movie! Suddenly, it's Mom, not Percodan, that's the substance Suzanne needs to learn to control. In Fisher's roman a clef, Suzanne's mother, Doris Mann, is a *nice woman*. She brings her daughter in detox comforting things like a quilt and cookies and a mother's love. When Shirley MacLaine, as the movie Doris, visits her daughter in detox, she brings the right cookies, but the wrong vibes.

Shirley's Doris is a selfish show-boater more interested in chatting up her fans than talking to her daughter. When conversations do occur, they bring poor Suzanne little comfort.

Is everybody happy? Author Carrie Fisher and her two stars, Shirley MacLaine and Meryl Streep, seem pleased about Postcards *from the Edge. Carrie's mom, Debbie Reynolds, may feel differently.*

You can't really be on somebody's side when you never get off their back, and Doris is constantly *at* Suzanne, criticizing and controlling her whenever possible, and acting the injured party when her daughter rebels.

How do you explain the vast differences between the book of *Postcards* and the movie, both of which are credited to Carrie Fisher as author? Well, it could be that Carrie has just gotten more in touch with the fury she feels towards her mom. But I have another theory about Doris Mann's werewolfian transformation. And my theory can be summed up in two words: Mike Nichols.

I can see the disbelief in your face, gentle reader. You think I'm being an anti-male paranoid again. You could be right. But as the saying more or less goes, just because I'm paranoid, that doesn't mean he's not out to get us.

From his first films, *Who's Afraid of Virginia Woolf?* in 1966 and *The Graduate* the following year, to his current nifty little number, *Postcards*, Mike Nichols has shown an unhealthy fascination for women. I sometimes take some convincing, but after a quarter-century of gorgons, I'm beginning to think that the boy doesn't like us much. Ms. Streep seems to be one of the few women he has fond feelings for. She, at least (in *Silkwood*, *Heartburn*, and now in *Postcards*) plays a sympathetic figure, the plucky victim.

Still, you might ask why I blame the changes in Fisher's story on Mr. Nichols. Why, because Mike has all but confessed to taking a hatchet to Mommy. For example, the production notes of the movie quote him as saying that, "as Carrie and I worked on the screenplay, it changed very much from the book. The mother-daughter story became the center in a way that it never was in the book." (And how!) The same presskit quotes Mike's co-producer, John Calley. He describes Nichols as "very collaborative . . . . He was deeply involved in the structuring and the writing of the script with Carrie . . . ."

"Mothers are something I've always been interested in," Nichols recently told the *New York Times*, adding to the evidence of his malice aforethought. Recalling a skit he once did with comedy partner Elaine May, he characterized the mother-child relationship with a bit of dialogue: "And I say, 'Mother, you've made me feel awful,' and she says, 'If that's true, you've made me the happiest woman in the world.'" Ba-dum-bump.

In keeping with that philosophy of motherhood, Nichols assisted Fisher the writer and MacLaine the actor in constructing a Mommie-Dearest of monumental proportions. The part was a snap for MacLaine. All she had to do to play Doris Mann was dust off the overbearing maternal virago she played in *Terms of Endearment* and insert a Steven Sondheim show-tune in the middle. Shirley still knows how to give a great performance giving motherhood a bad name.

Meryl Streep's performance as Suzanne is more doubtful. For one thing, Streep is too old for the part. "My character simply gave birth to her when she was 11 1/2," MacLaine recently quipped. And although she has a couple more years on Meryl than that, she is still (in all ways but biologically) too young to be Streep's mother.

But the age absurdities of the movie have less to do with generational differences than they do with who Suzanne is supposed to be. "*I'm* middle-aged," Streep says to MacLaine in one scene. And, more power to her, that's true. So I ask myself how likely it is that a movie studio would require a 41-year-old woman (Streep's real age) to go home and live with her Mommy while she shoots a movie (as proof that she will stay clean for the duration). Yet this is precisely the situation the filmmakers have set up for their comedy.

Need I add that this improbability is not in the book? (Suzanne does stay with relatives, her grandparents, while she shoots her comeback movie, but she does so because the film's location is in the Palm Springs area near their desert home.) The book's Suzanne is an adult woman of 29 turning 30 who lives alone when she's not living with a lover, just like you would expect of an adult.

The film presents a woman who is older than she should be acting even younger than her fictional equivalent. It denies the character Suzanne her adulthood. Streep is, we all know, a fine actress. She (and MacLaine) can make us forget about issues of chronological age, but Meryl's performance is still self-contradictory. The girl has way too much backbone. She never really projects raw insecurity. We see plenty of annoyance in Streep's Suzanne, but we seldom get a glimpse at all the pain she must be feeling again, now that her painkillers are gone. As for capturing the shaky look of someone new to sobriety, she doesn't even come close, except for the no-makeup scene where she wakes up from her overdose.

But, who knows, that may be Nichols at work, too. It is necessary for Suzanne, even as a "middle-aged" adolescent, to appear more stable, healthy, generous, and sympathetic than her monstrous mamma. Doris, consumed with her base jealousy of her good and beautiful daughter, plays a part right out of a fairytale about a wicked stepmother. But she is an even more frightening crone, the wicked *natural* mother.

I'd be the first person to admit that mothers and daughters often have troubled relationships. And undoubtedly there are some mothers out there who've done heavy-duty damage to their daughters—and sons. But where does daddy-damage fit into this picture? If the picture is *Postcards*, nowhere.

Fisher's (that is to say, Nichols') philosophy of paternal responsibility seems to be out of sight, off the hook. Yet Fisher's own experience with father-figures was, seemingly, far more disastrous than life with her unsinkable mom. Her natural father, Eddie Fisher, abandoned the family for the violet-eyed Liz Taylor when Carrie was a tiny tyke. In later life he had a closer relationship with controlled substances than he did with his daughter. Debbie's second husband, Harry Karl, was, at first, looked upon as the clan savior. He turned out to be its financial ruin. The so-called shoe tycoon took all of Reynolds's show-biz earnings—to supply his gambling habit, according to her.

The screenplay of *Postcards* nonetheless ignores the juicy possibilities of paternal iniquity completely. Mention is made of an abandoning father, but it is merely a passing mention. Dad isn't held accountable. Not Suzanne's natural father, nor the Barcolounger spud her mother is currently married to. Not all of the movie's men are angels, by any means. Dennis Quaid, in a cameo that got him third billing, plays a lothario producer who is less than honest with Suzanne about their relationship. But his inconstancy is obvious. We see it coming, and so does Suzanne. It doesn't break her heart, it just pisses her off. Quaid's scenes are just romantic and comic relief from the mother-daughter negativity.

In fact, Suzanne's only positive parent-like influence comes from a man, the perfect Hollywood father-figure, her director. Gene Hackman has only two scenes, but his character, Lowell, is a crucial one. In his first scene, he confronts Suzanne with her drug addiction—no co-dependent, he!—humiliating her in front of cast and crew. In his second scene, late in the film, he gives Suzanne both forgiveness and the courage to rebuild her life. It is Lowell who delivers the movie's punchline: "Your mother did it to you, and her mother did it to her...back to Eve."

Here, at last, is the gospel according to the Daddy/Director: The world is but an endless continuum of women doing damage to their young. The child must reject the mother's power to survive. Lowell advises Suzanne to say "Fuck it! I start with me." He further counsels her to "grow up" and "leave [her] mother." He assigns no blame to Papa. It's a conveniently misogynist view, to say the least, since statistics have long shown us that it is Daddy who is much more likely to abandon, beat, rape, and otherwise maim the lives of his children.

But, lest you doubt Lowell's sermon, Nichols makes sure to drive the point about mothers doing it to their daughters home in the next scene. Fisher has admitted it was written to Mr. Nichols's exact specifications. "[H]e handed me that prescription in triplicate and sent me to write the scene," is how she described the process to *Premiere*. Nichols told Fisher a story to illustrate what he wanted. It concerned a Pope stripped of his accoutrements of power, who had to put on his vestments and take up his staff to be able to face the world and condemn a man to burn at the stake.

Fisher, actress born of actress, knows how to give a director what he wants. She wrote the scene, but was apparently horrified by the filmed results. What Nichols wanted, and got, is very powerful, and straight out of a horror film. Doris lays in a hospital room after crashing her car while drunk. Stripped of her own clothes and make-up and wig, she is a powerless figure. Nearly bald, with no eyebrows, she is no longer beautiful, and, therefore, her magical spell as a woman and mother is broken. Doris is reduced to a gigantic baby. Cosmic retribution is complete as she must, once more, endure verbal abuse from her own cruel mother (Mary Wickes). Seeing her mother suffer a daughter's indignity frees Suzanne from Doris's toxic thrall.

And, lo, what the Director Lowell sayeth, so it shall come to pass: Each female shall suffer at the hands of her mother. "If I thought I made you feel like that," the humbled Doris tells Suzanne, "I'd kill myself." But that's exactly how Doris has made her poor daughter feel all her life. (And that's why Suzanne almost killed herself with drugs.)

But now Suzanne has seen the Pope without his miter, the emperor without his clothes, her mother without her serpent's poisonous tongue or accompanying lip rouge. No longer dominated by her mother, Suzanne will at last be able to live a drug-free life. She can now act and sing, feel joy, and fall for the doctor (Richard Dreyfuss) who pumped her stomach.

In the novel of *Postcards from the Edge*, Suzanne is unhappy to think that her mother might somehow feel responsible for her drug problems. "She thinks I blame her for my being here. I mainly blame my dealer, my doctor, and myself, and not necessarily in that order," Suzanne tells the reader. If only in the film Suzanne had been allowed to be that wise and that magnanimous.

But no. Mike Nichols wanted to use Carrie Fisher's talent for the one-liner to bring home his own sick joke about the mother who's happiest when her child feels their worst. The child-devouring mom is "not only a Hollywood type," Nichols assured the *Times*. Indeed, he wants us to experience the universality of mother-blaming.

And maybe it is universal. The same week that I saw *Postcards*, I saw the TV movie on Leona Helmsley (*The Queen of Mean*) that blamed her greed and nastiness on her mother. The movie's last line, as Leona (Suzanne Pleshette) is led from the courtroom after her conviction, is a voice-over of a plaintive little girl: "Mama, *look* at me!"

Personally, I question whether Leona's tax-evasion, late in life, was her mom's fault. And I resent the way Carrie Fisher adapted her own novel into an orgy of mother-blaming. Her defense may be the same as war-criminals, that she was just taking orders. But why did she have to take orders so well? Perhaps it is a hidden fury (as well as a big paycheck and renewed fame) that made Fisher distort her satire of Hollywood society into an attack on motherhood. Fisher isn't stupid. She's seen what the gossip-mongers do. If she weren't still consumed with mother-blaming herself, would she have written a movie that invites America to draw such ugly conclusions about her real-life mother? Why let us add Debbie Reynolds's star to the Hollywood Walk of Maternal Infamy?

I think that crucial scene between Suzanne and Lowell, the Father-Director, holds a clue. Right after he explains the great scheme of motherly villainy to her, he embraces her like a loving father and gives her the ultimate Hollywood blessing, the assurance that he will hire her again for another movie very soon. "Thank god!" Suzanne murmurs ecstatically, as she buries her head in Lowell's shoulder.

Mike and Carrie do some truth-telling in that moment. All that matters in Hollywood is winning your next job. Little Carrie may have sold her own novel and her own mother down the river in *Postcards from the Edge*, but she gave the great Father-Director, Mike Nichols, what he wanted. In gaining his approval, Fisher has no doubt assured herself of a successful career behind and in front of the cameras. Debbie must be very proud.

REBEL IN POLKA-DOTS
Mermaids

A feminist collective I belonged to in the mid-'70s included for a short time a wonderful woman by the name of Sally. Then in her forties, I remember the weather-beaten warmth of her smile and her sturdy, wide-legged stance (so well suited to her favorite wardrobe of denim and black leather, and her favorite conveyance of black motorcycle.)

Born in America's heartland to a traditional, conservative family, Sally had been a life-long feminist. The women's movement allowed her to give a name to the rebellion she had felt in her heart and expressed through mutinous deeds from earliest girlhood. Of course, she didn't call herself a "feminist" back in the '50s and early '60s. And no one else called her a feminist, either. They called her "unconventional" when they were being kind. And, mostly, folks didn't take kindly to Sally and her revolt-ing ways.

She made no apologies for her life, but when I knew her, Sally had one deep sadness. That was her relationship with her son, to whom she gave birth as a high-schooler. He hadn't coped well with having such a strong, "liberated" mother. He'd wanted a parent who stayed in one relationship, in one place. He wanted the kind of environment Sally had once escaped from. He couldn't appreciate the joyful renegade who was his mother.

Sally's son left home to join a fundamentalist cult where his lifestyle mimicked, in even more extreme form, the conservative, small-town life Sally had escaped. The community was rigidly patriarchal. Her son was in control of his wife and baby daughter. His authority was second only to the male minister who led the community and the male god those men had fashioned in their own fascist likeness.

One of Sally's biggest dreams was to ride into that community one night and spirit her granddaughter away. Shortly after she told me all this, Sally rode away from Cambridge on her black motorcycle. I never saw her again. I have no way of knowing if she ever did "liberate" her granddaughter. But I'd like to think that it doesn't matter. Barring complete brainwashing, Sally's granddaughter has no doubt tapped the rebellion in her own heart by now.

Opposition is a natural part of the parent/child relationship, especially within the separation process we tactfully refer to as adolescence. To rebel against parents you perceive to be old fuddy-duddies is easy enough, albeit sometimes painful. To rebel against parents who are themselves rebels is much trickier, and a lot more painful. I felt for Sally's misguided son (and for all our present-day teens of "hippie" parents) as I watched the coming-of-age story of Charlotte Flax, the heroine and narrator of the new film *Mermaids*.

Although Jewish, Charlotte (Winona Ryder) wishes she were a nun. Like armor against her mother's life, she wears prim black dresses and prudish expressions. And when she's not praying at the makeshift shrine she's erected in her bedroom, she can often be found poring over the life and martyrdom of some forgotten virgin saint. If all this doesn't sound like teen rebellion, that's because you haven't yet met Charlotte's mother, whom she always coolly refers to as Mrs. Flax.

Rachel Flax (Cher), like my friend Sally, was a woman ahead of her time, in her time of 1963. Jackie Kennedy, the ice princess in the Chanel suit, was one ideal. Another was the warm domesticity of the shirt-waisted Donna Reed. Mrs. Flax is tight polka-dotted sass in backless pumps. She is a hot number in a cold-war world. As for domesticity, Rachel Flax wants none of it. Cooking is "too big a commitment." She fixes her daughters "cheese-ball pick-me-ups" for dinner with miniature franks on the side, "and for desert, marshmallow kabobs."

Men are too big a commitment, too. Donna Reed may have depended on her doctor hubby, but Rachel Flax depends on no man. In fact, if a man gets too close and starts thinking about settling down, Rachel begins to think about breaking camp. If her latest lover takes her for granted or tries to take advantage, Rachel just picks out a new point on her trusty road atlas and pulls out for parts unknown. Charlotte can recall moving eighteen times in her fifteen years.

It's not an easy way to grow up. Charlotte devotes herself to her younger sister, Kate (Christina Ricci), and to the fine art

The Mermaids *are Charlotte (Winona Ryder), Mrs. Flax (Cher), and little Kate (Christina Ricci). This family of women takes care of themselves and each other. And not just on market day.*

of repentance. Yet as holy as Charlotte tries to be, she can't keep herself from indulging in extravagant lies and impossible crushes. She considers it a sign from God that the latest Flax home, in the southeastern Massachusetts town of Eastport, is just down the road from a convent. Yet when Charlotte finally gets to meet a kindly Mother Superior (Jan Miner), all she can think to ask is what color her bra is.

It's a question she never outwardly articulates. (Good thing!) But the audience hears it through Winona Ryder's voice-over of Charlotte's inner-voice. Such a film technique seldom works well. Voice-over narration usually represents the incompetence of filmmakers who don't know how to tell a story through their story. But screenwriter June Roberts (*Experience Preferred . . . But Not Essential*) knew what she was doing. And what she was doing is honoring the seriocomic spirit of Patty Dann's novel.

As the film's undisputed star, Cher's name appears above the title, but Roberts and director Richard Benjamin respected their original source enough to stay true to it, keeping their focus on the daughter. And Cher, who was expected to choose a star-vehicle after her break-through, Academy award-winning role in *Moonstruck*, shows real wisdom and magnanimity in *Mermaids*. As good as she is as the free-spirited Mrs. Flax, she is clearly more interested in doing good work in a good movie than she is in reminding us what a pop icon she is. Cher consciously allows Winona Ryder to dominate *Mermaids*.

Ryder is up to the responsibility, that's for sure. She is super as Charlotte. The voice-overs work because of Ryder's exceptional skill. Her Charlotte is a bright and very sensitive girl, but she often has a tough time expressing herself. Bursting with a jumble of emotions, she is struck dumb by the intensity of what she thinks and feels. That's why it's important that the audience get inside her head. Because the real Charlotte is so much more than the taciturn teen we see before us.

She strives to be pious and pure because she perceives this to be the antithesis of a mother who always looks "like a woman about to go forth and sin." But Charlotte is also fighting her own raging hormones—and it's a battle she's about to lose. The bashful caretaker at the Protectors of the Blessed Souls convent, Joe (Michael Shoeffling), seems like the perfect candidate for her first real romance. In this gentle, boyish 26-year-old, who spends most of his time with nuns, Charlotte can pursue sex and holiness at the same time.

Meanwhile, her mother pursues her own older man, the owner of the local shoe store, Lou Landsky (Bob Hoskins). Lou's wife abandoned him a while back, in the middle of vacuuming, but not before she'd frozen a lifetime's supply of roasts and casseroles. He'd like to share this bounty of put-by hot meals with Rachel and her children, if she'll only let him.

But Rachel learned to distrust men at an early age, when Mr. Flax stole her car and left her while she was in labor with Charlotte. What she's known of men since then hasn't improved their image in her eyes. And since she'd rather be "taken for a ride" by a car than a man, she has often hit the road rather than become too entangled. Rachel's only real relationship is that with her two daughters. With them she makes a family, a unit of strength and affection called "us." Her man of the moment has never rated inclusion.

Rachel never even caught the name of little Katie's father. He was but a fine specimen of a lad, hoping to win a place on the Olympic swim team, and she was his chambermaid who brought him more than towels. Rachel got what she wanted out of that brief encounter: Katie, her own little swimming champ. And she's expected even less from the men she's been with since. She'd rather work and live and support her daughters on her own.

Rachel Flax would be considered, by many, an unconventional woman today. In 1963, she would have been revolutionary. Through Cher's sympathetic portrayal, it is easy to see Rachel as a rebel without a cause; a feminist without that name for her anger and independence. Cher has said that she was attracted to the project—which never would have gotten the green light from Orion or any other studio without a major female star—because it reminded her of her own early life with her mother and sister.

That being the case, one would expect Cher's interpretation of Mrs. Flax to be either overly sanitized or mud-slung (according to her own feelings about her mom). It is neither. Her Rachel is a loving mother who is not always a "responsible" mother. She is a woman whose reflexive reaction to men is both fight and flight. It may be justified, but it is also compulsive. It does damage to her daughters and to herself.

Who could blame Charlotte for running away? (It is, after all, a skill she learned at her mother's knee.) She crashes her way, temporarily, into a perfect nuclear family and longs to stay in this home with a live-in father and sit-down meals. Yet Charlotte's friend Mary O'Brien (Betsey Townsend) comes from such a family and wants to grow up to be just like Mrs. Flax. Everyone, with the possible exception of Sinead O'Connor, wants what they haven't got.

Rachel wanted out of her staid, kosher background. She tells Lou that she left home as soon as she got her first paycheck. The night before her first big getaway, she stood defiant in her parents' kitchen, a cigarette in one hand and a ham sandwich in the other. Hers was a total break. Charlotte may be luckier.

Sexual awakening and family crisis teach Charlotte the valuable lesson that she is, indeed, her mother's daughter. Rachel learns an opposite lesson, that Charlotte is not her, and not hers. Her daughters aren't simple possessions, easily packed-up and moved. Charlotte forces Rachel to understand that it's not only her behavior and style of dress that differ greatly from her mother's, but also her needs. It's a hard lesson, but Rachel is learning to respect those needs.

Patty Dann has said that she chose the title for her novel because of the dual child/woman natures of Mrs. Flax and

Charlotte. I would add that this story, both in the original novel and in this fine screen adaptation, shows how difficult it is for a woman to be a part of—or fully separate from—this man's world.

The mythology of the mermaid, the virgin of the sea, is sometimes one of active villainy (as in the siren who lures the sailor to his death) and sometimes one of passive victimization (as in the fairytale heroine whose love of a mortal man is her doom). But the mermaids Cher and Winona Ryder and little Christina Ricci give us aren't interested in destroying men or themselves. And, to their surprise and relief, they discover that they don't want to destroy each other, either.

It will be interesting to see whether *Mermaids* finds an audience. Traditionally, movies about unconventional clans of women (like the exquisite Bill Forsyth film, *Housekeeping*) have sunk at the box-office with nary a ripple of interest. Cher is a real drawing card—and she's not exactly a performer from whom one expects good-girl femininity. Still, the anger tucked away in Rachel's bad-girl sashay is something many men, and some women, will find discomfiting.

"She did a bad impersonation of herself," said the man next to me at the screening. The college co-eds behind me who found *Mermaids* "cute" were also, I think, missing the point. At a time when women had so few options for autonomous life, Rachel Flax's life of openly expressed lust (and wanderlust) was a declaration of independence that put her at odds with whatever town she moved into.

The good news is that female rebellion grew as the '60s progressed. Eventually we learned that promiscuity (the "sexual revolution," if you prefer) wasn't the only, or even the best, way we women could declare our freedom. Rachel seems on her way to figuring that one out at the end of *Mermaids*. We don't get to see America catch up with Rachel Flax (since the film ends in 1964), but we do get to see her come together with her eldest daughter, which is almost as satisfying.

Rachel in her polka-dot sheath, and Sally in her jeans and black leather, were on the front-lines of a struggle that isn't over by a long-shot. They couldn't have been comfortable mothers to have, but they were still good mothers to have. Winona Ryder's Charlotte knows that in her heart. And if Sally's son never realized it, there's always that granddaughter. The next young woman you see on a black motorcycle might just be her.

WITH FRIENDS LIKE THESE . . .

One Too Many from Woody

Another Woman

If male filmmakers cared what I and other feminists thought about their work (and they most assuredly do not), I'd almost pity their predicament. They face what amounts to a no-win situation. If they leave women out of their movies, or use us only as trivialized support characters, damsels in distress, or beautiful objects of their male lust, they get blasted for their sexism. If they use us as major characters, we still love to pick holes in their portrayals of women, and we blast them anyway. Of course, all this blasting is done for good reason. It seems as though it matters little whether it's a bimbo bit part or a dramatic lead, male filmmakers can't seem to keep themselves from saying nasty things about women.

Woody Allen, one of America's most inventive and respected filmmakers, is no exception. While it's true that his New York-based films never look anything like the formula-ridden fluff that comes out of Hollywood (for which we are duly grateful), he hasn't treated us much better than the West Coast moviemakers he loves to sneer at. His films have become increasingly sophisticated and serious over the years. And so has his presentation of women. In his early films, which were always about a neurotic but adorable Jewish schlump played by Allen himself, the women were little more than cardboard.

Over the years, Allen's stereotypes haven't so much changed as expanded. These are still stock portrayals of women. They just get more screen time now. Take Allen's Jewish mothers. (Please!) They're all variations on the same bad joke. It takes him longer and longer to tell it each time he delivers it, but it never gets any better. These women were always mean shrews who undercut their loser husbands at every turn, and made their sons—usually played by Allen—wish they'd never been born. For example, in mid-career, *Annie Hall* (1977), his character's screeching mother bemoaned that "she married a fool." In *Manhattan* (1979), his most consistently anti-female film, the Allen clone, Isaac, worried about his son being raised by two lesbians because he felt that few people "survive *one* mother." And Isaac's own childhood memories inspired him to write short stories about Mom, "The Castrating Zionist." By *Radio Days* (1987), the mother figure had more depth—especially as portrayed by the marvelous Julie Kavner—but she is still a mean, frustrated, "castrating" shrew. Mom is more than just a one-liner joke now, but she is still a negative stereotype that feeds into both the anti-semitic and misogynist impulses of Allen's audience.

With Allen's love-interest female leads, the stereotypes also still operate. He may spend more time exploring the whys and wherefores of their neurotic, sexually-withholding attitudes toward men in each new film, but Allen's women are still frigid, disloyal, messed-up dames. It used to be that Woody's women existed primarily as straight-women for his sex-starved unpleasantries before the rolling cameras. Their parts weren't that important. Things are different since Woody has taken his misogyny behind the scenes. The Woody-playing-Woody-figure, once central to every movie, has been relegated to, at most, support roles, while his female characters now fill the frame and dominate the dramatic action.

It's a fact. Woody Allen films are now, more and more, studies of the lives of women. I'd like to think that this change came from a raised consciousness and the growing importance of women like Diane Keaton, and more recently, Mia Farrow, to his personal life and his public art. But that's wishful thinking. Films like the serious *Interiors* and *September*, and the more light-hearted *Hannah and Her Sisters*, owe less to the influence of his screen-acting significant others than to one of his male heroes, the ponderous Swedish filmmaker Ingmar Bergman.

Allen's fascination with female characters (usually in units of three) owes much to Bergman's later work, especially *Cries and Whispers* (1972), and *Autumn Sonata* (1978). In *Cries and Whispers*, three sisters, all in their own way sick, come together with a great deal of icy angst and precious little sisterly warmth. All three are failures at being real (nurturing, maternal, supportive of men) women. *Autumn Sonata* explores similar material, less successfully, except that this time the three women are a mother and her daughters.

Like Allen today, Bergman clearly found us gals fascinating creatures. And in the late '60s and '70s, when he was making films like *Persona* and *Autumn Sonata*, many women were so hungry for movies that showed women in a significant way that we temporarily mistook his fascination for tender feelings. On the contrary, if you look back, you can see a whole lot of anger there. Women were changing in Sweden when these films were created, and I don't think I.B. liked what he was seeing.

Similar changes were happening here in the U.S., of course. You could defend Woody Allen by claiming that he didn't personally feel that same anger (although a careful watching of *Manhattan* will probably convince you that he was mad at us uppity women); but rather he was merely emulating the emotional content of Bergman's films, just as he was trying to copy the Swede's visual style by using Bergman's favorite cinematographer, Sven Nykvist. But intentional or not, Allen's fascination for the female character doesn't feel anymore compassionate or true than that of his Scandinavian mentor.

In *Interiors*, a mentally unstable, cold and controlling mother (Geraldine Page) almost destroys her three daughters and husband. All three daughters (Diane Keaton, Mary Beth Hurt, Kristin Griffith) are unable to lead the full, creative lives they so crave. Nor are they able to integrate their femaleness into their lives. Keaton isolates herself from her children and her emasculated-by-her-limited-success-as-a-poet husband. Griffith is a coke-snorting flirt. Hurt, oppressed by her mother, rejects her own chance at motherhood by having an abortion.

The present day action of the film takes place at the family's beach house where everyone is gathered to witness the marriage of Dad (E.G. Marshall) to a crude but warm earth mother (Maureen Stapleton). At dawn, following Dad's wedding night, Hurt finds her mother lurking outside and decides it's a good time to rebuke her for never allowing into her "perfect" life "any room for any feelings." Hurt accuses Page of not just being a "sick woman," but also of bringing a "perverseness," a "willfulness of attitude" (Oh! Sin of Sins!) to her life as a wife and mother. Mom, thus renounced, calmly walks into the sea and drowns. Mother-blaming drives her to her death, to the evident relief of her entire family.

Hannah and Her Sisters, because it contains the presence of the still-neurotic, still-hilarious Allen, brings us a more upbeat treatment of very similar material. The three sisters, two of whom (Barbara Hershey, Dianne Wiest) are frustrated in their ambition for a creative life, are much more accepting of their dotty mother (Maureen O'Sullivan), first of all. And one daughter,

Hannah (Mia Farrow), is actually a creative and professional success. It's no coincidence that the successful daughter is also the only one who is, as Marabel Morgan used to call it, a Total Woman. That is, she is an adoring and involved mother of four sons who always subjugates her personal and professional needs to those of her husband (Michael Caine), children, and family. She sounds perfect. And she is almost the angel she looks. Her one fault, for which she almost loses the love of both her husband and her sisters, is that she is too much the "competent" Super Mom. Hannah "gives so much" and "needs so little in return" that she fills the hearts of all her nearest and dearest with anger and guilt.

When Hannah finally realizes how much her family resents her for being so together, she falls apart on cue. She confesses to her hubby that she is afraid of the dark. She whimpers that she feels "lost." That's all he needed to hear. He is instantly reconciled with his wife. Marriage also straightens out the lives of Wiest and Hershey.

Back in serious mode, *September* (1987) is again the story of three women and their relationships, but this time they are a mother, a daughter, and the daughter's best friend. The beach house of *Interiors* is now a Vermont farmhouse, but the stultified lives are the same. Again, these are still women who can't get their acts together. Watching them try, in their own whining way, is an excruciating two hours.

Elaine Stritch, *September*'s mother, like O'Sullivan's mother-figure in *Hannah*, is an overblown and faded actress. But while we are allowed to perceive O'Sullivan as a "harmless" drunk, there is nothing even vaguely innocuous about Stritch. Like her serious counterpart in *Interiors*, Mommy Stritch does real, regular damage to her daughter, played by Mia Farrow. Long ago, she destroyed Mia's childhood (in an episode Allen obviously based on the Lana Turner-Cheryl Crane scandal), and now Momma blithely wants to take her daughter's home away from her. The friend, played by Dianne Wiest, who spends all of her time fidgeting and rubbing her face, betrays Farrow, too. She sleeps with the man (Sam Waterston) Farrow claims to love.

The characters in *September* are even more despicable than those in *Hannah*. The women are even more isolated from one another. Everyone moons around in a round-robin of unrequited love, muttering over past injuries and failed ambitions. Their self-centered lives have little meaning and no honor. Yet Allen seems to take these people seriously. Is this film an indictment of their shallow, selfish lives? I've heard it said. But Allen never makes this clear to me. Without an earthy, uncouth figure like Maureen Stapleton in *Interiors* or an ethnic absurdity like Woody Allen in *Hannah* for contrast, you end up with a cinematic microcosm of life that makes these upper-class infants look like normal, sympathetic people.

My trouble is that I *don't* have sympathy for such characters. My reaction to them is similar to Cher's response to Nicholas Cage's protestation of love in *Moonstruck*. I want nothing better than to give them all a swift slap across the face and yell "snap out of it!"

My reaction isn't all that different to the women and men of Allen's new serious film, *Another Woman*. That's because the issues and the stereotypes are still the same, although the external plot is a little different. If *Cries and Whispers* and *Autumn Sonata* (with a touch of *Smiles of a Summer Night*), informed the creation of Allen's first two dramas, you could probably find similarities between his new film and Bergman's *Persona*, in which the lives of two women (or are they two women?) intersect in obscure and deeply psychological ways.

Another Woman is the story of Marion (Gena Rowlands), another of Allen's competent and controlled (and controlling) female leads. She is a successful academic in the appropriately inaccessible field of German philosophy. She thinks she has a swell life, but she prefers not to "delve." Of course, we know that any woman who dares to achieve on a professional level, who dares to live a "life of the mind," must be kidding herself if she thinks she has a happy, fulfilled life. *Another Woman* records Marion's process of self-discovery. And what Allen helps her discover is that her life is an empty, meaningless sham, and that all the people she thought loved her actually despise her.

Interestingly, Marion makes this discovery through the auspices of another, openly messed-up, woman. She is a psychiatric patient who makes daily visits to the practice next-door to Marion's new, sub-leased office. Seems that Marion can hear every word uttered in the shrink's office and when she hears the voice of Hope (Mia Farrow), she is compelled to hang on every word. Hope wonders about "ending everything" as she questions her own life choices and worries about her feelings of alienation. Her weepy anxiety opens Marion's eyes about her own life.

She thought she had a good life, but, boy, was she wrong! Marion (Gena Rowlands) discovers how bleak her life really is when she meets Another Woman, *ironically named Hope (Mia Farrow).*

Marion suddenly realizes that her own choices in life were the wrong ones. She becomes aware that the men in her life aren't as devoted to her as she thought. Her brother hates her. (Her sister-in-law assures her of this.) Her second husband can't stand to be alone in the same room with her. She ruined her chances for feminine fulfillment by aborting her only child as a young woman. This fact, Allen implies, somehow contributed to the suicide of Marion's first husband. The woman she remembers as the best friend of her youth (Sandy Dennis) goes into a paranoid-psychotic fit when they meet again. And her current best friend (Blythe Danner) is messing around with Marion's husband behind her back.

It is Hope, who is pregnant (and therefore fully a woman) and suicidal (and therefore in touch with her emotions), who sums it all up for her therapist. Not knowing that Marion is listening in the next room, Hope tells of meeting "a really sad woman" who "has nothing." She is able to dissect Marion quite easily, although they met only once. Marion's life is dust because she didn't "allow herself to feel" enough. And by not feeling enough, she "alienated everyone around her."

Woody Allen is, for all his New York sophistication, just an old-fashioned guy when it comes to women. He tells us, through Marion's spontaneously ruined life, that a woman's existence must be based in emotion and not in the mind. Professional achievements are meaningless for a woman, he seems to be saying. If she is "afraid of the feelings she'd have for her baby" or rejects "intense [consuming] passion" for a man, then she is nothing.

Some moviegoers bewail that Woody Allen is turning his back on comedy. Comedy or tragedy, I regret the fact that he is turning his serious cinematic attentions to women. We want films that tell our stories, but not when we view those stories through a filter of male anger and resentment. I don't care if Allen picked up his bad attitude from Ingmar Bergman or not. Snap out of it, Woody! Or tell the stories of your own kind, at least. Leave us women alone.

DADDY'S DAY

Betsy's Wedding

Forget all that make-believe stuff about a wedding being about two people pledging a life's worth of love and commitment to one another. Like so many things in this society of ours, a wedding is really about money and power. Which means that the lead character in a wedding is not the blushing bride or her stammering groom. The star of a wedding is the patriarch who pays for it all, the dad in the act of marrying off "daddy's little girl. "

At least that's Hollywood's view of weddings, and has been for forty years. *Father of the Bride*, Vincente Minnelli's 1950 smash sentimental comedy, made no bones about it. The bride may have been played by none other than Elizabeth Taylor, and her mom played by the exquisite Joan Bennett, but their parts were merely support player filler and their lives were but the setting for the real star, the title character, Stanley T. Banks, played with comic brilliance by Spencer Tracy.

Yes, *Father of the Bride* touches on the emotional issues (for the *father*) of "giving away" his only daughter (a. k. a. , Kitten) to another man. But matters of the heart are a secondary consideration. What Stanley really worries about is maintaining his prestige in the face of new in-laws and couple hundred family members, friends, and business associates. It's his dwindling bankroll he gets the most wistful about. It's breaking his heart to foot the bill for a "big flashy show that [he] can't afford."

Eddie Hopper (Alan Alda), the father of the bride in this summer's *Betsy's Wedding*, has the same problem Stanley Banks did forty years back. But his attitude towards the power games and the spending frenzy are much different. This is the '90s, after all. No one feels guilty about shooting their wad anymore. Shelling it out is what American life is all about.

You can't take it with you, and Eddie doesn't want to try.

His problem is that, from a financial viewpoint (the only one that matters), his younger daughter Betsy (Molly Ringwald) has picked the worst possible time to get married. Eddie is feeling a definite financial squeeze at the moment. His building contracting company is in trouble. A developer has just pulled out of a major project, leaving Eddie to go into hock to finish the job. And now Betsy is marrying into a family of rich investment bankers, and Eddie is driven by male pride to give his daughter the best wedding possible.

So Eddie turns reluctantly to his sleazy, successful brother-in-law, Oscar Henner (Joe Pesci) to help him out. Eddie wants a loan. What he gets is an unwanted deal with the mafia. And therein lies the major source of situation comedy in this mildly amusing but only minimally heartwarming movie.

I have always resented the way mafia figures loom large in every film about Italian-Americans. But who can I blame when paesanos like Francis Ford Coppola (now putting the final touches on *Godfather III*), Marty Scorsese (about to release *Goodfellas*) and Alda keep pushing the stereotype. Alda has been haled for getting back to his roots with this movie. But, if so, the poor dear must be pot-bound. Alda himself is the most bland, anal-retentive Italian I have ever seen. And he hires Joey Bishop to play the ghost of his Italian papa (who changed his Southern Italian surname to Hopper but never quite tells us why), and Molly Ringwald and Ally Sheedy to play his daughters. This is not exactly a Calabrese cast. At the same time, Joe Pesci, who looks and sounds like the Jersey-born, Bronx-raised Italian-American that he is, ends up playing a guy named Oscar Henner. Basta!

Perhaps Alda's odd notions of ethnicity have something to do with the "blended family" that he belongs to in real life and which he attempts to reproduce (in that annoyingly semi-autobiographical habit of the writer-director) in this movie. Madeline Kahn gets the thankless job of playing Eddie Hopper's Jewish wife, Lola. Kahn is a brilliant comic actor, but you'd never know it from the walk-on part Alda handed her. Her Jewish ethnicity is defined, solely, by the fact that she wants her future son-in-law to stomp a glass at his wedding. And the sad thing is that the rest of her character is defined with even less detail.

If Alda's ego dominates his real marriage the way he allows his character to eclipse poor Lola in *Betsy's Wedding*, then we owe Mrs. Alda our condolences. And while we're at it, someone should check the expiration date on Alda's credentials as a card-carrying feminist. The points he gets for loading his cast with talented women are all lost in his disregard for their character development. Without some meaningful dialogue and action, they might just as well by chorus girls.

The case of Kahn, as Eddie's wifie, is the most egregious. This marvelous actor is given practically nothing to do except wake Alda up when he (twice) tries to throttle her during nightmare sequences. Who is this woman? There are a couple of tantalizing hints that she is a far more fascinating creature than her husband. A couple of lines imply that she is an old leftist. And sharp viewers may pick up that Lola has her own professional life because she says something about needed family income being derived from a "nursery" (as in garden retailer, not childcare center) at one point.

But we never learn anything important about what this woman thinks or feels. For example, if Lola is a leftie, how does she feel about her eldest daughter becoming a police officer? We have no idea. Alda is too busy showing Eddie plotzing over his new relationship with the mob to tell us. As a male-directed male director, Alda allows Eddie Hopper to spend more time talking to the ghost of his dead father than he does conversing with his live wife.

In the background for the group shot because he's tall, Alan Alda steals all the screen time he can from Betsy's Wedding *co-stars (l-r:) Ally Sheedy, Molly Ringwald, Dylan Walsh, and Madeline Kahn.*

Betsy, the bride, remains in equal obscurity. If this movie was supposed to represent (as has been claimed by some) Ringwald's comeback, she should demand a recount of her on-screen time. Her character is delineated entirely by her atrocious taste as a fashion design student.

In one of the movie's few genuinely touching moments, Lola tells Betsy to "go for it" when the girl feels the need to gain some control of her own wedding by altering the expensive wedding gown her mother bought for her and considers perfectly beautiful as is. Unfortunately, Alda turns that nice touch into a cheap shot against his title character. He could have portrayed Betsy as an artistic, free spirit by means of some real character development. Instead he has the film's costume designer Mary Malin deck Ringwald out in a wedding gown that looks like a Busby Berkeley Bo-Beep on mescaline.

It's supposed to be symbolic of how stuffy and rigidly non-ethnic Betsy's fiance, Jake (Dylan Walsh), and his rich, Anglo mom and pop (Bibi Besch and Nicolas Coster) are that they are unable to appreciate Betsy's zany togs. But when Jake tells Betsy to "be creative, just don't let it show so much," he is, the viewer can easily tell, being too kind. What he should tell her is that the Fashion Police are on her trail and are planning to haul her off to work camp for twenty years of hard labor with a Butterick pattern, so she had better start making clothes that look like they're meant for the human body. Once more, a valid point (that men too often want to "change"—control—the women they marry) is lost in the vapidity of Alda's visual humor.

The female character that comes off the best in *Betsy's Wedding* does so because she has most of her scenes with the film's real scene-stealing male. Ally Sheedy is all grown up and playing a cop named Connie. She is Betsy's older sister, and she's depressed to see her little sister walking down the aisle when she can't even get a date. Her perfect match, in Alda's comic view, would have to be a guy who also packs a rod. So, presto chango, a mafioso-in-training named Stevie Dee (Anthony LaPaglia) is sent to oversee the day-to-day crimes at Eddie's construction site and is smitten at first sight with Connie.

Anthony LaPaglia is very funny and absolutely adorable as the courtly wiseguy who falls for a cop. He is, without doubt, the film's major asset. Alda must have realized this, since he inflated a bit part into a star turn. I certainly don't begrudge

LaPaglia his big break. But I do think that the fact that he is so readily able to steal the show, demonstrates how weak and, yes, sexist, this show really is.

Two male characters dominate a story that cries out to be a "woman's picture." And that is why I can only recommend *Betsy's Wedding* in comparison with what else is out there this summer. It almost feels like carping to complain about the level of male dominance that exists in this movie when you compare it to what else is available to us right now.

Scan even a twelve-theatre marquee. You can go see Arnie travel to Mars to bounce back and forth between a good woman and a bad woman. (*Total Recall* contains my nominee for the most frightening semisubliminal message of this movie season. When Arnie points his fat gun at his bad "wife," she tells him: "You wouldn't hurt me. After all, we're married." "Consider this a divorce!" snarls Arnie, as he calmly blows her to kingdom come.) Then there's the hero so macho he's metallic in *RoboCop 2* and the infantile biracial violence of the buddy boys in *Another 48 Hrs*. If you like the cars crashing in the movie you're watching to have numbers painted on their sides, you can go see Tom Cruise seek "control" in *Days of Thunder*. Your other major choices are to watch *Dick Tracy* spray his freakish enemies with machine gun fire, or you can stand in line with everyone else to see Bruce Willis die harder; we should be so lucky.

Betsy's Wedding is a feminist's dream compared to all those. But I still rue the fact that Alan Alda, modern sensitive guy, didn't give Kahn, Ringwald, Sheedy and Catherine O'Hara (as Lola's sister, Gloria Henner) the same chance to shine that he egotistically afforded his own character, and more generously allowed newcomer Anthony LaPaglia. It's dangerous to borrow so heavily from a classic like *Father of the Bride*. Using a model forty years old is liable to leave you looking not so sensitive, and not at all modern.

It's one thing for Vincente Minnelli to glorify the father figure at the expense of the women in his story. Times were different then. Patriarchy wasn't even a dirty word. But Alan Alda professes to know differently. And even with his woeful track record at the box office, Alda still has the Hollywood clout to get a movie with some meaningful women characters made. Clearly, even for un-macho fellows like Alan Alda, old habits die harder than even Bruce Willis. And patriarchy is still far from a dirty word with the boys of Hollywood.

More Hare-Brained Ideas About Women

Strapless

The majority of David Hare's work as a playwright, screen-writer, and stage and film director, has focused on the lives of women. Because of this, he has been hailed, more than once, as the great male hope for women actors. In a 1985 review of *Plenty* (which he wrote for the screen after the great success of his stage play of the same name) and *Wetherby* (a film he both wrote and directed) in *Ms.*, Molly Haskell dubbed Hare "a one-man renaissance of great women's roles."

High praise. And I wanted to believe it at the time. I still do. But the more I see of David Hare's work, left-leaning though it's reputed to be, the less I like it. His new film, *Strapless*, is another he both wrote and directed. It tells the story of an American doctor changed forever by her surrender to a peripatetic lover. Written as it was for an actor Blair Brown, for whom he felt a deep personal interest, the film vents less spleen, and is far more engaging than most of his work has been. But the conclusions it reaches about the way women must live their lives are just as suspect.

Giving women star-billing doesn't mean much if the characters they're given to play remain obscure, and their actions odious or foolish. Women are placed front and center in Hare's screen/plays, but they don't know what to do when they get there. Sometimes competent on a professional level, they seem unvaryingly ineffectual in coping with life.

I don't require saintly heroism in female characters, as long as they're interesting to watch. Hare's female characters don't even possess the magnetism of the hell-cat parts written as star vehicles for Bette Davis or Joan Crawford or Barbara Stanwyck. When the glorious Ms. Davis was a bitch (in movies too numerous to mention, although *Jezebel, Dangerous, The*

186

Little Foxes, and *All About Eve* come to mind), she was a Bitch Goddess. She made bad attitude breathtakingly attractive. We adored her. We were fascinated by her scheming ways, and we secretly wished we had the daring and allure to be just like her. She was so regal in her wickedness that we felt sure that even if she faced death or disgrace in the final reel, she would never, ever really be humbled.

Hare's heroines, on the other hand, likeable or not, are no one we'd aspire to be. And watching them, you get the feeling that they don't even want to be who they are. When they take a tumble, and they invariably do, they and we are somehow sure that they deserve it.

Plenty is the best known of Hare's screenplays. A difficult story to sell to an American audience to begin with (the film's climactic confrontation takes place during a dinner party discussion of the Suez Crisis), it was hindered rather than helped by the casting of Meryl Streep in the lead role. As adept as Streep is at accents, her portrayal of Englishwoman Susan Traherne was unconvincing and very cold. Meryl did what she could, although she apparently couldn't bring as much fire to the part as the stage Susan, Kate Nelligan. Director Fred Schepisi did his best, too, although he appeared to be stifled by the material. The biggest impediment was Hare's play, which sets up one woman's decline into madness as some half-baked metaphor for the final disintegration of the British Empire in the years following World War II.

Hare's literary conceit might have worked in an arty short story (although I strongly doubt it), but as the basis of a screenplay, it leaves much to be desired. Poor Susan makes little sense as a symbol of Empire, and even less as a flesh-and-blood woman. One of the few female members of the SOE (Special Operations Executive), a group of British operatives who worked behind enemy lines during the war, we are led to believe that Susan just couldn't re-adjust to the feminine domesticity expected of women in the '50s. And who could blame her? This movie seems to.

From the very start, every attempt by the audience to bond with Susan's character is rebuffed by Hare. This starts from the first moment we meet Traherne as a member of the French underground. She acts the cool and daring spy when she rescues a male comrade (Sam Neill), who parachutes, off-course, into her village. But when a Nazi unit approaches, she shows her real stripes and collapses into a hysterical invertebrate who must be silenced and saved by the more genuinely brave Neill.

Plenty, like *Swing Shift* (released a year earlier), fails to do justice to those women who were oppressed anew by the peacetime demand that all women should go home and multiply. Rosie the Riveter, Susan Traherne, and all the other women who got a glimpse of the outside world during the war, might well have felt some resentment at being pushed back into the kitchen after giving so much to the war effort, but if that's Susan's problem, Hare seems unable to articulate it. Only once, in a meeting of the Coronation Committee, of all things, does Hare's screenplay even hint at the sexism the single, working woman had to deal with every day.

Susan's penchant for losing control and behaving badly seems to come not from a feminist anger but from an overall weakness of character. And that weakness is far from captivating. She is such a cowardly, arrogant shrew, that the only sympathies the audience can muster go to the men whom Susan seems intent on making as miserable as she is.

Our hearts go out not to Susan but to the working-class hustler (Sting) she picks to father her child, and to the sweet, staid diplomat (Charles Dance) she marries. The one she tries to shoot, the other ruin. Her cruelties are well-documented, but we never even glimpse the secret soul (abuse as a child? Post-traumatic Stress Syndrome from the war?) of her torment.

There are a few lines that seem to indicate that society's failure to implement real social change after the war somehow contributed to Susan's personality disorder, but since we never see her work toward, or even meaningfully discuss, that change (planning dinner speech protocols and table settings for banquets celebrating the crowning of a new figurehead monarch hardly counts), this interpretation makes no sense at all. Unless poor Sue is supposed to symbolize the apathy of the Left as well the crumbling of colonialism, and that's way too much symbol for one perplexingly turbulent character to carry on her frail shoulders.

After watching *Plenty*, I wondered what the point was, since it was obvious that Hare meant for there to be one. And I kept wishing that the play were about Alice (Tracey Ullman), Susan's bohemian pal and sometime roommate. As a free-loving and career-hopping rebel, she was just as much at odds with her times, and her story (in hands other than Hare's, at least) would have been infinitely more entertaining. And Ullman, who is a warm and gifted actress, could have made us feel that struggle much more intensely than the chilly if brilliant Streep.

Vanessa Redgrave is another actor who is both cerebral and impassioned in her craft. She is the saving grace of Hare's even more abstruse film, *Wetherby*. But despite her brilliance, and an almost equally affecting performance by her daughter, Joely Richardson, who plays Redgrave's younger self, a friend watching the film with me complained that it was "like watching paint peel." Well, not quite. More on the order of watching a sunburn peel. It takes a shorter period of time, but is even more uncomfortable to watch.

Again, a woman is the central character. And once more the heroine is a miserable soul who seems to summon further miseries to herself. Did Jean (Redgrave) cause a younger man (Tim McInnerny), a stranger who crashed her dinner party the night before, to blow out his brains at her kitchen table? Did she at the very least have this calamity, and the related occupation of her home by a strange young woman, coming to her for not marrying her young airman lover decades earlier? Hare doesn't say, exactly, as he jumps hither and thither over thirty years, flashbacking from one character to the next. But in his own plodding, obscure way he seems to (wink, wink) think so.

Certainly the morose detective who plagues Jean for the cause of the suicide seems convinced that this woman is reaping what she has sown. He nonetheless seems inclined to sow a little something on the order of wild oats with her himself. His probing Q & A sessions do double duty as police procedure and as a peculiar rite of foreplay prior to screwing Jean on her hearth rug.

The insinuated moral of *Strapless* is very similar to that in *Wetherby*. Lillian Hempel (Brown) states it to her younger sister, Amy (Bridget Fonda) who's "always known" it. "You have certain feelings, then you have to pick up the bill." This is an acceptable (if depressingly fatalistic) message for a movie, except that Hare appears to be gender-specific when he delivers it. When the piper must be paid, it's the women, not the men, who must come up with the cold currency.

Lillian has spent forty years completely unaware of the emotional bottom line of relationships. An American oncologist practicing with the National Health Service, she is a caring doctor who knows enough not to get too attached to her patients. And her relationships with lovers are just as amiable and stand-offish, until a continental charmer with a child-like smile makes a move on her. Raymond Forbes (Bruno Ganz) approaches Lillian beneath a life-size statue of the crucifixion in a Portuguese church. It's an ominous portent, but Lillian doesn't get it. She prefers to accept Raymond's extremely disingenuous interpretation, that if they met in church, he "must be trustworthy."

Still, she senses his power to completely disrupt her life. So she stands him up for their first real date, and she refuses to read a letter from Raymond that follows her home to London. Then he appears on her doorstep with a handsome steed named Heartfree, and she realizes that she won't be able to resist his courtship (or "siege," as she accurately labels it) for long. His claims of being "totally in love" with her are backed by his honorable (to the point of Old World) intentions. He doesn't want a sexual conquest, he wants her hand in marriage.

To the viewer, if not Dr. Hempel, it is obvious that Raymond's romantic devotion is Too Good To Be True. For

A caress may prove that your lover has soft hands, but it's no guarantee that he has a kind heart. Lillian Hempel (Blair Brown) is played for a sucker by Raymond Forbes (Bruno Ganz), in Strapless.

very long, anyway. Indeed, no sooner are the two married, with Lillian preparing to settle down to an "ordinary" life of wedded bliss, than Raymond re-enacts the old American folk-tale of the husband who steps around the corner for a pack of cigarettes.

Setting up a woman of such common sense and professional competence as a total patsy is hard enough to take. But it's much worse to be told, as Hare's screenplay seems to preach to us, that giving herself completely, to the point of financial ruin and total heartbreak, is just what the doctor ordered for a woman like Lillian.

Dr. Hempel is a better sister, a better physician, and a better all-round human being after becoming a romantic dumpee. And Raymond's reputation never suffers for being a dumper, either. Both Lillian and an earlier wife, Annie (Rohan McCullough, who along with her son, played by Joe Hare, practically steal the movie in their single scene), retain tender feelings for their bigamistic mate. Both feel that their abandonment was somehow their own fault, for not providing Raymond with "permanent romance."

What we have here is a spot of romantic victim-blaming, combined with whopping big helping of villain glorification. When Raymond's old schoolmaster expresses to Lillian one of the few negative opinions about his old protegee, his wife encourages Lillian to "just ignore him." She, too, has only the fondest memories of Mr. Forbes. "Raymond loved women," she affirms. "That's very rare."

While I would agree with Mrs. Brodie that a man who truly loves women is rare, I was shocked that Hare would trot out that old fallacy about a womanizer being a man who loves women, and expect us to still buy it. The casting of Bruno Ganz, who was so perfect as the lovesick angel in *Wings of Desire*, is further proof that Hare means for Raymond—a liar, embezzler, and bigamist—to be viewed as a good guy-savior, in fact, for his self-contained heroine.

A compulsive love-em-and-leave-em con-artist is nobody's savior. Lady-killers like Raymond are the emotional equivalent of rapists. They are acting out anger, not love, when they seduce and abandon woman after woman. Still, I'm not surprised that Hare sees his lothario hero as wearing a halo. Hare may be a lefty, but his attitudes towards women are right out of the Stone Age. And if you still have any doubt, all you have to do is consider the meaning of the film's title. *Strapless* describes the gowns designed by Amy Hempel, but in Hare's lexicon the word means Much More. The strapless gown is but another of David's Hare-brained metaphors for the lives of women. "Let them stand up on their own," Amy says when she first designs her gowns. And later, when she and Lillian marvel at the finished product, she sighs, with some amazement, "They shouldn't stay up, but they do."

Women should indeed stand up for themselves. And we don't need the under-wires, bone stays, elastic ribs, and all the other elaborately false and painful constructs of men like David Hare to do it. His ideas of what women are and how we look are male fantasies, and do not reflect our reality or our aspirations.

Like Raymond Forbes, David Hare is acting out a lot of anger when he pays court to women in his movies and plays. Some would claim that the anger (even more vividly expressed in Hare's as-yet-unreleased film, *Paris By Night*, and in his latest stage play, *The Secret Rapture*) is meant for Prime Minister Margaret Thatcher.

Well, Maggie might deserve an artist's fury, but the rest of us don't. Audiences should tell David Hare and Raymond Forbes to peddle it elsewhere. Their attentions are unwanted.

NOT TOUGH ENOUGH
Cookie

Believing something is much worse than knowing it. It lasts longer. Things you know you can easily relearn. Things you believe are much harder to shake. We all have our articles of faith. One of mine is that if women had more social power and more cultural control the world would be a better place. The catch to this belief resides in another that contradicts it: power and control are not benign forces. As the story goes, power corrupts. I believe *that* one, too. And so does anyone who has bothered to look at what women have done in Hollywood, and what certain successful women have helped Hollywood do *to* women.

The movie *Cookie* is a good example of that success gone awry. Directed by Susan Seidelman (*Smithereens, Desperately Seeking Susan, Making Mr. Right*), written by Nora Ephron and Alice Arlen (*Silkwood*), and starring Emily Lloyd (who was heartbreakingly wonderful in David Leland's not so wonderful film, *Wish You Were Here*) in the title role, this was a movie I anticipated with great eagerness. Even more so when I learned that Ricki Lake (Tracy in *Hairspray*) had been cast as Cookie's best friend. This looked like a no-lose situation for moviegoers: a pop film both general audiences and feminist viewers could love.

Alas, my hopes were crushed again. *Cookie* will be a real disappointment for almost everyone. Billed as a comedy, general audiences will wonder where all the laughs are. The writing is far from hilarious (the costumes and set decoration got the biggest chuckles at the showing I attended) and the direction is so sluggish that it is hard to believe that this is the work of Susan Seidelman. But it gets worse. For feminists, this movie is an even greater failure since it is written, directed, and executive-produced by women who should know better, and from whom we expected better.

Like father, like daughter—even when the family trade is the mafia. Dino (Peter Falk) and Cookie *(Emily Lloyd) mug it up in Susan Seidelman's film, written by Nora Ephrom and Alice Arlen.*

Cookie is billed as the story of a "rowdy free spirit[ed]" eighteen year-old trade school drop-out punkster named Carmela Maria Angelina Theresa Voltecki. Cookie for short. Her mother, Lenore (Dianne Wiest), is a faded flower who runs her own dress shop by day and spends her evenings fluffing her pink pillows and faithfully waiting for her lover to come back to her. Cookie's father, Dino Capisco (Peter Falk), who never married her mom, is a leading labor racketeer from the Brooklyn mob. Cookie hasn't seen dear old dad since she was five. But then neither has anyone else. He's just been paroled after serving a thirteen-year prison sentence.

The theme of a daughter's rebellion against her father is the stuff of great movies. As a symbol of a woman's struggle against patriarchy, it can't be beat. Cookie's storyline seemed like the perfect vehicle since, in her case, the paternal authority Dapper Dino exerts is completely unearned. Dad is a stranger who shows up at her door demanding respect as king of the domestic castle and as a don of the local mafia. Potentially, *Cookie* was a dynamite movie. Yet it squanders all its possibilities.

It does this, primarily, by letting its viewpoint wander. Seidelman has claimed, in interview after interview, that she was drawn to the film because it is "seen from the point of view of this very free-spirited girl" and is therefore a new twist on an old formula. I don't know whether Seidelman is lying or just kidding herself, but I can tell you that Cookie is not the tough "very active and spirited" woman she's cracked up to be.

Except in the matter of wardrobe (Cookie's black leather jacket, embellished with drapery cord, belt buckles, cheap jewels, fake flowers, and decals, is a far cry from the Frederick's of Hollywood femininity adopted by most young women in her community), our heroine isn't rebellious, she's just bored. And as for the viewpoint of the movie being hers, I don't think so. The viewpoint is much more male than that. The key character and real star of the movie isn't Cookie, it is her back-from-the-slammer papa, Dapper Dino.

Since Peter Falk is a well-known star of both television and motion pictures, and has ten times the name-power of British newcomer Emily Lloyd, it may be natural for the film to shift in his direction. But I don't think the dynamics of this movie can be explained away that easily. In the way it was written, and not just in the way it was played, this is a movie about Daddy getting even. And a tale of the triumph of (a violent and greedy) patriarchy within both the family and The Family is not what I was looking for from this movie.

Cookie, the so-called rebel, is from the very beginning a girl waiting (nay, hoping) for Daddy to take control of her life. Dino's first meeting with his daughter since she was a youngster is one he forces upon her. Dino's goons kidnap Cookie and drive her against her will to Sing-Sing. More concerned about his parole than his only child's well-being, Dino demands that Cookie take a minimum-wage job at a counterfeit jeans sweatshop run by Dino's even more crooked ex-partner, Carmine (Michael V. Gazzo). Cookie mulishly mugs at Dino through the visiting-room plexiglass, but she does what she's told.

Later, when Cookie protests Dino's casual insult of her mother and remonstrates against his two decades of exploitation of Lenore, he slugs her. (For real, according to Lloyd, who reported that method-actor Falk hit her not the proposed once, but twice, with a force level far exceeding a "stage" slap.) She runs from him then, but soon she is passively accompanying him to mob Christmas dinners and driving his limo for him. This is rebellion?

Get past the sullen face and the cracking of bubble gum and you have a Daddy's Little Girl in Cookie. She is as desperate for his approval as he is reluctant to bestow it. One of Lloyd's best scenes allows her to let loose on her father for not treating her more like a son and equal. But at no time does she question why anyone would *want* to be the equal of such a man. Her eagerness to identify with her father is all the more misguided when you realize that this is the kind of man who exploits workers and kills his rivals without remorse.

Jonathan Demme's mafia comedy of last year, *Married to the Mob*, is a much better film. As a comedy it works better because Demme keeps his pace (to the occasional detriment of his story-telling) quick and cartoonish. Likewise many of the performances (especially Mercedes Ruehl as Tiger Tony's jealous amazon wife, Connie) are deliciously overplayed. The screenplay, written by men, is also more affirming of women, and less morally discomfiting, because Angela DeMarco (Michelle Pfeiffer) really does want to get away from The Family, first symbolized by her husband (Alec Baldwin), who kills people for a living but is a good provider, and later by his even more powerful and lascivious boss, Tony Russo (Dean Stockwell).

Her escape isn't easy. Her attempt to build a clean new life for herself and her son is viewed as a dangerous defection by the mob. And running from one system of organized male power and control lands her quite literally in the arms of another. The FBI wants Angela, too. And the Bureau's fresh-faced agent, Mike Downey (Matthew Modine), places Angela at the top of his personal most-wanted list.

Angela has no money and few of the skills needed to challenge the likes of the mob and the FBI. She knows it, and trembles (adorably) a lot—in a manner I found annoying when I first saw *Married to the Mob*. But for all of Angela's fearfulness and surface timidity, she still has a helluva lot more moxie and independence than Cookie Voltecki.

In the last scene of *Cookie*, our title heroine is accompanied by the same goons who once kidnapped her for her father. Except now, they are on the same side. The younger and handsomer of the two (Adrian Pasdar) is her lover. And the top patriarch, the godfather (Lionel Stander) of the mob, is looking her over in a way that conveys both approval and lust. This is the kind of happy ending three women with quasi-feminist credentials give us: a young woman being absorbed into a male power structure even more rigidly enforced than the one it mimics.

Cookie probably *is* a representative heroine of the eighties. Her ingenuity and eventual success remind me of the kind of woman who makes it to junior v.p. at Exxon. Or maybe an even more apt and depressing comparison is the kind of woman who gets to make movies in Hollywood. Women like Seidelman and Ephron and Arlen. The rest of us are supposed to watch these successful gals buy in (and sell out) to powers-that-be and applaud. I'm not applauding.

Cookie isn't worth a six dollar admission price. It squanders the talents of the women on the screen as well as behind it. Ricki Lake, one of the selling points of the movie for me, is completely wasted in a bit part used to illustrate that Cookie has a friend, without actually *showing* us the friendship. Other support performances by women, especially Dianne Wiest's iron-willed fluffhead and Brenda Vaccaro's hard-hearted wife who runs a chop-shop for stolen pooches, are given more screen time but no more depth.

If you're in the mood for mafia comedy with laughs and a rebellious women's viewpoint, check out *Married to the Mob* on tape or cable. Or, better yet, forget about the mafia altogether and go see Pauline Collins' tour-de-force performance as a 42-year-old homemaker falling in love with herself (and Greece) in *Shirley Valentine*. It's a marvelous women's film that gives us a '70s heroine instead of an '80s heroine.

Shirley wants to put more joy and freedom in her life, but gets little assistance from other women in her pursuit. Her "feminist" friend abandons her for a man just when she needs her most. And Shirley's grown daughter sputters with outrage at the thought that her old "Mum" should do anything by or for herself. The demanding and duplicitous men in her life are even less supportive.

Sisterhood may not provide any answers for Ms. Valentine, but she learns to resist the pitfalls of the romantic solution, too. Bitching is what this movie is all about. And Collins does it exceedingly well. It's Consciousness Raising 101, to be sure. But I think a little Consciousness Raising 101 is exactly what the movie-going public needs about now.

Shirley Valentine was written and directed by men, and it hurts me to recommend it over a movie written and directed by women. I want to believe that women can go to Hollywood and make movies that better serve women. But I'm beginning to doubt it. At one point in *Cookie*, Peter Falk's Dino raises a squawk about how he was screwed by his business partner while he was in prison. A friend encourages him "not to take it personally." How else should he take it, "as a group?", he asks.

I feel equally betrayed. And I ask the same thing of the trio of women behind this movie. Do I take *Cookie* personally or as a an abandonment of us all?

A REAL CLASS ACT

THE POOR STILL KNOW THEIR PLACE IN TINSELTOWN

● ●

Driving Miss Daisy, Stella, Stanley & Iris, and *Where the Heart Is*

Driving Miss Daisy is a hit. Critics loved it, awards are being heaped upon it, and (this is the real shock) regular folks are flocking to see it. This affectionate chronicle of the friendship and trust that grows, over twenty-five years, between two older Atlantans, one rich, white, Jewish, and female, the other poor, black, Christian, and male, has been certified a "heart-warmer" of a movie.

    Driving Miss Daisy is a handsomely mounted and beautifully performed film. Jessica Tandy (Daisy Werthan) and Morgan Freeman (Hoke) are both brilliant in Alfred Uhry's adaptation of his own Pulitzer prize-winning play. While so many movies glorify the violence people do to one another, *Driving Miss Daisy* is about compassion and caring.

    Or is it? After I wiped away my sentimental tears at the end of the movie, it became increasingly clear to me that *Driving Miss Daisy* glorified another, much more subtle violence—that inherent in the touching, lovely relationship between the two lead characters. *Driving Miss Daisy* gives us poor African Americans propping up the lives of rich white folks, and calls it a healthy relationship. It romanticizes, rather than challenges, the racial power politics it presents. Hoke is Miss Daisy's "best friend" by the end of the movie, but theirs is never an alliance of mutual regard and support between two equals. Daisy is not even a friend Hoke would choose. She is a "friend" forced on him by the economic necessity of feeding his family. What kind of a friendship is that?

    In the movie's final scene, Hoke visits Miss Daisy in the nursing home where she resides and tenderly hand-feeds her

The *"friendship"* of Daisy Werthan (*Jessica Tandy*) and her chauffeur, Hoke (*Morgan Freeman*), is *touching. It's also racist and elitist. White Americans made* Driving Miss Daisy *a hit.*

the pie on her dinner tray. Hoke's gesture of care-giving is very beautiful, but there is something ugly and disturbing about it and about Hoke's courtly, Uncle-Tomish devotion to Miss Daisy throughout the film. It is disturbing because the movie claims Hoke's slavish devotion to be Miss Daisy's right. And it invites us to think "Ah, that's the way people ought to be with one another."

Uhry is himself an owning-class Atlantan. And since Miss Daisy is based on his own grandmother (and Hoke on her chauffeur), it is understandable that he would not *seriously* question the morality of Daisy's relationship with Hoke. He pays passing lip-service to the civil rights movement, and fleetingly laments the evils of racism and anti-Semitism in his story. This is meant to absolve him. It is an exquisite example of American two-faced logic to say that racism is a bad thing, but the unequal master-servant relationship between Daisy and Hoke is a very good thing. It enriches the life of one, and ennobles the life of the other. And that is supposed to warm the heart.

Noble sacrifice of self. Purity of heart. Denial. These are

the positive traits most often assigned to women and people of color in movies. And I have found these elements of heroism suspect ever since the days the nuns used to try to sell me a bill of goods about how virgin martyrs were the feminine ideal. Assign this personality profile to an overachiever of the underclass and you deny them the impulse to change their own lives. Hollywood does it time and time again, sometimes recycling the exact same story, like *Stella Dallas*.

The 1990 version of *Stella* is the brainchild of producer Samuel Goldwyn, Jr., whose dad produced both of the earlier Hollywood adaptations of Olive Higgins Prouty's 1923 bestseller. Too bad no one warned Junior about trying to follow too closely in papa's footsteps. Plenty of women (and a few men) wept over Prouty's novel. Even more sobbed over the silent screen gem of 1925 and bawled over its 1937 re-make as a talkie. And a generation continued to sniffle and thrill over Anne Elstner's performance in the "true-to-life sequel...to the world-famous drama of mother love and sacrifice" over NBC's airwaves. The radio soap lasted from the late-'30's through the mid-'50's. That's a lot of tears. And frankly, Mr. Goldwyn, we're all cried out over this particular elitist tear-jerker.

The world didn't need a new "up-dated" movie version of Prouty's story. Especially not when the definitive film version of *Stella Dallas* will always be the 1937 melodrama directed by King Vidor, and starring the sorely-missed Barbara Stanwyck.

I may only feel this way because her death this past February is still heavy in my heart, but I think it goes beyond chutzpah to re-make a Barbara Stanwyck film of the caliber of *Stella Dallas*. It's meshugge. Stanwyck, living or dead, owns that part as far as I'm concerned. Moreover, even those unaware of the magnificence of Barbara Stanwyck, who have no idea that this story has been done to death already, will likely still wonder why anyone would make a movie like this today.

Stella is the story of a working-class woman who gives up her daughter to the girl's rich father for the girl's own good. Maternal sacrifice has always been a crowd-pleaser in movie melodrama, and the success of *Steel Magnolias* shows that it still packs them in. But even if you set aside the dangerous mother mythology that argues that motherhood is everything to a woman, and that no sacrifice is to great for a woman to make for her child, the story of *Stella Dallas* would still be poison. Hollywood has turned to this same plot again and again because it glorifies two traits a male, elitist culture most hopes to cultivate in its audience: the self-abnegation of women, and the self-hatred of the working class.

I have always made (too many) allowances for 1937's *Stella Dallas*. The way Stanwyck practically swaggers down the street in tear-stained triumph as the closing music swells gets me every time. Like Bette Davis, Barbara Stanwyck was incapable of playing a wimpy woman. And unlike Davis's finishing-school regality, Stanwyck's up-from-the streets moxie was clearly earned. Stanwyck makes the lies of *Stella Dallas* more palatable, and the time period made the lies more plausible.

It seemed that in a country staggering out of a deep economic depression, a single-mother like Stanwyck's Stella *might* make her wrenching choice out of an overall *lack* of choice. Stella might believe that her daughter would never attain a prosperous and happy life except through attachment to a rich, socially-connected man: first as such a man's daughter, and later as the wife of her father's younger equivalent. In the days when divorce was still a thing of scandal and stigma, before joint custody was a common occurrence, it's *possible* that a woman might see her only option as a mother to be one of all or nothing. But let's face it, Stanwyck, who was raised poor and never went beyond grade school, proved with her own life of hard-knocks how ludicrous the story of *Stella Dallas* was, even in the '30s.

Women are falling into poverty in ever-growing numbers today, but we still have more options than our grandmothers did 60 years ago. It is women's greater empowerment that makes a 1990 Stella such an anachronism. Even if Bette Midler's Stella has no hope of going beyond a life as a barmaid or a door-to-door cosmetics saleswoman herself, her daughter's collar is much more likely to be white. And screenwriter Robert Getchell admits as much to us.

As written by Getchell, Jenny (Trini Alvarado) is an A and B high-school student with a recognized talent for architecture. Her rich father, Stephen Dallas (Stephen Collins), has never lived with her, but since the filmmakers are far too cowardly to show an abandoning father, he is portrayed as doting on her just the same. He'd be more than willing to pay for the Ivy League education of her choice. So why is Stella forced to insure a better life for her daughter by driving her out of her life forever? The closest thing Getchell can offer as a reason for Stella's excessive self-sacrifice is that she is worried that Jenny will get involved with bad boys and drugs if she stays in her working-class community.

This is convoluted classist reasoning at its worst. Can Getchell actually think that owning-class boys have no behavioral problems and never take drugs? If so, he should hang out at a prep school on the tony side of town someday. His eyes would pop wide open. And, besides, since Jenny will soon be going away to college (where they also never act out or do drugs—ha, ha), her escape route is already waiting.

Getchell sticks to the basic plot of the old *Stella Dallas* in a way 1937's screenwriters Victor Heerman and Sarah Y. Mason would probably find touching, but which ruins his credibility as a man in touch with reality. His faithfulness forces him to stand by scores of class myths that make even less sense now then they did fifty years ago.

The worst of these myths goes "you just can't take a poor person out in public because they are just too tacky and rude and boisterous." A ridiculous insult in 1937, it caused some of the worst contradictions in Vidor's film. For example, in one scene Stanwyck knows enough about her estranged husband's staid, preppie tastes to rip the extra frills off of her dress when

Bette Midler, shown here with movie daughter Trini Alvarado, is Stella [Dallas]. *This paragon of maternal self-sacrifice was already a class anachronism when Barbara Stanwyck played her in 1937.*

she wants to impress him. Yet later she piles every piece of costume jewelry she owns onto an already garish outfit when she knows she is about to meet the country club maters of her daughter's high-toned new friends.

Stanwyck's self-destructive compulsion towards vulgarity was preposterous. But *Stella*'s filmmakers force Midler to play the same scenes in almost exactly the same way. If anything, she is even more of a social buffoon than Stanwyck's Stella. Midler not only dresses like a clown (or like The Divine Miss M. doing Chiquita Banana in an outfit complete with frou-frou head-dress), she even forces a resort waiter to do a medley of tropical dance numbers with her.

When your star is a woman of Bette Midler's divine madness, it must be very tempting to give her at least one gonzo musical number—especially when your plot is as feeble as this one is. But Stella is supposed to be a believable, even tragic, heroine. Her zany antics knock the props out from under what little credibility the character had, up to that point, built up.

Just because a woman only went to the tenth grade doesn't mean that she lacks the most basic social skills. If Stella were that aggressively gauche, how in heaven's name could she effectively sell products door to door? But if she's not a total social misfit, why is it necessary for her to completely divorce herself from a daughter she adores?

It's incomprehensible. And the total absurdity of the film's climactic sacrificial act makes *Stella* a complete failure as melodrama. John Erman, who did such a good job with the ground-breaking TV AIDS weepie, *An Early Frost*, assists Midler, Alvarado, and John Goodman (as Ed, Stella's old friend and suitor) in giving good performances. But *Stella*, as a piece of screen literature, is the kind of hopeless anachronism that makes an actor's good performance just a waste of time.

Martin Ritt's new film, *Stanley & Iris*, also does a number on working-class women. In it, a working-class widow, Iris (Jane Fonda), teaches an illiterate co-worker, Stanley (Robert DeNiro), to read. Now, what could even a cynical old feminist like myself find offensive in that?

Plenty, starting with the fact that the movie sells itself on such a trendy subject as literacy. I am just cynical enough to see the current national obsession with both illiteracy and drug abuse as a diversionary tactic of a government eager to keep its citizenry aiming their thousand points of flashlight wattage on a few emotionally-charged symptoms, in the hopes that the real systemic disease of social inequity will remain in total darkness, well out of public sight and collective mind.

Novelist Pat Barker wasn't interested in assisting in governmental sleight of hand. She told the truth whole in *Union Street*, her 1982 novel detailing the lives of seven working-class women in Northern England. *Stanley & Iris* may be based on Barker's novel, but it goes without saying that Hollywood is less willing to make an honest statement about the lives of the poor. Still, I expected more of the team that created *Norma Rae*—screenwriters Harriet Frank, Jr. and Irving Ravetch, and once-blacklisted director Martin Ritt—than the likes of this.

Gone is Barker's England. Frank and Ravetch give us Connecticut, where the poor are, by the looks of it, comfortably so. Gone also is Barker's feminist focus on women. Fonda's Iris is a nice woman who looks more like a California "professor's wife" than a New England laborer, but this movie isn't really about her or the women she works with at the baked goods factory. This film is so uninterested in the women characters it presents to us that it doesn't even bother, in one key instance, to keep track of their whereabouts.

Swoosie Kurtz, that paragon of modern character actors, plays the thankless role of Iris's sister Sharon. Sharon and her out-of-work and abusive husband, Joe (Jamey Sheridan), are living with Iris and her two kids as the film begins. Sharon is introduced as an important support character, but then is summarily dropped mid-way through the movie. Her mysterious disappearance is never explained. Robert Stack is sure to investigate any day now.

As for the filmmakers, they are much more concerned with a male character who doesn't even appear in Barker's novel. He is the Horatio Alger of the 1990's, the illiterate Stanley Cox. DeNiro (who is admittedly much more believable as a working-class character than the svelte, tanned, perfectly poised, and obviously privileged Fonda) does a wonderful job in the role. Barker's men, emasculated by their lack of economic and social power, abuse alcohol and their families for relief. Stanley is a saintly fellow, and a genius to boot.

The implication is that a lack of literacy is the only obstacle keeping Stanley from becoming king of the universe. All it takes is for Iris to teach him to read and he becomes an American success story. Ten easy lessons in your ABC's taught by a volunteer schoolmarm, and you too can be transformed from a homeless ditch-digger to an inventor/engineer with a

Stanley (Robert De Niro) will shortly turn in this bike for a new car. Iris (Jane Fonda) teaching him to read launches him on the road to success. Too bad reading never did her that much good.

big house, a new car, and a bright future. If you're a man, anyway. Upward mobility is not that easy for the women of the story. Social ascent is the same for Iris and her kids as it is for Stella and hers. Female success means attaching yourself to the right paterfamilias. Iris can read War and Peace, but like Stella, she's incapable of uplifting her family on her own. She's stuck in her cake factory. And her literate and intelligent daughter, Kelly (Martha Plimpton), seems destined for the same life. Only the lightning-quick rise of Stanley can save them from their blue-collar morass.

In *Norma Rae* (1979), Sally Field could only come into her own power through the mentoring of Ron Liebman, but she was still the valiant hero of her own story. She learned self-acceptance not by sleeping with a more powerful man, or by becoming middle-class, but by fighting the good fight for herself and for her co-workers at the mill. That *Stanley & Iris* should be made by the exact same writing and directing team eleven years later is proof of how badly Hollywood is backsliding in its treatment of women and working-class characters.

The filmmakers refuse to empower Iris. And they refuse to honestly deal with the issue of abortion. Much of Pat Barker's chapter on Iris King in *Union Street* details the family crisis when Iris's youngest daughter is discovered to be five months pregnant. Doctors refuse the girl an abortion, and a desperate Iris and her daughter must turn to a neighborhood woman for help. When I said that Barker tells the truth whole, I meant it. The scene in which a terrified and exhausted young girl gives birth to a live fetus is unflinching in its horror and sadness.

In *Stanley & Iris* there is, of course, no abortion. Kelly doesn't even consider it an option. She wants to continue her pregnancy and keep her baby, and does so, happily enough, after a brief conflict with her mother. After the birth of her daughter, young Kelly quits school and goes to work at the same factory as her mom.

Am I the only person who finds this plot development just as incomprehensible as Stella's big sacrifice? Why would a loving mother like Iris spend countless hours educating a man she barely knows, and yet be so seemingly content to see her own daughter drop out of high school to work what she believes to be a dead-end job? Can it be that she, like the filmmakers, believes Stanley to be a human being of greater value than her own woman-child? At least Iris's sacrifices pay off for her family one way or the other. She can't help herself, but by helping a man make it big, she insures a happy ending for herself and her kids. What does Stella get for her efforts? The knowledge that her daughter is living on easy street without her. Because Stella never really attaches herself to Stephen Dallas, the owning-class man of the piece, she is left alone, out in the rain, at the movie's end. But let's be fair to Hollywood, they aren't picking on Stella because she's a woman. Not entirely, anyway. They isolate and discard her just as much because she is a member of the underclass.

Stella is an American pariah. But poor men, even white ones played by Christopher Plummer, aren't always treated better by Hollywood. In John Boorman's new movie, *Where the*

Heart Is, Dabney Coleman plays a rich demolitions expert and land developer who is also a concerned father. Worried that his three spoiled, grown children will never become independent enough to make their own fortunes, he dumps them one evening in an abandoned building, informing them that they must thence forward live by their own wits. There is no wit in this fiasco of a farce, but there is plenty of elitism.

Coleman's kids know nothing about making do, but you can bet your Beamer that they will be well on their way to independent wealth after just a few weeks on their own. They are, after all, the deserving rich. For them, fortunes are easily made or restored. Their aura of entitlement insures them all a fairy-tale happy ending. Everyone in this disgusting tale finds both success and romance by the time the credits roll except for one character. Care to guess who that character would be?

Where the Heart Is contains only one lead character who is portrayed as genuinely homeless and destitute. And he, alone, stays that way. In the movie's last scene, an enchanted dance party, that character is the one character without a lover. And in the end, as in the beginning, he is the one character without a name. Without money, even a white man can be stripped of his identity and value. There is little doubt of how worthless the filmmakers find him. They have their rich protagonists dub him, affectionately, of course, "The Shit" and "Shitty."

The silver screen of the '90s continues to present a world populated by the people born with silver spoons in their mouths and the people who spoon-feed them their pumpkin pie. The rich are entitled to stay that way. And the poor—especially women and people of color—are entitled to sacrifice themselves for their betters. Hoke brings comfort and companionship to Miss Daisy. Stella Claire gives Stephen Dallas the daughter she prizes above all else. Iris King gives Stanley Cox the means of upward mobility. (Why not give it away? It never did her any good.)

Unlike Hollywood, I no longer admire the Haves for their selfish *joie de vivre*, or the Have-Nots for their selfless nobility. I want to see movies wherein the Hokes and the Stellas and the Irises and the "Shitty's" of the world get what they need and want in the final reel. I want them to stop making life easier for those who already have it way too easy. I want them instead to use their hearts and minds to make life better for themselves, their children, and their communities. That's the kind of movie *I'd* certify as a "heart-warmer."

Index

A Cry in the Dark, 2
A Dry White Season, 61–66
A Guy Named Joe, 22
A Man in Love, 68
A Question of Silence, 126
A Taxing Woman, 67–68
A World Apart, 46, 63, 79
Absolute Beginners, 18
Accused, The, 115–120, 154
Adjani, Isabelle, 2
Adlon, Eleonore, 71–72
Adlon, Percy, 69, 71–72
African National Congress, 48
Airplane!, 23
Alcott, Louisa May, 48
Alda, Alan, 3, 181–185
Alexander, Jane, 139
Alexander, Jason, 12
Alien, 100
Aliens, 100
All About Eve, 187
All My Children, 81
Allen, Woody, 27, 174–180
Alley, Kirstie, 152
Alvarado, Trini, 203
Always, 22
American Graffiti, 54–55, 59
An Early Frost, 205
An Unsuitable Job for a Woman, 103
Anderson, Eddie "Rochester," 26
Annie Hall, 174
Another 48 Hrs., 185
Another Woman, 178–180
Arlen, Alice, 193, 197
Armstrong, Gillian, 69
Arsenic and Old Lace, 135
Attenborough, Richard, Sir, 50, 61
Atwood, Margaret, 2
Aunt Julia and the Scriptwriter, 32
Autumn Sonata, 175–176, 178
Awful Truth, The, 35

Baard, Frances, 53
Baby Boom, 2, 37, 114, 154
    TV Show, 151
Bagdad Cafe, 69–73
Baldwin, Alec, 12, 196
Bancroft, Anne, 28
Barker, Pat, 206, 208
Barr, Roseanne, 128–131, 133, 198
Barron, Zelda, 59
Barry, Tony, 122
Barrymore, Drew, 39
Bates, Kathy, 145

Batman, 15
Beaches, 10, 76–81
Beart, Emmanuelle, 37
Begley, Ed, Jr., 131
Bellamy, Ralph, 11
Benedek, Barbara, 10, 146, 148,
    154–155
Benjamin, Richard, 168
Bennett, Joan, 181
Berenger, Tom, 112
Bergen, Candice, 133
Bergman, Ingmar, 175, 178
Bernstein, Sharon, 1
Besch, Bibi, 184
Betsy's Wedding, 3, 181–185
Big, 37
Big Chill, The, 148, 154
Bigelow, Kathryn, 101, 105, 109
Biko, Steve, 50–51
Bill & Ted's Excellent Adventure, 32
Bishop, Joey, 182
Blankenship, Beverly, 124
Blind Date, 41
Blithe Spirit, 21
Blondell, Joan, 21
Blue Steel, 101–107
Body Double, 82
Boorman, John, 208
Boothe, Clare, 93–94, 97
Borden, Lizzie, 118
Bortman, Michael, 113
Bosco, Philip, 87, 104
Brando, Marlon, 61
Brennan, Eileen, 31
Brickman, Paul, 143, 146–148
Bridges, Jeff, 39
Brindley, Michael, 124
Brink, Andre, 64
Broadcast News, 37
Bronson, Charles, 125
Brown, Blair, 186, 189
Brown, Clancy, 103
Brown, Julie, 16–19
Bruckheimer-Martell, Bonnie, 81
Buchanan, Simone, 122
Burns, Mark R., 130, 132

Cage, Nicholas, 178
Caine, Michael, 177
Calhoun, Monica, 70
Calley, John, 161
Camille, 77, 81
Camille Claudel, 2
Campbell, G. Smokey, 70

Carrey, Jim, 18
Carrie, 136
Casual Sex?, 37
Cates, Phoebe, 55
Chances Are, 38–39
Chapman, Leigh, 107, 109
Chariots of Fire, 64
Checker, Chubby, 51
Cher, 37, 167–171, 178
Clayton-Cragg, Carolyn, 49
Close, Glenn, 21, 154
Coffey, Charlie, 16
Coffey, Scott, 58
Coleman, Dabney, 209
Collins, Pauline, 197
Collins, Stephen, 203
Connery, Sean, 34, 86
Cookie, 193–197
Coppola, Francis Ford, 182
Cosby, Bill, 26, 64
Cosby Show, The, 151
Costa-Gavras, 62, 147
Coster, Nicolas, 184
Coward, Noel, 21–22
Crane, Cheryl, 177
Crawford, Joan, 93, 97, 186
Cries and Whispers, 175, 178
Cross My Heart, 37
Crossing Delancey, 37
Cruise, Tom, 148, 185
Cry Freedom, 50–51, 61, 63
Cukor, George, 93
Curtis, Jamie Lee, 101–103, 105–106
Cusack, Joan, 87, 146
Cyborg, 101

Dance, Charles, 188
Dangerous, 186
Dann, Patty, 170
Danner, Blythe, 179
Dark Victory, 77
Dart, Iris Rainer, 80
Date with an Angel, 37
Davis, Bette, 77, 81, 158, 186, 203
Davis, Geena, 17
Days of Thunder, 185
Dead Calm, 4
Death Wish, 125
Death Wish 4: The Crackdown, 125
DeMarco, John, 107, 109
Demme, Jonathan, 86, 196
DeNiro, Robert, 4, 205–206
Dennis, Sandy, 179
Desperately Seeking Susan, 131, 193
Dick Tracy, 185
Diner, 55
Dirty Dancing, 54, 59
Dirty Harry, 125
Dirty Rotten Scoundrels, 83
Doherty, Shannen, 138

Dona Flor and Her Two Husbands, 20
D'Onofrio, Vincent Phillip, 90
Donoghue, Mary Agnes, 80
Douglas, Michael, 146
Downey, Robert, Jr., 39
Dr. Strangelove, 138
Dreyfuss, Richard, 22, 119, 164
Driving Miss Daisy, 89, 200–201
Dukakis, Olympia, 84, 96
Dukes, David, 39
Dunne, Irene, 35
Dutka, Elaine, 1
Dzundza, George, 107

E.T., 63
Earth Girls are Easy, 16–19
Eastwood, Clint, 15, 125
Eating Raoul, 135
Eddie and the Cruisers II, 15
Edwards, Blake, 41–43
Elizondo, Hector, 11
Elmes, Rowen, 65
Empty Nest, 151
Ephron, Nora, 193, 197
Erman, John, 205
Evers, Medgar, 57
Experience Preferred . . . But Not Essential,
    168
Extremities, 126

Fahey, Jeff, 107
Falk, Peter, 32, 194–195, 197
Farrow, Mia, 175, 177, 178
Fatal Attraction, 116, 146
Father of the Bride, 181
Fawcett, Farrah, 39
Ferrell, Conchata, 89
Field, Sally, 4, 96
First, Ruth, 46–48, 51, 53
Fisher, Carrie, 21, 158, 161, 164–165
Fisher, Eddie, 163
Flagg, Darron, 70
Fletcher, Louise, 104
Fonda, Bridget, 55, 189
Fonda, Jane, 4, 205–206
Footloose, 136
Ford, Harrison, 37, 82, 87
Ford, Margaret, 122
Forsyth, Bill, 171
Fossey, Dian, 2, 82
Foster, Jodie, 115, 117, 119
Frances, 2
Francis, Connie, 56
Frank, Harriet, Jr., 3, 206
Freeman, Morgan, 200
Friday the 13th, Part VII, 76
*Friday the 13th, Part VIII: Terror in Times
    Square*, 15
Full House, 151
Furness, Deborra-Lee, 122, 124–125

Gaby—A True Story, 31
Gallagher, Peter, 32
Ganz, Bruno, 190–191
Garbo, Greta, 81
Gazzo, Michael V., 195
Gere, Richard, 5, 9
Getchell, Robert, 203–204
Ghost, 1, 4–5, 20–26
Ghost and Mrs. Muir, The, 20
Ghost Dad, 20, 26
Ghostbusters II, 15
Gibson, Mel, 101
Gish, Annabeth, 55, 89, 91
Glimcher, Arnold, 113
Glover, Danny, 101
Goddard, Paulette, 93
Goddess in Progress, 16
Godfather III, 182
Goldberg, Whoopi, 4, 22, 25
Goldblum, Jeff, 18
Goldman, Emma, 14
Goldwyn, Samuel, Jr., 23, 202
Goldwyn, Tony, 23
Gone with the Wind, 96
Good Mother, The, 112–115, 117, 120
Goodfellas, 182
Goodman, John, 205
Gorillas in the Mist, 2
Gorris, Marleen, 126
Graduate, The, 28–29, 161
Grafton, Sue, 100
Grant, Cary, 27, 35
Gray, Spalding, 79
Griffith, Kristin, 176
Griffith, Melanie, 37, 82, 85–87
Griffith, Tracy, 115
Gruer, Merav, 48
Gung Ho, 68

Haas, Lukas, 39
Hackman, Gene, 163
Hairspray, 59, 193
Hamilton, George, 56
Hammond, Kay, 22
Handmaid's Tale, The, 2–3
Hanks, Tom, 37
Hannah and Her Sisters, 175–180
Hannah, Daryl, 37, 96
Hannah, Page, 55
Hare, David, 186–192
Hare, Joe, 191
Harker, Susannah, 65
Harling, Robert, 94, 97–98
Harrison, Rex, 22
Hart, Delores, 56
Haskell, Molly, 186
Hazel, 151
Heard, John, 79
Hearn, Ann, 119
Heart Like a Wheel, 118, 154

Heartburn, 161
Heathers, 4, 134–139
Heaven Can Wait, 20
Heckerling, Amy, 152
Hedren, Tippi, 85–86
Heerman, Victor, 204
Hellbound:Hellraiser II, 76
Hello Again, 26
Helmsley, Leona, 165
Hemingway, Margaux, 125
Hemingway, Mariel, 125
Hepburn, Katherine, 35
Here Comes Mr. Jordan, 20
Hershey, Barbara, 31, 47, 52, 77–
    79, 81, 176
Hitchcock, Alfred, 85
Hoffman, Dustin, 29
Home Alone, 4
Hoskins, Bob, 169
Hot to Trot, 76
Housekeeping, 171
Howard, Arliss, 146
Howze, Perry, 39, 89
Howze, Randy, 39, 89
Hunt, Linda, 132
Hunter, Holly, 22
Hurt, Mary Beth, 176
Hutton, Timothy, 37

I Love You to Death, 32
Immediate Family, 3, 148, 154
Impulse, 106–109
Indemnity Only, 100
Interiors, 175, 176–178
Interview, 63
Irving, Amy, 37
Itami, Juzo, 67

Jackson, Michael, 64
Jaffe, Stanley R., 116
James, P.D., 103
Jezebel, 186
Jodrell, Steve, 124–125
Jones, Amy, 89
Jones, Gillian, 124
Jones, Jennifer, 21

Kahn, Madeline, 182, 185
Kaplan, Jonathan, 118, 154
Karate Kid III, 15
Kaufmann, Christine, 70
Kavner, Julie, 175
Keaton, Diane, 112–115, 175, 176
Kidman, Nicole, 4
Killing Fields, The, 52
King, Stephen, 112
Kiss Me Goodbye, 20
Kline, Kevin, 50
Klute, 39
Knight, Michael E., 37

Korsmo, Charlie, 143
Krabbe, Jeroen, 47
Krige, Alice, 39
Kurtz, Swoosie, 206
Kurys, Diane, 68
Kuzwayo, Ellen, 53

La Rue Cases-Negres, 62
Ladd, Alan, 124
Lady and the Tramp, 146
Lake, Ricki, 59, 193
Lange, Hope, 32
Lange, Jessica, 2, 142–143, 146–148
Lansing, Sherry, 116
LaPaglia, Anthony, 184–185
Larroquette, John, 32
Lavin, Linda, 40
Lawton, J.F., 10
Leatherface: Texas Chainsaw Massacre
      III, 15
Legitimus, Darling, 62
Lehmann, Michael, 135
Leigh, Jennifer Jason, 12
Leigh, Vivien, 28
Leland, David, 193
Lesotho, Albee, 50, 52
Lethal Weapon, 101
Lethal Weapon II, 15
License the Kill, 15
Liebman, Ron, 207
Lipstick, 125
Little Foxes, The, 187
Little Women, 47
Llosa, Mario Vargas, 32
Lloyd, Emily, 193, 195
Locke, Sondra, 106, 109, 125
Lombard, Carole, 35
Long, Shelley, 26
Look Who's Talking, 3, 152–153
Looking for Mr. Goodbar, 112
Loos, Anita, 93
Los Angeles Times, 1, 63
Love Letters, 89
Luce, Clare Booth. See Booth, Clare
Luce, Henry, 93, 97

McIntyre, Vonda N., 99
MacLaine, Shirley, 96, 158–159, 161
Made in Heaven, 37
Madigan, Amy, 100
Mandoki, Luis, 31
Madonna, 131
Magnuson, Ann, 37
Making Mr. Right, 37, 193
Manhattan, 175, 176
Marnie, 86
Married to the Mob, 130, 196–197
Marshall, E.G., 176
Marshall, Garry, 10
Martin, Steve, 157

Mason, Sarah Y., 204
Mason, Tom, 143
Masterson, Mary Stuart, 39, 154
Maxie, 21
May, Jodhi, 47, 52
McCullough, Rohan, 191
McGillis, Kelly, 37, 119
McGovern, Elizabeth, 32
McInnerny, Tim, 189
McNally, Terrence E., 16
Men Don't Leave, 142–149
Menges, Chris, 50–52
Mermaids, 167–171
Miami Blues, 12–14
Micki and Maude, 41
Midler, Bette, 77–78, 203, 205
Miller, Sue, 112–113, 115
Mimieux, Yvette, 56
Miner, Jan, 168
Minnelli, Vincente, 181, 185
Mission, The, 52
Modine, Matthew, 196
Modise, Thandi, 53
Mokae, Zakes, 64
Monroe, Marilyn, 86
Moonstruck, 36, 169, 178
Moore, Demi, 3, 4, 22
Moses, William R., 91
Mr. Belvedere, 151
Mrs. Soffel, 69
Ms., 186
Ms. 45, 125
Mtintso, Thenjiwe, 53
Murfin, Jane, 93
Murphy Brown, 16
Murphy, Eddie, 64
Music Box, The, 147
Mvusi, Linda, 48, 52
My Fair Lady, 10–11
My Two Dads, 151
Mystic Pizza, 37, 39, 89–91

Naked Gun: From the Files of Police Squad!,
      The, 23, 83
National Lampoon's European Vacation, 152
Naughton, James, 113
Near Dark, 105
Neeson, Liam, 113–114
Neill, Sam, 4, 187
Nelligan, Kate, 187
New York Stories, 27
New York Times, 10, 77, 113
Ngoyi, Lilian, 53
Ngubene, Emily, 66
Nichols, Mike, 28, 34, 82–83,
      86–87, 161–165
Nightmare on Elm Street 5, 15
Nimoy, Leonard, 113–115
1969, 54
Norma Rae, 3, 206–208

Now, Voyager, 77
Nowhere to Hide, 100–101
Ntshinga, Thoko, 64
Ntshona, Winston, 64
Nugent, Frank S., 77
Nykvist, Sven, 176

O'Connor, Sinead, 170
O'Donnell, Chris, 143
O'Hara, Catherine, 185
Olivier, Laurence, 28
One Life to Live, 150
O'Neal, Ryan, 38
O'Sullivan, Maureen, 176–177
Overboard, 10, 37, 152

Page, Geraldine, 176
Pakula, Alan J., 39–41
Palance, Jack, 70, 72, 134
Palcy, Euzhan, 61–65
Paradise, 151
Parenthood, 3, 151, 152, 157
Parents, 135
Paretsky, Sara, 100, 109
Paris By Night, 192
Parton, Dolly, 95
Pasdar, Adrian, 196
Patinkin, Mandy, 21
Patty Hearst, 2
Pena, Elizabeth, 103
People Magazine, 34
Perkins, Elizabeth, 37
Persona, 176, 178
Pesci, Joe, 182
Pfeiffer, Michelle, 196
Philadelphia Story, The, 35
Pick-Up Artist, The, 41
Pink Cadillac, 15
Pinter, Harold, 2
Playboy, 99
Plenty, 187–188
Pleshette, Suzanne, 165
Plimpton, Martha, 207
Plummer, Christopher, 208
Portrait of Jennie, 20
Positive I.D., 126
Postcards from the Edge, 1, 158–165
Pounder, CCH, 70
Power, Tyrone, Jr., 55
Premiere, 116, 164
Prentiss, Paula, 56
Pretty Woman, 4–5, 8–14
Prince, 64
Prochnow, Jurgen, 65
Prouty, Olive Higgins, 202
Pygmalion, 10, 10–11

Quaid, Dennis, 163
Queen of Mean, The, 165

Radio Days, 175
Raitt, Bonnie, 143
Rambo III, 76
Rascoe, Stephanie, 126
Ravetch, Irving, 4, 206
Read, James, 79
Reagan, Ronald, 60
Red, Eric, 101
Redgrave, Vanessa, 189
Reeves, Keanu, 32
Reynolds, Debbie, 158, 165
Ricci, Christina, 167, 171
Richardson, Joely, 189
Richardson, Natasha, 2–3
Ringwald, Molly, 182, 185
Risky Business, 148
Ritt, Martin, 4, 205–206
Ritter, John, 41
Robards, Jason, 139, 151
Roberts, Julia, 5, 8, 89, 96
Roberts, June, 168
RoboCop 2, 185
Rocket, Charles, 17
Roman Spring of Mrs. Stone, The, 28
Rose, The, 78
Roseanne, 16, 133
Ross, Herbert, 94, 97
Rowlands, Gena, 178
Roxanne, 43
Ruehl, Mercedes, 196
Russ, Joanna, 99
Russell, Rosalind, 93, 97
Russell, Theresa, 106
Russo, James, 126
Rutherford, Margaret, 22
Ryder, Winona, 4, 134, 138–139, 167–171

Sägebrecht, Marianne, 69–72
San Giacomo, Laura, 14
Sarandon, Susan, 29–31, 61, 66
Sargent, Alvin, 30
Savan, Glenn, 31
Schepis, Fred, 187
Schlondorff, Volker, 2
Scorsese, Martin, 182
Screen Actors Gill, 1, 5
Secret Policeman's Other Ball, The, 18
Secret Rapture, The, 192
See You in the Morning, 39–41
Segal, George, 152
Seidelman, Susan, 37, 129–132, 193, 197
September, 175, 177
Seventh Sign, The, 3
Shag, 54–60
Shame, 121–127
Shane, 121
Shaw, George Bernard, 10–11
She-Devil, 129–133, 198
Shearer, Norma, 93, 97

Sheedy, Ally, 182, 184–185
Shepherd, Cybill, 38
Shepard, Sam, 95
Sheridan, Jamey, 206
She's Back, 21
Shirley Valentine, 197
Shoeffling, Michael, 169
Shull, Richard B., 32
Shy People, 79
Silkwood, 2, 161, 193
Silver, Joan Micklin, 37
Sisulu, Albertina, 53
Skerritt, Tom, 95
Skin Deep, 41, 41–43
Slater, Christian, 136
Slovo, Joe, 48
Slovo, Shawn, 46–48
Slumber Party Massacre, 89
Smiles of a Summer Night, 178
Smithereens, 193
Sobukwe, Robert, 52
Something Wild, 82, 86
Sophie's Choice, 39
South, Margaret Jennings, 81
Spader, James, 29–30
Spielberg, Steven, 22
Splash, 37
Square Dance, 139
Stander, Lionel, 196
Stanley & Iris, 4, 205-208
Stanwyck, Barbara, 77, 186, 203, 205
Stapleton, Maureen, 176
Star Trek V, 15
Stark, Ray, 94, 97
Starting Over, 39
Steel Magnolias, 3, 95–98, 202
Stella, 202–205
Stella Dallas, 77, 81, 202–205
Stevens, George, 121
Stewart, Jimmy, 35
Sting, 188
Stockwell, Dean, 196
Storke, Adam, 91
Strapless, 186–192
Streep, Meryl, 2, 5, 129, 133, 158,
        161–162, 187, 189, 198
Stritch, Elaine, 177
Strugatz, Barry, 130, 132
Suchet, David, 50
Sudden Impact, 125
Sugar Cane Alley, 61–65
Sugarbaby, 69–70
Surrender, 41
Sutherland, Donald, 61, 63–66
Suzman, Janet, 65
Swayze, Patrick, 22
Sweet Dreams, 2
Swing Shift, 188

Tally, Ted, 30

Tampopo, 67–68
Tandy, Jessica, 200
Taylor, Elizabeth, 163, 181
Taylor, Lili, 89
Terms of Endearment, 161
Thigpen, Lynne, 107
Three Coins in the Fountain, 91
Three Men and a Baby, 3, 152
Three Men and a Little Lady, 3
Topor, Tom, 116–117
Topper, 20
Topper Returns, 20, 20–21, 26
Total Recall, 185
Townsend, Betsey, 170
Tracy, Spencer, 181
Travolta, John, 153
Truffaut, Francois, 62
Tune in Tomorrow . . ., 32–34
Turner, Lana, 177
Twins, 83

Uhry, Alfred, 89, 200
Ullman, Tracey, 188–189
Union Street, 206, 208

Vaccaro, Brenda, 197
Van Damme, Jean-Claude, 101
Vidor, King, 202, 204
Vieira, Asta, 113
Village Voice, 133

Wade, Kevin, 85, 86
Walker, Kim, 137
Wallace, George, 57
Walsh, Dylan, 184
Ward, Fred, 12
Warner, Jack, 11
Washington, Denzel, 50
Waters, Daniel, 135
Waters, John, 59
Waterston, Sam, 177
Wayans, Damon, 18
Weaver, Sigourney, 2, 82
Weldon, Fay, 130, 132
Welland, Colin, 64
West, Mae, 27–28, 133
Wetherby, 189
Where the Boys Are, 55–56
Where the Heart is, 208–209
White, Diane, 133
White Palace, 29–31
Who's Afraid of Virginia Woolf?, 161
Wiest, Dianne, 176, 194, 197
Willis, Bruce, 152, 185
Winfrey, Oprah, 129
Wings of Desire, 191
Wish You Were Here, 193
With Six You Get Eggroll, 39
Women, The, 93–94, 96, 97
Woods, James, 154

Working Girl, 37, 82–87
Wright, Teresa, 115

Young, Robert M., 126, 151
Young, Roland, 21
Yours, Mine and Ours, 39

Zobel, Joseph, 62
Zucker, Jerry, 23